Wordsworth's Biblical Ghosts

Wordsworth's Biblical Ghosts

DEEANNE WESTBROOK

palgrave

First published 2001 by PALGRAVE™
175 Fifth Avenue New York, N.Y.10010 and
Houndmills, Basingstoke, Hampshire RG21 6XS.
Companies and representatives throughout the world

PALGRAVE is the new global publishing imprint of St. Martin 's Press
LLC Scholarly and Reference Division and Palgrave Publishers Ltd
(formerly Macmillan Press Ltd).

ISBN 0-312-24014-7 hardback

Library of Congress Cataloging-in-Publication Data
Westbrook, Deeanne
Wordsworth's Biblical ghosts / Deeanne Westbrook.
    p.   cm.
  Includes bibliographical references and index.
  ISBN 0-312-24014-7
  1. Wordsworth, William, 1770–1850—Religion.   2. Religion and
literature—England—History—19th century.   3. Religious poetry,
English—History and criticism.   4. Bible—In literature.   I. Title.
PR5892.R4 W47   2001
821'.7—dc21

                                        2001021320

A catalogue record for this book is available from the British Library.

Design by Letra Libre, Inc.

First edition: September, 2001
10 9 8 7 6 5 4 3 2 1

Printed in the United States of America.

For Andy

Andrew Westbrook
1964–1997

. . . impatient as the wind

CONTENTS

Acknowledgements

My research for this book has validated and deepened my respect for the community of Wordsworthian scholars, with several of whom I have carried on an interior and lopsided dialogue over the last several years. Their scholarship has furnished a foundation for my work, and their informed and thoughtful texts enter my analyses at every turn. I am grateful to my generous colleague, Carol Franks, who read and helped edit the chapters as they were emerging, and to the fine editors at Palgrave, Kristi Long and her staff. Finally, my mentor in this endeavor has been Romantics scholar, editor, and generous lady, Marilyn Gaull, whose encouragement and support I treasure.

Abbreviations

Letters
: *The Letters of William and Dorothy Wordsworth: The Later Years.* Ernest De Selincourt, ed. Oxford: The Clarendon Press, 1939.

Oxford P. W.
: *The Oxford Authors: William Wordsworth.* Stephen Gill, ed. Oxford and New York: Oxford University Press, 1984; reprinted in. 1987.

Prelude
: *The Prelude 1799, 1805, 1850.* Jonathan Wordsworth, M. H. Abrams, and Stephen Gill, ed. New York and London: W. W. Norton & Company, 1979.

Pr. W.
: *The Prose Works of William Wordsworth.* W. J. B. Owen and Jane Worthington Smyser, ed. 3 vols. Oxford: The Clarendon Press, 1974.

P. W.
: *The Poetical Works of William Wordsworth.* Ernest De Selincourt, ed. Oxford: The Clarendon Press, 1952.

Preface

The Bible became the single most influential document of the Romantic period, the most popular book in the first age of popular literature.

—Marilyn Gaull 176.

Wordsworth's interest in biblical narrative should not be seen as separate from his reflection on the origin and ends of poetry.

—Allen Bewell 120

Every sacred truth not one's own becomes a fable, an old song that requires corrective revision. . . . Wordsworth alone found the new way, our way alas, to ruin sacred truths.

—Harold Bloom, *Ruin the Sacred Truths* 125, 130

William Wordsworth discovered in biblical texts both a basis for his revolutionary poetics and models for his extraordinary poems, whose excellence and innovations owe much to his idiosyncratic and ingenious biblical readings and borrowings—his "corrective revision," the new way to ruin sacred truths. For a number of years I have taught a course in the Bible as literature, along with courses in English Romanticism. Over time, as I read the Bible side by side with Wordsworth, I experienced a series of recognitions of what I want to call the *presence* of the Bible in Wordsworth's poetry and my sense that an understanding of the extent and effects of that presence was required for a richer appreciation of Wordsworth's poetry and poetics. By *presence* I wish to suggest something more and other than the well-acknowledged biblical influences—his biblical allusions or his adaptation of biblical plot and language—although these constitute aspects of the phenomenon that I have in mind. The presence with which I am concerned is pervasive and subtle as white noise and at the same time invasive as a haunting by a not-altogether-congenial ghost. A case in point is the lyric, "Three years she grew in sun and shower" (discussed in chapter 3), in which Wordsworth's Nature is possessed by and assimilated to Ezekiel's lustful, proprietary, and homicidal God. Once recognized, this startling alien presence transforms one's understanding not only of this poem, but of the remaining Lucy poems as well, by providing a glimpse of yet one more "speaking" face—perhaps the true face, perhaps only a disguise—for Wordsworth's enigmatic, shape-shifting Nature.

Many of Wordsworth's biblical ghosts are philologists, both imposing and imposed upon in Wordsworth's texts, exhibiting like Wordsworth a keen interest in language, whether divine or human, and its powers. Such spirits are made to serve the nineteenth-century poet's clear recognition that mind and world, life and death, are word-stuff; that, in Umberto Eco's analysis, "being is something that is said," and, "as it is thinkable, being manifests itself to us right from the outset *as an effect of language*" (*Kant and the Platypus* 22). For example, in Book 2 of the *Prelude,* one finds Wordsworth grappling *to express* this relationship between language and being, between substance (the profane form or image) and essence (pure being represented in the silence of the heavens that can only be captured in sound, the ur-language associated with breath, the originary breathing expressed as "Let there be . . . ," spirit-words that echo still from the rock beneath which the boy William stands, the "ghostly language of the ancient earth" [1805 2:321 - 9]). Wordsworth, taking his cues from the Bible, recognized the fact that, again in Eco's words, "for being to exist, it is necessary to say as well as to think" (*Kant and the Platypus* 22). And that saying takes Wordsworth to the very limits of language, to a boundary where substance becomes essence and something becomes nothing.[1]

In what follows, I want to make the case that reading Wordsworth will be markedly enriched by an awareness of an omnipresent, agonistically sublime biblical presence. I speculate that somewhere on his own road to Damascus Wordsworth was halted and his vision drastically altered by the Book of Books. Wordsworth's style, forms, subjects, and poetics all are suffused—often unobtrusively, yet undeniably—with the poetic matter of the Bible. An important corollary to this proposition is that biblical sacrality, mystery, and metaphysics adhere like lint to its language, images, themes, and forms as these undergo intertextual processes—processes by which the nineteenth-century poet transports them across millennia, interprets, transforms, deforms, and adapts them to his own purposes. I shall argue that the debate over Wordsworth's "religion" in the early texts[2] is in part a result of the interpretative difficulties presented by metaphysical lint.

An example will illustrate what I have in mind. In Book 1 of the *Prelude,* Wordsworth invokes the parabolic figure of the false steward as a metaphor for the failed poet (270).[3] When given attention, the brief and seemingly casual allusion is found to distend and complicate the poet's present narrative situation and "secular" text with implications of both a grand poetics and a fearful metaphysics. Through the allusion, the English scene is figured in the "kingdom of heaven," the setting of the parable, where eternal matters, including (eternal) life and death, are at stake in the steward's failure. Moreover the poet's situation itself becomes parabolic of that in the earlier parable, and shares the extraordinary difficulty of interpretation posed by the genre.[4] Like other parables, the tale of the false steward is marvelously suggestive and at the same time ultimately indecipherable. It is a narrative in which incommensurates are forced into conjunction, a narrative about spiritual economics and the kingdom of heaven, wherein a "hard" businessman (presumably a figure for God) confronts a terrified "false" steward. Out of fear, the steward has failed to invest the lord's "talent" and thus to earn appropriate "usury." He explains his failure: "I knew thee that thou art an hard man, reaping where thou hast not sown. . . . And I was afraid, and went and hid thy talent in the earth" (Mt. 25:24 - 5).[5] The steward's rather astonishing description of the "lord" as hard and acquisitive nevertheless proves accurate, for as punishment the lord takes back his one "talent," hands it to another who will invest it, and banishes the steward to "outer darkness" and endless sorrow. The English homonyms *talent,* a coin, and *talent,* a superior natural endowment, complicate Wordsworth's parabolic reading of the biblical parable and imply that both steward's coin and poet's aptitude are in any case not theirs at all, but the property of some mysterious other who expects the talents to be "invested" and multiplied so that he may reap where he has not sown and who imposes the harshest of penalties for failure. In such a figurative setting, the poet's lapse is not just regrettable, but fatal. Further implications for Wordsworth's poetic theory lie in the fact that poetic talent, like the coin, is really the "lord's," and that the poet is merely a temporary guardian of some grander, eternal poetics and universe-engendering linguistic power.

Much of the evidence is fairly subtle. For example, according to Lane Cooper, the poet uses the word *Bible* only four times in the poetry, and in his study of Wordsworthian allusion, Edwin Stein finds only about forty biblical "echoes" (10). While I believe that the figure of forty actual allusions or echoes is too few, Stein's relatively small number indicates that

the biblical presence with which I am concerned is indeed ghostly—
elusive enough that it has frequently gone unnoticed. Usually, though, the
presence rests beneath the surfaces of texts. I have come to imagine a sort
of biblical underlayment of Wordsworth's thought and practice, a textual
subduction layer that with the passage of time melds with the overlying
matter. Once fused with it, the biblical material here and there forces its
way to the surface, becoming "visible" as overt allusion (as in the example of the false steward). Nevertheless, even when it remains submerged,
its presence and influence manifest themselves as figurative tremors,
ironic adjustments of word and image, and telling deformations in virtually all the poetic strata of language, figure, theme, and form.

To make a thorough case for a ubiquitous biblical presence in
Wordsworth's works is, of course, impossible. At best in a book-length
project I can demonstrate merely the likelihood that my thesis is valid.
My intention in the following pages, therefore, is to identify some of the
more significant types of biblical presence and to illustrate their effects.
As a theoretical basis for my analysis, I identify and discuss in chapter 1
three pertinent critical foci of consideration—intertextuality, poetics,
and metaphysics. Chapters 2 and 3 address Wordsworth's poetics and
practice as these are entangled in and revisionary of the New Testament
doctrine of Incarnation. Chapters 4, 5, and 6 consider Wordsworth's
adaptation and appropriation of biblical forms of narrative discourse—
the biblical etymological tale (focusing on *Poems on the Naming of Places*), the
parable (focusing on *Michael*), and mystical allegory (focusing on "Nutting"). Finally and, I suppose, appropriately enough for this sort of study,
my last two chapters, chapters 7 and 8, examine what I call Wordsworthian apocalyptics (in the plural), where I take up the several forms in
which biblical apocalyptic themes, images, and ideas are manifest both
theoretically and poetically.[6]

CHAPTER I

INTRODUCTION
POET IN A DESTITUTE TIME

The relevance of biblical criticism to literary theory can, in historical terms, scarcely be overestimated.

—Stephen Prickett, *Words and* The Word 198

The case has been well made that the Bible was of profound influence on Wordsworth's poetry and poetics.[1] Further, that Wordsworth worked within the tradition of God's two books—the Bible and nature—is made explicit throughout his poetry. The two-book tradition is central, rather than peripheral—a key concept, for example, in one of Wordsworth's major metapoetical texts, Book 5 of the *Prelude*.[2] Wordsworth's fascination with the book, the language, the speaking face of nature is apparent, as is his resort to the Bible for themes, models, language, and inspiration.[3] Although his language is not so overtly biblical as that of Christopher Smart and William Blake before him, the Bible is still for Wordsworth the crucial influence on his emerging and revolutionary poetic theory and practice.[4] What Wordsworth found in these two books was at once model, method, mystery, language, and encompassing all of these, a metaphoric field through whose parts and relations both his thought and vision might be discovered and articulated.

Having acknowledged all this, my purpose in this introduction is to make explicit what is implicit in acknowledging the Bible as a Wordsworthian source of poetic theory and poetry; in succeeding chapters I shall examine more closely than has previously been done some specific ways in which the reading of individual poems is enriched by a clearer recognition of Wordsworth's ways of appropriating the devices of biblical texts. Biblical language and images are pervasive in the poetry, and details of these will enter my discussion, as will the New Testament doctrine of the Incarnation (chapters 2 and 3), but my chief focus in succeeding chapters is on the ways in which Wordsworth adapts the forms or genres of biblical discourse to his poetic enterprise. These forms include etymological tales, prophecy, allegory, parable, and apocalypse. On close examination it is apparent that the Bible serves as a kind of poetic primer for Wordsworth—not only a source of poetic language or a compendium of images, figures, and types, but, most important, a paradigm of authentic poetic genres, originary and timeless. Wordsworth's strong reliance on the Bible as poetic paradigm left him in the often difficult, often audacious, position of translator, interpreter, and redactor of some of the most powerful texts ever written.

My argument calls forth three interrelated critical matters that I shall address in this introduction: intertextual issues, arising with particular immediacy when the intertext is the "authoritative" Book of God; the poetic issue, concerned with the ways in which Wordsworth's poetics is influenced by both biblical criticism and his own reading of biblical language, doctrine, and genre; and the metaphysical issue, raising again a problem whose solution must be fundamental to any reading of the poems—the problem of Wordsworth's "religion," and the debate over whether his orientation is secular or religious. Separating these issues for discussion disguises the fact that none of them acts alone. It is from the dynamics and chemistry of their confluence that an astonishing Wordsworthian artistry is born. The imbrications of these three issues—the intertextual, the poetic, and the metaphysical—will, therefore, necessitate a certain amount of circling back as the discussion progresses.

INTERTEXTUALITY

I look about, and should the guide I chuse
Be nothing better than a wandering cloud,
I cannot miss my way.

—Prelude 1:17–19

Intertextuality may exist at the level of word, phrase, and sentence, or at the level of whole text, genre, or form. The former, classical sense of intertextuality, attributed to Julia Kristeva, encompasses quotation, allusion, and paraphrase, indicated, as Gérard Genette says, by "the literal presence (more or less literal, whether integral or not) of one text within another" (81–2). (The epigraph to this section, for example, alludes to God, guide of the Israelites through their long wandering, as pillar of cloud, and makes the phrase "be nothing better than a wandering cloud" evocative and ironic in the extreme.) It is this sort of intertextuality that Edwin Stein examines, using the terms "echo" and "echoing" to cover Wordsworthian allusion (3). Of some 1,300 instances of quotation, echo, and allusion, referring to some 150 writers, Stein finds that about 500 allude to Milton (Wordsworth's most frequently echoed source) and about 40 to the Bible (10).[5] Stein's figure of 40 biblical echoes is, I believe, too few, even ignoring intertextuality at the level of form. The underestimation can be attributed to the fact that Wordsworth's biblical allusions are often quite subtle, oblique, or well disguised.[6] Moreover, distinguishing Miltonic from biblical allusions is an intricate process. At times both Miltonic and biblical allusions are interwoven within a single passage, as in the preamble to the *Prelude*. In the opening 19 lines, as Stephen Gill notes (*Oxford P. W.* 728), Wordsworth interweaves allusions to both *Paradise Lost*, describing the exile of Adam and Eve, and Exodus, announcing the Israelites' escape from the "house of bondage," the two allusions creating an irresolvable ambiguity concerning the speaker's situation: Has he escaped from bondage? Has he been exiled from Paradise? Or are this escape and this exile alike? At this point I want simply to assert that the Bible operates as an important intertext even in this classical sense, or what might be called the micro-level of intertextuality.

Genette has both micro- and macro-levels of intertextuality in mind when he uses the terms "transtextuality" and "textual transcendence," which he defines as "everything that brings [the text] into relation (manifest or hidden) with other texts." Under the higher category "transtextuality," Genette includes both *intertextuality* in Julia Kristeva's sense and *metatextuality,* "the transtextual relationship that links a commentary to the text it comments on" (81–2), a relationship that includes both literary retelling or revision and literary criticism. Genette's "metatextuality" is the most accurate term for Wordsworth's practice of adapting biblical forms. In a similar vein, Michael Riffaterre offers a useful way of thinking about the relation of text to text. "Literariness," he says, depends not so much on the meanings of individual words, phrases, and sentences, as on "a relation between form and content, or even on a subordination of content to form." Therefore, "Literariness . . . must be sought at the level where texts combine, or signify by referring to other texts rather than to lesser sign systems" (56). What Stein calls "echoes," Riffaterre calls "connectives." The function of connectives is to serve as "signposts" (operating at the level of word or phrase). The connective presents a difficulty or a mystery or an obscurity in the text that "only an intertext can remedy." An illustrative case is my identification of the phrase "voice of waters" in Wordsworth's "It was an April morning," which points to Ezekiel's vision on the banks of the Chebar (chapter 3). At the same time that the connective poses a problem, it will also "[point] the way to where the solution must be sought"; it is thus of a "dual nature"—it is "the problem seen from the text" and "the solution to that problem when [its] other, intertextual side is revealed." The important point to be made from this view of signposts or connectives is that they implicate whole texts in the intertextual process: "The connectives combine the sign systems of text and intertext into new semiotic clusters, thereby freeing the text from its dependency on usage and existing conventions, and subordinating its descriptive and narrative devices to a signifying strategy unique to the text" (58).[7] Interpretation and understanding await the intertextual solution to the problem posed by a signpost that serves to annex the entire text to which the signpost points. This whole-text implication in the intertextual allusion is the subject of my discussion, for example, of *Michael* (chapter 4), a poem whose complexity and difficulty can be better appreciated when the ghostly presence of the intertext or pre-text (Luke 15) has been recognized; and of "Nutting," a poem that, I argue, is Wordsworth's revision of the Song of Songs (chapter 5).

Riffaterre's connective is thus like Stein's echo, but one with clear semiotic and semantic, as well as formal, implications. The connective is transformative of both text and intertext as they become merged into a new semiotic cluster. This notion of reciprocity and mutual transformation of text and intertext is central as well to J. Hillis Miller's analysis of the intertextual relationship that he presents by means of the metaphor of a parasite-host relationship ("The critic as host"). Both Riffaterre and Miller attempt to understand how meaning is created or changed by the intertextual gesture. To be sure, the imported text, the intertext, is a complex, unstable linguistic field whose presence in the new text produces a rich, equivocal display that helps create the meanings of the later text; however, when that cited language or intertextual allusion attempts to go home again, to its original text, it will return subtly altered, speaking as it were with an accent and affecting the meaning of its original text. Each citation amounts to an interpretation that, applied to the intertext, alters or creates the meaning of that earlier text at the same time the earlier text, not just the citation, enters and interprets the later text. One might say that the intertextual allusion is a foot in the door, and that the remainder of the text can and must follow. The process is exponentially complicated by the inclusion of multiple "connectives."

Intertextuality and its effects are central concerns in this study of Wordsworth's choice of the Bible as intertext. Evidence of that intertextuality exists at both the micro- and macro-levels. Wordsworth's adaptations and interpretations of biblical language and forms are original and audacious. Whereas both Milton and Wordsworth interpret biblical texts through their intertextual invitations, their methods and results are quite different. Although he does not, of course, use the term *intertextuality,* John Dryden in his analysis of translation is clearly interested in the relationship of text to text. His categorization of the types of translation is useful in distinguishing Milton's intertextual practice from Wordsworth's. Dryden reduces all translation to three categories:

> metaphrase, or turning an author word by word, and line by line, from one language into another. . . . Paraphrase, or translation with latitude, where the author is kept in view by the translator, so as never to be lost, but his words are not so strictly followed as his sense; and that too is admitted to be amplified, but not altered. . . . [And] imitation, where the translator (if now he has not lost that name) assumes the liberty, not only to vary from the words and sense, but to forsake them both as he sees occasion; and taking only some general hints from the original, to run division on the groundwork, as he pleases. ("Preface to the Translation of Ovid's Epistles" 1:237)

Milton, although unorthodox, works to "justify" not only the ways of God to men, but the intertexts themselves. His work may be termed "paraphrase," in Dryden's sense. His textual transgressions, while remarkable, purport to take their "authority" from the biblical texts and from the tradition of biblical exegesis. Although constrained by his faith, Milton nevertheless revises and interprets and, indeed, remakes Christian mythology, a remarkable feat. Wordsworth's practice, by contrast, is that of "imitation" in Dryden's sense. He takes "general hints from the original," disguises his enterprise and covertly reworks the biblical texts, in the process interpreting them and radically transforming and deforming them. Milton's paraphrase is seldom paradoxical or ironic; Wordsworth's imitation often is. Dryden describes Wordsworth's "translation" of biblical texts when he says of imitation that it is "an endeavour of a later poet to write like one who has written before him, on the same subject; that is, not to translate his words, or to be confined to his sense, but only to set him as a pattern, and to write, as he supposes that author would have done, had he lived in our age and in our country" ("Preface to Ovid's Epistles" 1:239). When the intertext is the Bible, Dryden's phrase, like "one who has written before," suggests the reach of Wordsworth's enterprise and raises apparitions of biblical authors: Moses, the "first" author; David, poet-king; Solomon, philosopher-king; Ezekiel, God-maddened prophet; the visionary John of Patmos; St. Paul;

Jesus, prime author of parables—and behind them, God, as Holy Spirit, muse, divine author, and ultimate precursor.

That Wordsworth recognized not only his debt to Milton's originality (in taking the biblical texts as his intertexts), but also his own unique and quite different project, is suggested in Wordsworth's announcement of his own projected work, published as "Prospectus" to *The Excursion* (an early fragment from *Home at Grasmere*, ll. 959–1049). Of this passage it has been said that it "stands as the manifesto of a central Romantic enterprise against which we can conveniently measure the consonance and divergences in the writings of his contemporaries" (Abrams 14) and that it is the "most defiantly unorthodox manifesto of a naturalistic humanism" (Bloom and Trilling 143). In the "manifesto" Wordsworth quotes and echoes Milton's *Paradise Lost*, invoking Milton's text as intertext, and also Milton's muse, Urania, or, in a telling gesture, "a greater Muse," in order to transcend the self-imposed limits of Milton's poetry (of paraphrase), the established boundaries of the Miltonic cosmos (bordered by the veil of the biblical "Heaven of heavens"), and Milton's conception of the divine (the terrifying "Jehovah—with his thunder"), whom the later poet will pass "unalarmed" ([ll. 979–4]). Whereas Milton's intertextual work is circumscribed by religious awe and the demands of personal faith, Wordsworth's is virtually unrestricted, opening on an unknown, unbounded realm of mind, a space that the poet would create through his verse for his own explorations and wherein the only landmarks to be found, the only bridges across the abysses, are the poet's chosen intertexts. Thus, the biblical and Miltonic transtextuality (in Genette's sense) and intertextual connectives (in Riffaterre's sense) of the "Prospectus" passage fill up the Wordsworthian text and transform it, while at the same time they are themselves interpreted and altered. As Miller's metaphor of the host suggests, one who opens his door to such guests makes at once a generous and sinister gesture: his guests may consume him or eat him out of house and home; or, on the contrary, he may serve the guests for lunch; or host and guests may sit companionably at the feast. However it goes, a new semantic and semiotic unit is formed by text and intertext, making them uneasy contemporaries who "hold communion" as meanings and signs flash from text to text, revealing both host and guest in a new light.

POETICS

There are also various other reasons why repetition and apparent tautology are frequently beauties of the highest kind. Among the chief of these reasons is the interest which

the mind attaches to words, not only as symbols of the passion, but as things, active and ef-
ficient, which are of themselves part of the passion.
                   —Wordsworth, "Note to 'The Thorn,'" *Oxford P. W.* 594

It has been well demonstrated that Wordsworth's revolutionary poetics is pervaded by biblical influences.[8] The biblical model affects virtually every aspect of Wordsworth's theory: his notions of poetic diction, style, and subject; of the poem and poet; and of poetic figuration, inspiration and composition. His and others' choice of the biblical model resulted in a radical swerve in poetic theory from that of neoclassical poets and critics, who looked to Greek and Latin models for the principles of poetry and who conceived of poetry essentially as entertainment.[9] By contrast, as Murray Roston demonstrates, biblical literature "had a sacred function to perform, and one which raised it to the level of a priestly task." Romantic poetry "stood closer to the prophetic tradition, catching fire from its sparks" (39). The biblical prophet was an inspired man speaking to men, using a language charged with passion, spirit, and purpose, but nevertheless a common, concrete language drawn from everyday activities and scenes; Ezekiel's call to prophesy, for example, is couched in the most concrete of terms: "And [God] said to me . . . 'eat this scroll that I give you and fill your stomach with it.' Then I ate it; and it was in my mouth as sweet as honey" (Ez. 3:3). Recognizing the shift from classical to Hebraic models in the years between the Augustan and the Romantic periods illuminates many aspects of Wordsworth's poetics (whose first formal articulation appears as the "Advertisement to *Lyrical Ballads*" [1798]) and makes apparent the profound influence on poetic theory exerted by the biblical texts. Wordsworth has spoken of these aspects of his theory in both prose and verse, and I shall review some key points here.

POETIC DICTION AND THE WORD

Recognizing that Wordsworth's revolutionary impact on poetic language owes much to his discovery of the Bible as poetry, it is nevertheless important to remember that he owes a substantial debt to Robert Lowth's biblical criticism—not only for its calling attention to the art of biblical poetry, but also for the specific attributes he singles out for discussion and praise. As Prickett shows, Lowth's *Lectures on the Sacred Poetry of the Hebrews* not only redefined the conception of biblical poetry, but "in the long run, they were to redefine the notion of 'poetry' itself." Lowth, Prickett argues, like Wordsworth after him, "implicitly rejects the stilted conventions of Augustan poetic diction, and praises instead the 'simple and unadorned' language of Hebrew verse, that gains its 'almost ineffable sublimity' not from elevated terms, but from the depth and universality of its subject-matter" (*Words and* The Word 41–2). Also for Lowth as for Wordsworth, the "poetic" was not a quality peculiar to verse; rather it was a "vent for over-charged feelings, or a full imagination" (*Words and* The Word 46). These concepts not only encourage a reconsideration of poetry and the poetic but, coming as they do from the realm of biblical studies, do so in a context in which the biblical poets are seen as exemplars. It is therefore not surprising that Wordsworth's theoretical arguments against the style of the preceding age often draw on biblical examples and follow in many respects Lowth's lead.

As is clear throughout his critical prose, Wordsworth objects to the frequent "classical" personifications, the periphrastic devices, the "arbitrary and capricious habits of expression" (*Pr. W.* 1:124), the distancing devices ("a tissue of false thoughts, languid and vague expressions, unmeaning antithesis, and laborious attempts at discrimination" [*Pr. W.* 2:80]), and the tendency of poets to let the couplet have its way, imposing upon the sense of the verse. He wishes to adopt "the very language of men," which requires that he avoid what, he says, "is usually called poetic diction" (*Pr. W.* 1:130). As he explains in his Appendix to the "Preface," the early poets wrote "from passion excited by real events; they wrote naturally, and as men: feeling powerfully as they did, their language was daring and figurative." As Wordsworth saw it, "Poetic diction" was developed by later poets who, lacking the passion of the earlier ones, "set themselves to a mechanical adoption of those figures of speech [and] applied them to feelings and ideas with which they had no natural connection." As a result an artificial language was produced, "differing materially from the real language of men in *any situation.*" The artificiality increased and resulted in a perversion of taste. "Abuses . . . were imported from one nation to another, and with the progress of refinement this diction became daily more and more corrupt, thrusting out of sight the plain humanities of nature by a motley masquerade of tricks, quaintnesses, hieroglyphics, and enigmas" (*Pr. W.* 1:160–2). Significantly, Wordsworth illustrates this corruption of taste by comparing a passage from Proverbs with the versification of the same passage by Samuel Johnson. The biblical passage begins, "Go to the ant, thou Sluggard, consider her ways, and be wise: which having no guide, overseer, or ruler, provideth her meat in the summer and gathereth her food in the harvest" (Pr. 6:6–8). Johnson's version begins,

> Turn on the prudent Ant thy heedless eyes,
> Observe her labours, Sluggard, and be wise;
> No stern command, no monitory voice

Prescribes her duties, or directs her choice;
Yet, timely provident, she hastes away
To snatch the blessings of a plenteous day;
When fruitful Summer loads the teeming plain,
She crops the harvest and stores the grain.

A closer look at Johnson's translation reveals Wordsworth's specific objections to "poetic diction." In addition to rendering the proverb in (obligatory) iambic pentameter and rhymed couplets, Johnson has nearly doubled the number of words from the original (in place of 32 words he has 57). Whereas the Proverbs passage has no adjectives, Johnson has liberally sprinkled his lines with largely empty modifiers (*prudent, heedless, stern, monitory, timely, provident, plenteous, fruitful,* and *teeming*), none of which is figurative, only two of which (*fruitful* and *teeming*) might be considered descriptive, rather than expository, and none of which calls up a concrete image. Through such modifiers, Johnson's poetic scene is personified as a moral, animate entity, and even the summer is personified. As a result of Johnson's "poetic diction," the impatient admonition of the original text is muted, becoming in Johnson's passage witty, preachy, and slack. Wordsworth understands that for Johnson, as for many of his contemporaries, the strictures of poetic principles and forms dictate the sense of the poetry.[10]

As he calls into question established conventions of poetic diction, Wordsworth in effect brings poetry and prose closer together. In this matter, too, he is influenced by Lowth's reevaluation of biblical texts, which were perceived as "poetic," whether in prose or in verse. Moreover biblical verse was built on the principles of parallelism with its incremental and climactic use of repetition, a style that in no way resembled the mannered artfulness of eighteenth-century poetry. An example may be seen in Wordsworth's important "Note to 'The Thorn'"[11] as he defends repetition against a charge of tautology on the grounds that passion itself is repetitive; language being inadequate, a speaker will repeat the words that seem to suffice; and in any case, repetition and tautology "are frequently beauties of the highest kind" (*Oxford P. W.* 594). Wordsworth says that the beauty of repetition and its effective use "might be shewn by innumerable passages from the Bible and from the impassioned poetry of every nation." He cites several verses from the Song of Deborah as instances of the beautiful and efficacious use of repetition, including the justly famous description of the death of Sisera at the hands of Jael: "At her feet he bowed, he fell, he lay down: at her feet he bowed, he fell; where he bowed there he fell down dead" (*Oxford P. W.* 594). Such biblical language can serve as a model for the experimental poetry

Wordsworth is defending, for it is free of "poetic diction," far removed from the restrained, mannered, and at times verbose versifying authenticated by Pope, practiced by a host of eighteenth-century poets, and at the beginning of the nineteenth century still dictating poetic standards, although the work of the pre-Romantics, as Roston argues, had made inroads into the neoclassical citadel of poetic propriety (143–71). As Wordsworth implies, and as Coleridge explicitly argues, Wordsworth's poetic program to write poetry in the real language of men led him to biblical language.[12]

LANGUAGE: ITS DEFICIENCIES AND POWERS

Having rejected the conventions of well-entrenched poetic diction, however, Wordsworth was left with a "real" language, potent yet curiously inadequate, which resisted the poet's best efforts of expression. Faced with this fact, Wordsworth crafted a genuinely modern poetics,[13] cognizant, on the one hand, of the inadequacy and mutability of language and, on the other, of its life, its *thingness,* its materiality, its figurative force, and its power to create knowledge and refashion reality. A source for this new poetics was, once again, biblical literature, this time the New Testament doctrine of the Incarnation. A common eighteenth-century metaphor for language was that it was the "dress of thought." A thought, this metaphor implies, exists separately from the language used to articulate it and thus can appear in several sorts of dress—"what oft was thought but ne'er so well expressed"—suffering no real change as its costume changes. Wordsworth rejects this notion of equivalency between thought and a variety of possible expressions of it. Instead, he argues an early version of the twentieth-century idea that the medium is the message, turning to the fourth gospel's remarkable figuration of Jesus as the Word that becomes "flesh" and dwells among us. Wordsworth's adaptation of this trope to his own theory has been aptly called his "incarnational poetics" (Haney 2). It is here, at the heart of his poetics, that the crucial metaphorical move joins Word and word, God and poet, divine texts (the Bible and Nature) and human texts, thought and language.

In his incarnational poetics Wordsworth has implicitly recognized what he refers to in the "Essay, Supplementary to the Preface" as an "affinity between religion and poetry" (*Pr. W.* 3:65), an affinity (with a change in emphasis) explored by Kenneth Burke in his study *The Rhetoric of Religion:* "If we defined 'theology' as 'words about God,' then by 'logology' we should mean 'words about words.' Whereupon thoughts on the necessarily verbal nature of religious doctrines suggest a further possibility: that there might be fruitful analogies between the two realms. Thus statements that great theologians have made about the nature of 'God' might be adapted *mutatis mutandis* for use as purely secular observations on the nature of *words.*" There should be, Burke continues, "a correspondence between the theological and 'logological' realms" (1–2). The example of the Incarnation is for Burke the "first analogy, that between 'words' (lower case) and 'The Word' (in capitals)" (11). It is likewise, for Wordsworth, the first and organizing analogy. One of his key articulations of incarnational poetics (and his rejection of the idea that language is the "dress" of thought) occurs in a well and often wisely discussed statement in the *Essays Upon Epitaphs*[14]:

> Words are too awful an instrument for good and evil, to be trifled with; they hold above all other external powers a dominion over thoughts. If words be not (recurring to a metaphor before used) an incarnation of the thought, but only a clothing for it, then surely will they prove an ill gift; such a one as those possessed vestments, read of in the stories of superstitious times, which had power to consume and to alienate from his right mind the victim who put them on. Language, if it do not uphold, and feed, and leave in quiet, like the power of gravitation or the air we breathe, is a counter-spirit, unremittingly and noiselessly at work, to subvert, to lay waste, to vitiate, and to dissolve. (*Pr. W.* 2:84–5)

The remarkable passage begins with Wordsworth's assertion of the "awful" power of language not to "dress" thought, but to dominate it.[15] At the same time, words are associated with good and evil, good with *incarnation* (the Word), and evil with *dress* ("counter-spirit," with a devilish power "to lay waste, to vitiate, and to dissolve"). Thus evident in the passage is an apparent dualism (at once Christian and poetic, represented by Jesus and Satan), as well as the doctrine of the Incarnation: words (like the Word) must be the incarnation, not the dress, of thought. Nevertheless, as the passage continues it expresses resigned recognition, again in biblical terms—this time invoking the Fall—that assuming body or materiality (being incarnated) in words renders thoughts (like humanity and the embodied God) mutable, fallible, and mortal: "thoughts cannot . . . assume an *outward life* without a transmutation and a fall" (*Pr. W.* 2:85; emphasis supplied).

This passage, dating from 1810, is in intriguing ways a prose restatement of a figurative demonstration of these concepts that Wordsworth had made years before in Book 5 of the *Prelude*. While the entire book bears on "poetics" (including the relation of thought to language, "dress," embodiment, mutability, and death), one incident recounted there is particularly compelling. It concerns an abandoned pile of clothes, a ghastly search, and a "risen" body. This aspect of incarnational poetics and the episode of the drowned man of Book 5 is explored in chapter 3.

BIBLICAL NARRATIVE: THEMES AND FORMS

Less explicit but nevertheless crucial to Wordsworth's poetics is his habit of adapting the themes and genres or forms of biblical texts to his poetic enterprise. What Wordsworth appears to have found particularly congenial in the biblical forms—in particular, etymological or allegorical narratives, parables, and prophecies—is their emphasis on and demonstration of the power of language. Emerging from the various biblical genres is a view of language as efficacious—as a system able to create and shape reality, to extend human knowledge, to embody the visionary and the metaphysical, and to rescue from oblivion—all ideas integral to Wordsworth's poetics. Biblical language is that which of necessity attempts to reach beyond the realms of ordinary speech in order to articulate the heretofore unthought and unknowable—the mysterious nature of the "kingdom of heaven," for example, or things "hidden from the foundation of the world." Its methods are figure and condensation, metaphor pushed into narrative motion, which thus brings new epistemological possibilities into the world.

Wordsworth appropriated biblical models because he discovered in them that the radical rhetoric of Bible talk operates not only at the level of the word or the syntax of the sentence, but also at the level of text— narrative, song, prophetic utterance. His several revisions of biblical parables attest to this discovery. For example, one finds allusions to or revisions of the parable of false steward in Book 1 of the *Prelude* in the poet's failure to "multiply his talent" (269–71); of the good Samaritan in the discharged soldier narrative in Book 4:400–504; the parable of the lost sheep in Book 8:222–311; the parable of the prodigal son in *The Excursion* 4: 275–375 (Jeffrey 641); and, most elaborately, in *Michael,* discussed at length in chapter 5. Certainly Wordsworth appears to have agreed with Lowth and his translator that Lowth's biblical criticism is applicable to poetry in general. Lowth's translator introduces the *Lectures* by claiming that their utility "is by no means confined to that single object [Hebrew poetry], [for] they embrace all THE GREAT PRINCIPLES OF GEN-ERAL CRITICISM, as delivered by the ancients, improved by the keen judgment and polished taste of their author [Lowth]." In Lowth's work will be found, the translator says, "all the best rules of taste, and of all the principles of composition, illustrated by the boldest and most exalted specimens of genius . . . which antiquity has transmitted to us: and which have hitherto seldom fallen under the inspection of rational criticism" (Lowth, "The Translator's Preface" 1:1–2).

Among the narrative forms of particular interest to Wordsworth were parable (mentioned above), allegory, and etymological tale. Allegory is fundamental, as that term was now to be understood through Lowth's analysis. Chapter 4 begins from Wordsworth's motto for the *Poems on the Naming of Places,* suggesting that these poems are allegorical, and explores the relationship between them and the etymological tales of the Old Testament. The new understanding of metaphor and allegory acknowledges, but revises, the old notion that, as Thomas Percy puts it, the "literal sense" of a work (the Song of Solomon, in particular) conceals "sublime truths" (vi).[16] Certainly Wordsworth employed something akin to this theory of accommodation (the ancient notion that God "accommodates" his mysteries to human understanding by speaking in simple human terms of divine matters and mysteries) and extended it to poetry in general. Wordsworth's statement to this effect appears in the "Essay, Supplementary to the Preface," where he asserts that "The commerce between Man and his Maker cannot be carried on but by a process where much is represented in little, and the Infinite Being accommodates himself to a finite capacity" (*Pr. W.* 3:65). Wordsworth exploits this idea in his own poetry by interpreting God's accommodation to "finite capacity" in the second of God's two books, Nature, as his motto for the *Poems on the Naming of Places* indicates: "[Some minds] find tales and endless allegories / By river margins, and green woods among" (*P. W.* 2:486). Nature, as book, accommodates its divine mysteries to finite human capacity by representing much in little—*endless* allegories on the banks of rivers and in the woods—the "reading," interpretation, and communication of which is left to the poet-prophet, one singled out to receive Nature's message and convey it to others as poetry. Chapter 6 explores "Nutting" as a mystical allegory defined in connection with Lowth's discussion of the Song of Solomon. That chapter further explains the relationship of allegory to metaphor in the medium of narrative, recognizing the notion of allegorical levels of meaning, whose relationships and meanings depend on a radically polysemous and equivocating language, and acknowledging that knowledge of new or unknown semantic realms advances by means of metaphor, whose vehicles are made to participate in the dynamics of narrative.

METAPHYSICS

The [Romantic] artist is the man who goes out into the empty space between man and God and takes the enormous risk of attempting to create in that vacancy a new fabric of connections between man and the divine power.
—J. Hillis Miller, *The Disappearance of God* 13–4

This realization [that the objects of belief are unavoidably fictive] need not lead to non-belief. Indeed, critical self-consciousness suggests that all awareness is in some sense fictive. In this situation, belief seems both impossible (since its object has "disappeared") and inevitable (since we must believe in order to understand anything).

—Mark C. Taylor 212

In this section I am not primarily concerned with Wordsworth's "religion" per se, or lack of it. Useful studies explore this subject from different perspectives. For example, J. R. Watson's *Wordsworth's Vital Soul* approaches Wordsworthian "religion" from an anthropological standpoint, preferring the term *sacred* to *religious,* and calling upon ideas of Claude Lévi-Strauss, Mircea Eliade, Martin Buber, and others to argue "that much of Wordsworth's imaginative activity is governed by structures which are close to those of religious experience, and that this is a major reason for Wordsworth's continued importance" (13). Nancy Easterlin's *Wordsworth and the Question of "Romantic Religion"* takes a psychological/sociological stance, from which to argue that Wordsworth's poetry is characterized by a "partial consciousness of the conflict between metaphysical striving and creative writing that results in some of the distinctive stylistic and formal innovations of romanticism" (31). Prickett's *Romanticism and Religion* explores Wordsworth's philosophical ideas (Platonist and Naturalist) and finds an irresolvable contradiction: "in the very midst of the unity Wordsworth so successfully affirms . . . [there appears to be] a no less fundamental dichotomy that lies so deep as to be apparently inseparable from the same qualities that make him the greatest poet of his age" (82).

I am interested in a point of generally common agreement among critics that at the heart of the relationship between Wordsworth's ideas, philosophical and religious, and his poetry exists an irresolvable tension, contradiction, paradox, or "two-sidedness," a characteristic that at times results in critical reservations about either his "philosophy" or the value of the poetry.[17] As Prickett puts it, "Few poets can have been hailed as truly great with so many misgivings as Wordsworth has been." He points out that almost from the beginning critics such as John Stuart Mill and Matthew Arnold (both of whom admired Wordsworth and had been deeply affected by the poetry) were "among the quickest to deny the power of his philosophy and the validity of the kinds of religious experience he was credited with having opened up" (*Romanticism and Religion* 70). Easterlin ascribes this separation of Wordsworth from the philosophers to "a conflict between religious and aesthetic aims" (31). And Keith G. Thomas finds "an increasing tension, in general terms, between epistemology and metaphysics, what the mind knows and how it knows" (22).

While individual critics differ about just where the tension lies, the consistency with which readers talk about tension dictates that one take that tension or two-sidedness as given. J. Hillis Miller says that "any thoughtful reading" of Wordsworth's poems results in "an encounter with the blankness of an irresolution" (*Linguistic Moment* 68). I will claim that the tension resulting from such irresolution is sheer craft, productive of and necessary to both the metaphysics and the art. The contradiction, tension, two-sidedness—call it what one will—is generated in and by the poet's attempt to render or to create in words the quite literally ineffable. The result is a characteristic linguistic torsion, a language under stress—powerfully evocative, equivocal, and polysemous. Moreover, this torsion that results from Wordsworth's constant testing of the limits of language is one of the poetry's great virtues. One reason for the tension lies in the fact that Wordsworth's metaphysics arises from his attempt or series of attempts to articulate what might be called the contradiction or paradox inherent in the post-Enlightenment (especially post-Kantian) world of ideas and in the almost oxymoronic term "modern religion." I am, therefore, interested in the rhetorical/linguistic interaction in the poems and the emergence of a metaphysics in or through the poetic, the ways in which these act and interact as mutual cause and effect, and the ways in which Wordsworth's dependence upon the biblical intertexts helps constitute that central paradox.

The epigraph from Miller comes from a work in which he speaks of the disappearance of God coincident with the age of Wordsworth at the dawn of the modern era. In similar terms Martin Heidegger speaks of the "default of God," a time when "the divine radiance has become extinguished in the world's history." The era, he says, "is defined by the god's failure to arrive" (91), which absence produces "destitute times." He says, "To be a poet in a destitute time means: to attend, singing, to the trace of the fugitive gods. This is why the poet in the time of the world's night utters the holy" (94). Theophilosopher Mark C. Taylor agrees that "the *disappearance* of the distinct or separate form of the holy becomes the *appearance* of a radically new experience of the sacred. This new religious experience becomes possible only with the death of the transcendent God" (3). Without a doubt, the Wordsworth of the Great Decade, greatest of poets in this "time of the world's night," does experience a new order of sacrality, an experience that hovers always between belief and disbelief. Even acknowledging that "there hath passed away a glory from the earth," still the poet seeks traces of the absent divine, and attempts by whatever linguistic and rhetorical means he can discover to utter the holy. Yet the Wordsworthian holy is elusive, so difficult to capture in language, that it appears in the poems as a great shape-shifter, capable of appearing at one time as a powerful all-encompassing but "disturbing" presence (as in "Tintern Abbey"); at another, a terrifying and monstrous "mode of being" (as in the boat-stealing episode in Book I of the *Prelude*); or an appropriating, death-dealing "poet" in "Three years she grew"; and at still another, an "eternal mind," a longed-for being with whom communion has been irretrievably lost, but who continues to "haunt," whose nonabsent absence occasions that attempt to follow the traces of the fugitive god, "which we are toiling all our lives to find, / In darkness lost, the darkness of the grave" ("Intimations Ode").

THE POET AS PROPHET

> *And I saw a new heaven and a new earth: for the first heaven and the first earth were*
> *passed away.*
> —Rev. 21:1; emphasis supplied

> *I seemed about this period to have sight*
> *Of a new world, a world, too, that was fit*
> *To be transmitted and made visible*
> *To other eyes. . . .*
> —Prelude 12:370–73; emphasis supplied

In following those traces, Wordsworth in general accepted biblical literature and biblical author(s) as models for poetry, the poet, poetic inspiration, and composition. The biblical background is so omnipresent as often to go unnoticed—the white noise of the texts. In the epigraph, for example, the apocalyptic promise of a new earth and new heaven, "seen" by the prophet of Revelation, almost enters into the *Prelude* passage in which the poet has *seemed* to see a new world, which not-quite-vision almost bestows on the poet the prophetic function of transmitting the new world to "other eyes." In his chapter 3, entitled "Poetry and prophecy: The language of the Great Code," Prickett questions the critical tradition culminating in M. H. Abrams' *Natural Supernaturalism*, which accepts as "*the* distinguishing hallmark of Romanticism" a "process of displacement and secularization" described by Abrams as the reduction of a three-part system of creator, creation, and creature (as exemplified in Augustine's *Confessions*) to a two-part system of creation (nature) and creature (human mind), in which process the attributes and functions of God are "inherited . . . by the two remaining components of Augustine's triad, nature and the human 'soul' or 'mind'" (Abrams 90). Prickett is not comfortable with this position, calling attention not to contrasts, but to clear parallels between the *Confessions* and the *Prelude:* "what strikes the reader about the *Prelude* is not so much its secularity, as a kind of disconcertingly inappropriate religiosity that suddenly obtrudes itself into the narrative for no very obvious reason" (*Words and* The Word 97). After analyzing several passages in which Wordsworth and others claim the prophetic role, Prickett comments, "Though it is argued just a little too vehemently to be a critical commonplace, the identification of the poet with the prophet of old so permeates Romantic thought that it is easy to lose sight of just how dramatic a critical revolution lies behind it" (102). On the face of it, this identification of poet and prophet denies Romantic secularization: "This is, given its historical context, not so much the language of secularization, but of religious revival" (Prickett 104).[18]

How can Wordsworth's poetry and poetics lead two careful, thoughtful critics to such radically different conclusions, both persuasive in their ways? Is Wordsworth poet or prophet? Is he involved in a process of secularization, or of religious revival? The question is not quite answered by Miller's assertion that "The central assumption of romanticism is the idea that the isolated individual, through poetry, can accomplish the 'unheard of work,' that is, create through his own efforts a marvelous harmony of words which will integrate man, nature, and God" (*Disappearance of God* 14), because, for one thing, the existence of God, or the divine, in any traditionally understood form is in question, and the "unheard of work" necessitates creating the divine as well. Nor does Abrams' analysis eliminate the divine (or supernatural or metaphysical concepts) from Wordsworth's thought. Rather, as suggested, these are absorbed into creation and creature, Nature and mind, immanent and uncanny. It has been said that one effect of the Enlightenment was to permit the emergence of a "specific dimension of the uncanny": "To put it simply, in premodern societies the dimension of the uncanny was largely covered (and veiled) by the area of the sacred and untouchable. It was assigned to a religiously and socially sanctioned place. . . . With the triumph of the Enlightenment, this privileged and excluded place . . . was no more" (Dolar 7). Homeless forms of the holy are set loose. That old heaven and earth, with its "personal form" of strength or terror—Jehovah on his "empyreal throne" surrounded by a "quire / Of shouting angels" (*Home at Grasmere* 980–3)—made places for the sacred (heaven, hell, temples, and other sacred precincts associated with worship), which (with small reservations) constituted the "religiously and socially sanctioned place." Crafted of words by ancient and recent prophet-poets, heaven and hell and the temples associated with them become in post-Enlightenment times quite literally irreconcilable with the universe as reconstituted in the Newtonian revolution and the philosophy formulated for this new world.

Part of the prophet-poet's task now would seem to be to follow the trace of the absent divine and in language to reconstitute a divinity or a metaphysical presence who might make a home in a Newtonian universe that by its nature is inhospitable to the holy. To make visible to others a "new world," requires nothing less than the creation of that world—"I had a world about me—'twas my own, / I made it"—and the "incarnation" of that world in words, the prophet's function. "Some called it madness; such indeed it was, . . . / If prophesy be madness" (*Prelude* 3:142–51). For Wordsworth, at least, the world of words, made of its linguistic structures and metaphoric identities, is *the* world, thoughts made flesh, but nevertheless crafted of parts whose adequacy and stability are always in question. Wordsworth's paean to the writers of romances suggests his understanding of the power of language to create reality. It is through these old romances that we feel

> With what, and how great might [their authors] are in league,
> Who make our wish, our power, our thought a deed,
> An empire, a possession. *Ye whom time*
> *And seasons serve—all faculties—to whom*
> *Earth crouches, th' elements are potter's clay,*
> *Space like a heaven filled up with northern lights,*
> *Here, nowhere, there, and everywhere at once.*
>   (*Prelude* 5:550–57; emphasis mine)

Despite this power of language to incarnate wishes and thoughts, to work the elements like clay, and to create a light-filled "space like a heaven," it is nevertheless always capable—always on the verge—of becoming counter-spirit, "unremittingly and noiselessly at work, to subvert, to lay waste, to vitiate, and to dissolve." Evidence of this subversive inclination lies in the resonance of the *nowhere/everywhere* contrast, a paradoxical pair that tends to invoke the God described by Hermes Trismegistus as "a circle whose center is everywhere and whose circumference is nowhere." What manner of place is this? Is it a world of romance (secular), or a place suffused with, filled by, some new order of the sacred or overseen by some supernatural uncanniness?

To return to the problem posed above, part of the difficulty in deciding whether Wordsworth's impulse is religious or secular lies just here in the linguistic recalcitrance, the power of language to slip its bounds, and as counter-spirit to say the unthought, not to create, but to dissolve and destroy. Supposing that Wordsworth's thought is secular, for him to "embody" that thought in the language of religion (*God, priest, prophet, vows, heaven, blessings,* and so forth) and of specific religious texts and doctrines is to call into his works on the skirts of the intertexts their ancient meanings, something of their order of the holy, their now wandering ghosts and gods, and the spirit realm they once called home. Hence Wordsworth through his language reanimates the universe crafted by science and mathematics, from which God has disappeared, investing it with an uncanny spirit. More than any other writer, Wordsworth is responsible for reinvesting the Newtonian Nature with a terrible modern holiness and restoring the ghost to the Newtonian machine, albeit a ghost that is all "spirit"—breath, inspiration, speech, words. That is, he makes language the joint between religious and secular. Imaginatively to identify or call into being a mysterious entity and to name it "Wisdom and spirit of the universe," "Nature," "Universal Mind," "presence," or even "God" is to employ the power of words to recall that which no longer "is," which never was, or which has "disappeared," into another incarnation; to invite this being into close proximity, into "thingness" in the realm of language, where it then becomes accessible to a virtually limitless number of predicates, thereby capable of acting and suffering in narrative. Which is originary—the imagination/thought/naming process, or the "real thing" itself? The poet will not decide the issue:

> To unorganic natures I transferred
> My own enjoyments, *or,* the power of truth
> Coming in revelation, I conversed
> With things that really are. . . .
> (*The Prelude* 2: 410–13; emphasis supplied)

What is being described, and which answer is preferred—psychological projection *or* (divine) revelation? Are they the same? Is one a metaphor for the other? The poetry does not rule out any possibility. As Wordsworth suggests, there is somehow no beginning, because language, vision, spirit, body, mystery, and being are unaccountably contemporaneous and congruent: "Visionary power / Attends upon the motions of the winds / Embodied in the mystery of words" (*Prelude* 5 619–21). Which is primary? Vision, spirit-winds, body-words, the mystery of their coexistence? Is this claim secular, or religious? One is tempted to say that like the Arab-Quixote figure in Book 5 of the *Prelude* it is "Neither and both at once."

In Wordsworth's shifting and equivocal world of words, metaphysical rhetoric is the most difficult language of all. As Kenneth Burke has argued, the language of metaphysics is radically metaphorical; it is always borrowed from the human realms of nature, society, politics, and language itself (these orders of terms covering "the world of everyday experience, the empirical realm for which words are preeminently suited" (14–15); these borrowed terms are then adapted through rhetorical devices to that which is always beyond the physical or greater than the natural. Rhetorical operations such as analogy or metaphor are useful, as is the small but powerful negative morpheme. Thus the effable ("capable of being expressed in words") becomes paradoxically the Ineffable— that is, that entity incapable of being expressed in words, even as it is named. Similar terms are *the Invisible, the Incomprehensible, the Immortal, the Immutable, the Timeless,* all suggesting through negative morphemes that which exceeds the natural or the physical, presenting the *super*natural or *meta*physical forms of the natural conditions of visibility, comprehensibility, mortality, mutability, and time. In considering this sort of linguistic operation, a passage in the *Prelude* comes to mind. It concerns the description of a theatrical production in which Jack the Giant-Killer dons his magic "coat of darkness" and becomes "invisible," "from the eye / Of living mortal safe," and "atchieves his wonders." Faithful, credulous, the audience "perceives" the wonders embodied in and accomplished through language, for Jack wears a black cloak, and "the word / INVISIBLE flames forth upon his chest" (7:303–10), the negative morpheme making Jack "metaphysical" in denying visibility by very visible means. Wordsworth ironically comments that he is delighted "To watch crude Nature work in untaught minds, / to note the laws and progress of belief" (297–9).

The astonishing maneuver of Wordsworth, I would argue, is actually to reverse this rhetorical process that Burke describes (of pressing empirical terms into metaphysical roles), by taking from his biblical and other intertexts certain language originally borrowed from the empirical realms to speak of supernatural matters. Now, having passed through the old texts, the "natural" language has been charged with metaphysical and supernatural associations (even when, as in parable, it purports to speak of "this world"). When Wordsworth presses it again into the service of a new poetry for a radically changed nature, the charged language brings its metaphysical intimations which invest the ordinary matters of which it now speaks with a kind of sacrality and spirit.

This argument differs from that of Abrams, whose point in *Natural Supernaturalism* is that a Romantic process, exemplified in Wordsworth's poetic practice, of "progressive secularization" involves "the assimilation and reinterpretation of religious ideas, as constitutive elements in a world view founded on secular premises" (13). My argument shifts the focus from ideas to language. I would say that Wordsworth's biblical language is like photographic film that has at some time been exposed, but is now used again for new photographs. These "double negatives" when developed reveal the newer pictures ambiguated and in a sense haunted by the ghostly images of the original exposures against which or through which one is forced to "see" them. A case in point is the story of the lost sheep recounted in the *Prelude* (8:222–311).[19] On its surface the tale is perfectly ordinary and secular, the story of a father and son who go look-ing for a lost sheep. But complicating the interpretation is a constant awareness of the biblical parable, that other "exposure," along with its context, meanings, and interpretations, which not only render the pre-sent "natural" tale equivocal, but invest it with metaphysical implications. In the biblical parable, the narrator is Jesus, and the sheep is a sinner whose recovery occasions "making merry" in both earth and heaven; in a parallel parable in the same chapter (Luke 15), the lost (or prodigal) son is likewise a sinner whose return occasions great joy. In Wordsworth's re-vision, however, one must ask how to understand, for example, the fact that the son is lost while looking for the sheep? What is implied by the fact that the sheep is lost forever in the raging stream, while the boy is found? Having called into his text the ancient and mysterious tale, Wordsworth cannot write/rewrite the parable without parabolic mean-ing. Metaphysical lint clings to the biblical language and genres when Wordsworth transports them back from the intertexts into his seemingly naturalistic tale, a condition that produces an astonishing irony, equivo-cation, and tension as the text flickers between secular and religious im-plications and between natural and supernatural realms. These notions of linguistic double-exposure and metaphysical lint, while they do not re-solve the question of Wordsworth's secularity or religiosity, do account for the tension readers perceive and the quite different readings offered by critics like Abrams and Prickett.

My conclusion is that an understanding of several complexities is en-hanced by a focus on language, rather than ideas, philosophical or reli-gious. Wordsworth's language resists efforts to settle the question of a religious or secular orientation, because it artfully and faithfully enacts the dilemma of a poet in a destitute time; to attempt to "resolve" the questions implicit in the language, to say it is either this or that, is to do violence to the art. One matter is clear: occupying, as he did, a pivotal place in history, Wordsworth refashioned poetry; he started over. Harold Bloom is unequivocal on this point: "Wordsworth . . . can be said to have invented modern poetry, which has been a continuum for two full cen-turies now." Bloom concludes that Wordsworth "inaugurated the bless-ing/curse" of modern poetry, "which is that poems are 'about' nothing," by which he means that "Their subject is the subject herself or himself, whether manifested as a presence or as an absence" (*The Western Canon* 239). Bloom makes an important point, but more needs to be said in this context, for *nothing* is one of those slippery, Burkean words formed of a negative (the no thing, that which falls short of, exceeds, evades, or transcends thingness) and laden with metaphysical implications. In many ways, it is the ultimate linguistic form of the metaphysical. And while Bloom does not elaborate (simply asserting the nothingness of the artist as the subject of art), Wallace Stevens offers a kind of gloss, describing a familiar Wordsworthian "listener, who listens in snow, / And, nothing himself, beholds / Nothing that is not there and the nothing that is" ("The Snow Man"). That is, Stevens suggests at least two (and probably three) orders of *nothing* along with their presence or absence, all pertinent to this analysis: first, the self as nothing, *no thing* because immaterial as consciousness "is" immaterial; second, the Nothing of Nothings, *No thing* (with a capital) that is absent (not there) yet seen (beheld); and, third, the *no thing,* that is present and seen, nature as specular image of the beholder whose nothingness this present nothing reflects. (After all, what does a snow man—water-become-snow-become-man-image—"behold" in the snowy landscape?) Taylor's chapter, "How to do Nothing with Words," is pertinent both to the metaphysical issue I have been exploring and to Bloom's claim of poetic originality for Wordsworth. As Taylor explains, this metaphysical nothing "is the unthought that we are now called to think. The nothing that remains to be thought is not simply the opposite of being but 'is' *neither* being *nor* nonbeing" (205). Wordsworth's readers are called to think the unthought, the nothing and the Nothing that lie beyond the end, beyond the failure of the god (that Nothing) to appear. I shall take up this problem of representing nothing in chapters 7 and 8, which concern themselves with Wordsworthian apocalyptics.

   To sum up this introduction, I have argued for a reconsideration of the impact of biblical texts and criticism on Wordsworth's revolutionary poetry and poetics and have separated for consideration three interrelated, language-centered issues that such a reconsideration entails: the intertextual, the poetic, and the metaphysical. Succeeding chapters will develop the points I have introduced here and relate them to specific texts.

CHAPTER 2

The Word as Borderer

INCARNATIONAL POETICS—THE THEORY

And the word became flesh and dwelt among us. . . .

—Jn. 1:14

Visionary Power
Attends upon the motions of the winds
Embodied in the mystery of words.

—*Prelude* 5:619–21

I n taking up the matter of Wordsworth's incarnational poetics, I am admittedly retracing well-traveled ground. Frances Ferguson's *Wordsworth: Language as Counter-Spirit* offers one of the early and best discussions of the subject. In that work Ferguson calls attention to the eternal difficulty encountered in any discussion of language—the absence of a nonlinguistic control "against which to measure language" (1)[1]—and provides invaluable exploration of Wordsworth's linguistic speculations in support of the claim "that Wordsworth thought seriously and coherently about language in both his prose and poetry" (xi). Ferguson emphasizes the poet's departure from the often-discussed metaphor of Romantic organicism in his positing of the epitaph as a metaphor for poetry (xii),[2] a metaphor that, Ferguson claims, exists in tension with the notion of "linguistic 'incarnation.'" He comments, "Although Wordsworth might seem to offer 'language-as-incarnation' as a replacement for the eighteenth-century notion of 'language-as-dress,' both the *Essays upon Epitaphs* and Wordsworth's poetry generally prompt a reevaluation of what linguistic 'incarnation' might be" (xvi). Ferguson finds that the "'fallings from us,' the 'vanishings' within the life of the individual, and the multiple miniature deaths which figure as a part of that Wordsworthian life suggest that neither human incarnation nor linguistic incarnation is a fixed form which can be arrived at and sustained" (xvi). Finding that a correlation between language and death becomes a "complex dialectic" in the third "Essay upon Epitaphs," Ferguson observes that "To insist upon language as incarnation in essays devoted to epitaphs is a strange tack, because the incarnation of language comes into direct opposition with the factual deaths, the de-incarnation of the actual human beings who are memorialized in the epitaphs" (30–31). A difficulty here and elsewhere seems to lie in the assumption that the meaning of "language as incarnation" is self-evident. There is a questionable logic in speaking of Wordsworth's *de-incarnation* of the dead. Death in either Christian theology or Wordsworthian poetics does not imply de-incarnation or disembodiment. The embodied states for the dead that find a variety of expressions in Wordsworth's poetry are, in chief, three: first, deprived of perception, breath, and movement, the dead may achieve a denser, nonpersonal order of embodiment or materiality when they are assimilated to nature, as is Lucy, "Rolled round in earth's diurnal course / With rocks and stones and trees" ("A slumber did my spirit seal"); second, they may achieve a denser, but still "personal" order of embodiment (as does the statued form of the drowned man or the book that *is* a Shakespeare or Milton [*Prelude* 5:163–5; 480–1]); finally (and usually seen in conjunction with one of the two possibilities just described), they may be *reincarnated*. As I shall argue below, during a significant period of his poetic career Wordsworth entertained two ideas of reincarnation—both as reembodiment of the soul and the more figurative reembodiment in words as things—or as Wordsworth says, the dead need "not wholly perish" if they are privileged to speak, to find reincarnation in the matter of words (*Home at Grasmere* 903). In addition, Wordsworth also seems to entertain from time to time another possibility—the traditional Christian notion of transmutation of the body from *physical* body to *spiritual* body, as in the case of Lucy Gray. The notion of incarnational poetics is certainly, as Ferguson finds, implicated with life and death, with living bodies, dead bodies, and dead-but-living bodies, but the matter is complex and works variations and reversals on biblical, theological, and philosophical expressions of the mystery of the Word become flesh.

The most extensive recent discussion of Wordsworth's incarnational poetics is that of David P. Haney, from whom I borrow the term. Haney performs important work by tracing theological and philosophical ideas of the Incarnation from Augustine to Hegel in an argument that seeks to place Wordsworth's practice within the history of the sign, seeing it as a sort of major fault in semiological geology, dividing the Lockean sign (of which the speaker is the master) from structural and poststructural signs (of which the speaker is the slave) and, in fact, initiating changes that helped shape the modern conception of the sign (34). He emphasizes that radical shifts in linguistic theory were precipitated by both British empirical and German Kantian and post-Kantian philosophies. Augustine, he says, "had revitalized language and linked it to the concept of the Incarnation by means of the inner word," but Wordsworth, "true to his empiricist heritage and mindful of the Kantian dilemma, revitalized it by seeing language incarnated as 'living thing,' as part of the animated material world . . ." (24); further, Wordsworth's presentation of incarnational language "has no choice but to remain in the often frightening contingency of the material world" (25). Haney notices that this requirement forces a "reversal in the priority of sight and hearing" (25) from the Augustinian notion of the true, shining, *visible* "inner word," which assumes the "flesh" of articulate sound, to the *heard* "outer word," which Augustine saw as merely a sign of the word that gives light inwardly" (24). Goals of Haney's discussion are, he says, "to preserve the theological bases of Wordsworth's thought *and* to rescue this side of his thought from charges of naive logocentrism." These goals are not incompatible, he claims, unless "we confuse incarnational thought with the thought of representational adequacy, which . . . post-Saussurean critiques of Wordsworth have done" (20). Instead, he argues—correctly, I believe—that Wordsworth struggled to articulate a "nondualistic process of incarnational generation of meaning" (18).

Nevertheless, raising the issue of semiotics and Wordsworth's place in the history of the sign (and even acknowledging Wordsworth's influence on modern semiotics), Haney curiously denies that Wordsworth engages semiotics in his incarnational poetics. In Haney's view, what incarnational poetics offers is "an alternative to semiotic representation, not . . . a fundamentally semiotic theory of representational adequacy" (32). I would suggest, rather, that Wordsworth's theory *is* semiotic, and that what he does is to elaborate the Lockean notion of signs to include nonverbal forms, recognizing the inevitable role of language (as only one kind of sign system) to interpret and "translate" into or "embody" in words various kinds of nonverbal signs, including aural and visual natural signs (the cloud and smoke that signal rain and fire as well as the ambiguous, difficult "ghostly language of the ancient earth" or the "speaking face" of nature).[3] In approaching natural signs, Wordsworth worked at a time when the natural code was still in the process of being radically revised in culture's semiotic encyclopedia through the scientific and social revolutions of the preceding century.[4] Telling evidence of Wordsworth's awareness of the impact of the Newtonian revolution on that revision is to be found in the fact that the dream metaphor for nature's "book" in the *Prelude* is *"Euclid's Elements"* (an archetype for Newton's *Principia Mathematica*), a work that "held acquaintance with the stars, / And wedded man to man by purest bond / Of nature, undisturbed by space or time" (5:104–6). Wordsworth suggests something of the remote immensity and geometrical precision of this post-Newtonian book of nature, whose significance is in question and whose signs require interpretation and reinterpretation. Nature's system of signs is traditionally seen as a code to be read for what it reveals of transcendent mystery. A tradition of recognizing natural semiotics arises from the Old Testament's understanding that "The heavens declare the glory of God; and the firmament sheweth his handywork" (Ps. 19:1), and extends to medieval Neoplatonism's finding that "the entire sensible world is . . . a book written by the hand of God" wherein "all visible things" carry "symbolic instruction" as figures for the "declaring and signifying of things invisible" (Eco, *Semiotics and the Philosophy of Language* 103), to Milton's calling heaven "the Book of God" wherein humankind might "read his wondrous Works, and learn / His Seasons, Hours, or Days, or Months, or Years" (*Paradise Lost* 8:66–9), to Wordsworth's book of nature figured as *Euclid's Elements*. However, in Wordsworth's figure (a natural sign, a stone, which is a book) is clear evidence of a shifting, even a breaking, of the old natural code in his curious blending of the transcendental (where the effects of space and time [those Kantian pure forms of sensible intuition] are not felt), the "invisible," and the empirically scientific (mathematics and astronomy).[5] If nature's stony matter is a book (a code) with significance to be read and interpreted for insights into the universe, its creator, and the place of humans within it, Wordsworth must from his vantage radically revise the old "readings." And while not dismissing them, he must, in a way, call into question those interpretations, interrogating as in his time of crisis "all passions, notions, shapes of faith" (*Prelude* 10:889). At the heart of Wordsworth's effort to read the code of a radically changed nature are the recognitions, first, that verbal signs are inadequate but nevertheless indispensable to the task they must perform and, second, that the poet as he interprets and translates nature's code cannot depend on "literal" language, but must resort to verbal image and rhetorical trope, particularly metaphor, whose effects in any semiotics are simultaneously ambiguous, disruptive, creative, and regenerative. The entire book lies open before him, and he must identify its signs and then read them.[6] In a sense, Wordsworth must create a reading by which the emergent new world of science, along with whatever mysteries may lie within, beneath, or beyond it, may be known.

In the process, and working within the inherited labyrinth of words, associations, and texts, he invents or reinvents the notions of *nature, book,* and *things invisible.* [7]

Keith G. Thomas's careful analyses of the evolution of Wordsworth's language-centered epistemology are helpful in understanding the nondualistic process of which Haney speaks and Wordsworth's semiotics (with its figural base and multiple codes). Thomas, interested in Wordsworth's philosophy, traces his evolving epistemology from Alfoxden Notebook fragments through "Tintern Abbey" and the *Prelude* to the *Excursion.* While not specifically addressing the subject of incarnational poetics, Thomas's work offers insights into the poet's struggle with language and other sign systems, natural and human, their embodiment, and the implicit epistemology resulting therefrom. As Thomas shows, in Wordsworth's emphasis on the heard "word," he attempts to enunciate not only the reception and translation of what he thinks of as nature's language, what he calls the "power of sound," and "sounds that are / The ghostly language of the ancient earth / Or make their dim abode in distant winds" (epigraph), but also the human response, the soul, responding to the code, remembering "how she felt," but not "what she felt" (*Prelude* 2:335–6).[8] This unintelligible language from an unspecified source, transmitted through an obscure medium, brings messages encoded in the visual or auditory aspects of nature—the ancient earth, the distant winds. Nevertheless these "incommunicable powers" are able to "shape" the soul and "move" human thought, as in this passage from the Alfoxden Notebook:

> To his mind
> The mountain's outline and its steady form
> Gave simple grandeur and *its presence shaped*
> *The measure and the prospect of his soul*
> *To majesty,* such virtue had these forms
> Perennial of the aged hills nor less
> *The changeful language of their countenance*
> *Gave movement to his thoughts and multitude*
> *With order & relation.* (Quoted in Thomas 30; emphasis supplied)

The visual outline, form, and presence of the mountains, along with their speaking face (the "changeful language of their countenance") are signs that affect or, more accurately, *effect* thought—initiating, quickening, and giving "movement" to it, along with seemingly poetic attributes of "order & relation." It is such signs and their movement through thoughts that must then be incarnated, embodied in human words. The primary language of signs spoken through and embodied in nature (its sights and sounds) must enter, as unintelligible image, into the mind, moving and shaping thought and feeling, and then undergo a second semiotic cycle as the poet struggles to read and translate, searching through his cultural and personal "encyclopedias" to "make Breathings ['breath things'] for incommunicable powers" (*Prelude* 3:187–8), finally giving that originally nonverbal code (the not-yet-articulated or inarticulate Word) "flesh" in the materiality, the thingness, of human speech and text.

The language of nature, a ghostly or spiritual code, is the polar opposite of the incarnate word. As it is without body, its oxymoronic "inarticulate" words are perceived as affecting and quickening images conveyed to the mind as impressions by the physical senses (affecting *how* it feels but unable to convey *what* it feels), these to be "read" as signs by the mind, the bodiless soul, for the message lies "far hidden from the reach of words" (*Prelude* 2:185). Unintelligible and therefore in their ghostly form incommunicable, nature's signs require figurative embodiment (or "birthing") in the "flesh" of human language. In the process, the poet expands epistemological horizons in order to accommodate the cognitive accretions.

Louis Marin, in his exposition of the theories of the Port-Royal logicians, demonstrates why the Incarnation, especially as expressed in the Eucharist, is a key *linguistic* notion. It provides what he calls "a *chassé-croisé,* or back-and-forth movement, between language and image," whereby "language acquires from the image its force and mimetic form, while the image acquires from language its normative and juridical form." This movement is like the one with which Wordsworth is concerned in the lines quoted above, where there are two kinds of codes, and two kinds of embodiment: first, as image speaks to and moves thought, thought "reads" the signs and embodies them in words; then this language in its turn makes the mountains "mean," permits them to be known in heretofore unacknowledged ways. Marin says that the movement between language and image "finds a motive, if not a basis, in a specific sign and in the utterance that produces it—in the eucharistic sign and its consecratory utterance":

> By virtue of its very production and as a result of the pragmatic nature of the context in which it is uttered, this sign plays on both registers [language and image], although it is always excessive vis-à-vis the one as well as the other. With respect to language, the excesses of the eucharistic sign are evident when the utterance that produces it ("This is my body") is uttered by the authorized individual under the appropriate circumstances

[the priest performing the ritual]. The sign then has the power to transform a thing [the bread] that is shown by means of the demonstrative *this* into a body that is signified by the word *body.* This body belongs, not to the person who utters the formula, but to Him whose words are cited in it, that is, Jesus Christ. (xiv–xv)

This back-and-forth movement with its mutually constituting speaker, word, and thing evades the sort of dualism through which, as Haney argues, modern critiques have viewed the matter. Wordsworth's expression of this sort of nondualistic poetics is found in the *Essays upon Epitaphs.* Wordsworth's notion of incarnational poetics does not describe all language or all poetry, certainly not that poetry described as "tainted by the artifices which have overrun our writings in metre since the days of Dryden and Pope." Rather, incarnational poetics describes poetry that, Wordsworth says, is characterized by "Energy, stillness, grandeur, tenderness, those *feelings* which are the pure emanations of nature, those *thoughts* which have the infinitude of truth, and those *expressions* which are not what the garb is to the body but what the body is to the soul, *themselves a constituent part and power or function in the thought . . .*" (*Pr. W.* 2:84; emphasis supplied). Wordsworth stresses here the intricate coexistence and interaction of feelings as emanations of nature, true thoughts, and incarnational language, words that are "what the body is to the soul" and that themselves form "a constituent part and power or function in the thought." Thomas De Quincey expands upon this notion that language is inextricable from thought and offers perhaps the clearest explanation of the resistance of poetic incarnational thought to dualistic understanding. If thought and language existed in a dualistic system,

if language were merely a dress, then you could separate the two; you could lay the thoughts on the left hand, the language on the right. But generally speaking, you can no more deal thus with poetic thought than you can with soul and body. The union is too subtle, the intertexture too ineffable— each coexisting not merely with the other, but each in and through the other. An image, for instance, a single word, often enters into a thought as a constituent part. In short, the two elements are not united as a body with a separable dress, but as a mysterious incarnation. (De Quincey 10:230)

De Quincey's claim is not simply that what is said is of a piece with how it is said, but, echoing Wordsworth's assertion that incarnational language constitutes a "part and power or function in the thought," that poetic images and thoughts (or concepts) are joined in a "subtle," "ineffable" (unspeakable) union with language—both before and after they are uttered. The echoes between Wordsworth's claims and De Quincey's analysis are not accidental. De Quincey understood Wordsworth and his work as few others of his time did. Certain aspects of incarnational thought find helpful expression in De Quincey's notion of *involutes,* a term of his own coinage, which suggests the inextricable and clearly nondualistic relationships among language, thoughts, feelings, perceptions ("perplexed combinations of concrete objects"), and meaning (De Quincey 1:39). Poetic language has no option but to attempt to express not thought, not feeling, not image (concrete object), but the significance of the compound experience, the involute, in which the parts are "incapable of being disentangled." In the Wordsworth passage cited above, the mountains, concrete objects perceived as images, offer feelings of "simple grandeur," shape the "measure and the prospect of [the] soul," and give movement, multitude, order, and relation to thought through their "changeful language." That is, as De Quincey puts it, "thoughts and feelings pass to us through perplexed combinations of concrete images" (De Quincey 1:39). An image or word does not represent thought, but "enters the thought as a constituent part," and participates in the "mysterious incarnation."[9]

Finally, this incarnational background would not be complete without mention of Alan Bewell's analysis of Wordsworth's place in what he calls "the history of death." Bewell opens his discussion with a point that, while obvious, is easy to lose sight of, namely that "Since we cannot experience death and also describe it, it is necessarily primarily a product of representation." As heirs of millennia of "elaborate fictions" representing death, which have filled "this unknowable gap with heavenly and spectral worlds," the Romantic poets "most frequently view death as a cultural phenomenon, which derives its specific character and coloration from human beings." As a result, "theirs is not the story of how death came into the world as a condition, but instead how it came into being as an idea" (187). While Bewell's interest is in demonstrating Wordsworth's use and revision of various Enlightenment ways of understanding death and traditions of thinking about death, rather than in incarnational poetics per se, his argument is pertinent to this study. Bewell finds that Wordsworth's interest in death is part of a wider concern with language-made realities—with custom and tradition—and the ways in which human understanding, behavior, and existence are shaped within and by those realities. Metaphysical "realities," including death, resurrection, and afterlife are a part of that linguistic/textual tradition, aspects of "custom." Bewell focuses his argument in a discussion of the "blind poet" of the "Intimations Ode," observing

In the figure of the blind poet struggling to see once more through words, Wordsworth found a means of *linking the themes of death and resurrection with the poetic issue of remaking language.* If the dead reside as much in language as in the grave, then a far greater death occurs when language is no longer a celestial soil but a grave of custom, "heavy as frost, and deep almost as life" (229–30; emphasis supplied).

Bewell observes that in his personal crisis Wordsworth nevertheless strives to give "intense expression to a larger cultural problem—that of the life and death of tradition":

> The figure of the blind poet, struggling with words that no longer allow him to see a glory now "past away," *dramatizes Wordsworth's belief that a tradition and poetry, which had its origin in Virgil's [messianic] prophecy, had become ossified and needed to be remade.* . . . From this perspective, the theme of resurrection that informs the poem ["Intimations Ode"] is less a theological than a poetic and cultural issue. (230; emphasis supplied)[10]

Bewell has begun what I find a persuasive argument, one which I wish to pursue in connection with Wordsworth's incarnational poetics: That the Wordsworthian desire to "sing a nobler song"[11] arises from the perception that the inherited poetic fashionings of life and death will not suffice; they are no longer relevant to human experience at the turn of the nineteenth century—a "destitute time," in the world from which "there hath past away a glory." Although after 1806 Wordsworth moves gradually toward orthodoxy in his view of an afterlife and his revisionary efforts are reduced to occasional reversions, the transition is slow. As early as 1802, in "To H. C.," and 1804 in the stanzas added to the "Intimations Ode," Wordsworth entertained the notion of reincarnation as an alternative not only to death, but to life in the traditional heaven. In 1810, in the first of the *Essays upon Epitaphs,* he is still entertaining his own version of reincarnation, whose shape may be seen in recurring imagery. Similar imagery links "To H. C.," the additions to "Intimations Ode," and the 1805 lyric "Stepping Westward" with the speculations about reincarnation in the first essay. In all of these life is seen as a cyclical and endless journey (in three of these, as a voyage over water) moving through time into eternity and returning again to the realms of time, figured in or associated with the movement of the sun. In the first essay, for example, Wordsworth remarks,

> As, in sailing upon the orb of this planet, a voyage towards the regions where the sun sets, conducts gradually to the quarter where we have been accustomed to behold it come forth at its rising . . . so the contemplative Soul, travelling in the direction of mortality, advances to the country of everlasting life; and, in like manner, may she continue to explore those

cheerful tracts, *till she is brought back, for her advantage and benefit, to the land of transitory things—of sorrow and of tears.* (Pr. W. 2:53; emphasis supplied)

"To H. C." presents the "Faery Voyager" as one who is in the process of returning to time from eternity; he has brought his fancies "from afar." In the "Intimations Ode," the Platonic Soul/Star "that rises with us . . . / Hath had elsewhere its setting, / And cometh from afar." The "immortal sea" is both origin and destination of the Soul/Star, figured in the sun that rises and sets and rises again. By the poem's end, this star is again setting, apparently beginning another cycle of exploration through the "cheerful tracts" before rising once again: "The Clouds that gather round the setting sun / Do take a sober colouring from an eye / That hath kept watch o'er man's mortality." In "Stepping Westward," the journey is over land, but the eye of the traveler, as in "Intimations Ode," is on the sky— and "such a sky"—and the direction, like the sun's, is westward:

> The dewy ground was dark and cold;
> Behind all gloomy to behold;
> And stepping westward seemed to be
> A kind of *heavenly* destiny.

The question the Scottish woman asks, "What you are stepping westward?" echoes significantly for the speaker, imbues with "human sweetness" "the thought / Of travelling through the world that lay / Before me in my endless way." The endless way, like the path of the sun, has no destination other than eternal return. Implicit in each of these texts is the heterodox notion of reincarnation—one of several alternatives to Christian orthodoxy and the received traditions that Wordsworth entertains poetically during and beyond the Great Decade. Key tropes and figures of those traditions, central of which is the Incarnation, with its associated ideas of life, death, and the creative power of the Word-become-flesh, need to be reevaluated and reinterpreted in order to participate in the Wordsworthian enterprise—the remaking not only of poetry, but of man, nature, and human life.

Following the work that has been done, my purposes in taking up the matter at this time are modest ones. I want to extrapolate from the various analyses a definition of "incarnational poetics" and examine more closely than has been done Wordsworth's actual practice of it. I want to demonstrate that while incarnational poetics is a consistent focus for Wordsworth, his actual theory and practice are not, strictly speaking, consistent or coherent, but experimental, exploratory, and heuristic. At what we now recognize as a crucial new beginning in intellectual history, he is like Noah sending out birds looking for signs of dry land. Some of them present ambiguous signs or no signs; one flies to and fro; one returns without signs; dry land is suggested in the dove's returning with an olive leaf, but is finally signaled by mere absence, a negative sign, the failure of the bird to return (Gen. 8:6–12). At each new trial Wordsworth's poetics remains partial as it examines the implications of its own claims in different figures and from different perspectives.

Nevertheless, common to the many exploratory trials and central to Wordsworth's poetics is his constant reiteration of a theme implicated in the notion of language as incarnation: that language can evade the either/or of natural states so as to bring into existence, to embody, some new or transformed thing, some new space and time, some new condition. This newness is made possible by what I refer to as the linguistics of the borderland, of which Wordsworth offers a critical analysis in the "Preface to Poems" (1815). Speaking of the "Imagination . . . employed upon images in a conjunction by which they modify each other," Wordsworth offers the example of the old leech gatherer, whom the poet has compared to "a huge stone," a thing that seems "endued with sense, / Like a sea-beast crawled forth":

> Such seemed this Man, not all alive or dead,
> Nor all asleep, in his extreme old age.
> *   *   *   *   *
> Motionless as a cloud the old Man stood,
> That heareth not the loud winds when they call,
> And moveth altogether if it move at all.

Wordsworth goes on to explain the dynamics by which the descriptions of opposing images, brought into conjunction, act upon each other to create something new (to which Wordsworth refers as an "intermediate image") together with a space where the intermediate image in its intermediate condition can exist, "not all alive or dead," neither, and yet both at once:

> The stone is endowed with something of the power of life to approximate it to the sea-beast; and the sea-beast stripped of some of its vital qualities to assimilate it to the stone; which *intermediate image* is thus treated for the purpose of bringing the original image, that of the stone, to a nearer resemblance to the figure and condition of the aged Man; who is divested of so much of the indications of life and motion as to bring him to the point where *the two objects unite and coalesce in just comparison.* (Pr. W. 3:33; emphasis supplied)

When the "two objects unite and coalesce" through the medium of language, something absolutely new comes into being to make a home in this linguistic borderland. Wordsworth declines to comment on the effects of the additional image of motionless cloud on the central image, but from what he has said it is clear that with the addition of the cloud a vertical dimension opens in the verbal borderland: the space and time of the old stonelike/sea-beastlike man, seeming "not all alive or dead," are expanded when opposing word-images of a light, high, ethereal cloud and a heavy, earth-bound, densely material stone come into conjunction through the "intermediate image" suggested by the word *motionless,* whereby the motionless old man, not all stone or sea-beast, nor all cloud or stone, is seen to occupy a newly minted point and moment not only between life and death, but between heaven and earth and between time and eternity, where he assimilates to himself their oxymoronic characteristics. This language-crafted and paradoxical space-time is occupied not only by the old man, but, as I want to demonstrate in what follows, by numerous other Wordsworthian figures; by the poem; and, not least, by the poet himself.

Jonathan Wordsworth's fine discussion of what he calls Wordsworth's "preoccupation with border states" (3), while different in focus from mine, is helpful in thinking about the linguistic borderland in which I am interested, especially when considered in connection with Bewell's "history of death" and his notion that Wordsworth's concern with the metaphysical "realities" of death, resurrection, and afterlife is an aspect of his broader recognition that language-made realities constitute, for good or ill, tradition's legacy—the customary verbal constructs that dominate thought. Jonathan Wordsworth identifies as characteristic of the border state a suspension, a stillness, an "extreme passivity," wherein figures "approach, or seem to approach, a boundary that is the entrance to another world" (4). To cross into "another world" it is necessary to traverse the realm of words and texts, for as Bewell points out, all we know or can know about other worlds and border crossings is necessarily a product of representation. To see a border as a line is to maintain a division, this world always separate from that other world. To create a four-dimensional borderland, as Wordsworth did, is to create a linguistic space-time hospitable to the contradictions between the facts of this world and representations of that other world, with room for metaphysical exploration without transgressing the ultimate line between life and death.

My concern is with the special Wordsworthian incarnational language and rhetoric of the borderland. In this and the succeeding chapter I shall demonstrate the ways in which Wordsworth works with multiple sign systems through language and its figures to recreate not only poetics, but in the newly "read" and complementary semiotics of natural signs, the world itself and, with it, representations of life, death, and "afterlife."

Through my analyses I will stress the Wordsworthian enterprise of paradoxical verbal embodiment of things, places, and times. While such embodiment is distinctively unnatural, or antinatural, or even, in a special
sense, supernatural, in the poems of the Great Decade it is still confined
in the borderland, at the linguistic margins of nature.[12] In the natural
world, life and death are mutually exclusive states; in the poetic borderland they "exchange particles" so that a thing may endure in a stony permanence and, like the old leech gatherer, may be "not all alive or dead."
The chief topographical features of Wordsworth's borderland are its
metaphorical stones, which in their dense materiality are capable of embodying words as epitaphs or poems, and hence breath or spirit.

TOWARD A DEFINITION OF INCARNATIONAL POETICS

As I have not found a definition of "language as incarnation" or "incarnational poetics" (although certain of its aspects can be discerned from what
scholars say of it), I therefore offer one that I will attempt to validate as I
go: Wordsworth's incarnational poetics, founded on the radically figurative
"linguistics" of the Incarnation, is a theory that, focused on the power of
poetic language, insists that words can become flesh, body, things. As written language, poetry acts at once to interpret, translate, and create meanings implicit in all other sign systems, including the natural world.
Wordsworth's poetics is an evolving, nondualistic (Haney's term), "involuted," and implicitly semiotic theory that attempts to account for the "intermixture" or subtle union in poetry of not two, but four mutually
influential constituents: the world, perceived as visual or aural signs, *images,*
or Lockean ideas of perception, *thoughts,* including Lockean ideas of reflection and a Wordsworthian imaginative creativity, the *emotions* or *feelings* associated with, carried in, or arising from images and thoughts, and *words,*
where words themselves are understood as things (*"Things* active and efficient, which are of themselves part of the passion" [*P.W.* 2:513]). It is a non-
Lockean theory in many respects, but particularly in that it emphasizes the
activity (along with the passivity) of the mind and its perceptions as well as
the active role of language—in thought, in knowledge, and in the mind's
shifting active and passive transactions with nature.[13] Further, its foundational figure (the Incarnation) and the resulting epistemology suggest for
poetic language as for the divine Logos an ill-defined substructure, an elusive feeling, power, thought, or spirit that may be felt as an immanent
"presence," invoking a suspicion of a metaphysics whose possibilities are
seeded in the theory's foundational metaphor—the Word made flesh. Two
orders of incarnation invest the poetics: the physicality of human language,
and the "matter" of the natural code, or nature's language.

I also want to specify one of my working premises: Wordsworth was
first and foremost a wordsmith, a poet; his approaches to philosophical
and theological matters were through the doorway of language, the "mysteries of words," and words, as he says in the *Essays upon Epitaphs* "are too
awful an instrument for good and evil, to be trifled with." Good and evil,
certainly matters of theological or philosophical attention, are, for
Wordsworth, concerns of language, that powerful system that participates in, colors, and is capable of actually constituting knowledge and
thought, understanding of the world, and behaviors in it. In the passage
on incarnational poetics, Wordsworth couches his poetic theory in figures drawn from both biblical and mythological sources, and it is in this
context that he introduces the basis of his own poetics, emphasizing, to
use De Quincey's term, the "intertexture" of language and thought, suggesting the relation of both to nature or reality, and distinguishing words
as embodiment or incarnation from words as clothing or garments. Parallel to his earlier claim about the ways in which the scene and its "language" shape the soul and move thought, here Wordsworth claims a
similar but even greater power for words:

> [Words] hold above all other external powers a dominion over thoughts.
> If words be not . . . an incarnation of the thought, but only a clothing for
> it, then surely will they prove an ill gift; such a one as those possessed vest-
> ments, read of in the stories of superstitious times, which had power to
> consume and to alienate from his right mind the victim who put them on.
> (*Pr. W.* 2:84–5)

Wordsworth speaks of words, as he does of nature, as "external powers."[14]
Human thought is poised between and subject to two powerful external
influences, both in a sense linguistic—natural signs (the language of nature) and human words. His metaphor here for words that exert a negative, dominating influence is "only clothing," a metaphor drawn not from
theology or philosophy, but from myth and folklore—the poisoned or enchanted cloak, like the one that destroyed Heracles or like Jack the
Giant-Killer's charmed and vision-altering cloak of darkness satirized by
Wordsworth in Book 7 of the *Prelude*. At the same time, Wordsworth's
mention of incarnation calls into the mix various biblical texts, including
Paul's assertion that "Jews demand signs and Greeks seek wisdom, but we
preach Christ crucified" (1 Cor. 1:22–23). Of this text, Haney observes
that "this declaration establishes the fundamental difference that Chris-
tianity bases its thought not on apprehension of abstract truth (Greek
'wisdom') or representational structure (Jewish 'signs'), but on the *event*
of the Incarnate God's transition into a very mortal life." This distinc-

tion, Haney says, "holds from Paul to Wordsworth, despite the many per-
mutations undergone by thought about meaning between early Chris-
tianity and Romanticism" (20).

The event of the Incarnation finds its fullest expression in the first
chapter of the Gospel of John and establishes in part the paradigm for incarnational poetics: The original or creative Word (as God, companion
of God, creative thought of God) is to Jesus (the Word become flesh) as
human thought should be to words, whose advent and materiality have
the power to "uphold, and feed, and leave in quiet." Wordsworth draws
further figures from nature (understood as another incarnation of God's
thought and speech—the "breath of God" [*Prelude* 5:222]) to characterize
"good" words: they are "like the power of gravitation or the air we
breathe." Language that is mere clothing for thought cloaks it, obscuring,
altering, and poisoning. Wrong words turn back to thought, victimizing,
"alienating from [their] right mind[s]," both speaker and hearer, writer
and reader.[15] As garments, words are of the nature of disguise, and therefore dangerous, "a counter-spirit, unremittingly and noiselessly at work,
to subvert, to lay waste, to vitiate, and to dissolve" (*Pr. W.* 2:84–5). Good
words, thought incarnated, are associated with life; bad words, thought
dressed in garments, are associated with death.

LIFE AND DEATH

Wordsworth's poetics is marked by that typical Wordsworthian "two-
sidedness" discussed in the introduction: his theory holds in suspension
contradictory implications and does not flinch from the demands of its
own foundational metaphor—that of body. The theory at times is able to
repudiate its own laws and tropes in order to engage the metaphors of a
competing theory of language subsumed under the metaphor of clothing.
Moreover, the theory is capable of conflating the two competing, figuratively expressed theories (words as body, words as clothing) through the
metaphor "body *is* clothing" (of the soul).[16] To complicate the matter further, in Wordsworth's treatment, the concept of language remains settled
in neither *body* nor *clothing* as simple metaphors; rather language occupies
a point in a metaphoric network that can be "read" horizontally (forward
and backward) and vertically (up and down), whereby, for example, language is book is body is garments, or garments are body is books, which
are stone (a potential body) and shell (a cast-off body), which are again
books, works of sage or bard, which are also caskets for both immortal
verse (words, breath, spirit) and dead bodies, which are themselves nevertheless clothing for the bodies that clothe souls, yet that are, again and
always, language.

The metaphor of body is central and recurring in different senses throughout the figurative network, and its ambiguity (as both living incarnation and dead corpse) furnishes the central aporia of Wordsworth's theory. An important point emerging from such metaphorical networks and the centrality of body is that incarnational poetics implicates and renders inextricable both life and death. As a theory of art, incarnational poetics places the poem strategically and precariously in that ambiguous region at their shared boundary.[17] That border-space of life-and-death is glimpsed in the motionless old leech gatherer of "Resolution and Independence" (discussed earlier), who seems stonelike, neither "all alive nor dead" (l. 71); in the aged thorn that "like a stone" is overgrown with lichens; and in Martha Ray, who is mistaken for a "jutting crag"; or in the portrait of a horse in a rejected passage of the five-book *Prelude.* Like the old man, the horse is motionless, "Insensible and still," all "breath, motion gone, / . . . all but shape and substance gone." All of these—the old man, the thorn, the woman, and the horse—obdurately hold a position between the tenuousness of expiring life and the inanimate permanence of stone. As such, all are "eternal" sufferers, yet the transformation of that suffering into poetry and its embodiment in words reveals an inherent beauty, a beauty that releases not sorrow but that pleasure to give which, Wordsworth says, is the "one restriction" under which the poet writes— "the necessity of giving immediate pleasure to a human Being possessed of that information which may be expected from him . . . as a Man" (*Pr. W.* I:139). They are representative of words as "living *things.*" The horse, Wordsworth says, is "A borderer dwelling betwixt life and death, / A living statue or a statued life" (*Prelude* 498).[18] Positioned between life and death, and embodying the qualities of both, the old man, the thorn, Martha Ray, and the horse are breathing, stony artifacts, tropes for the poem and poetic language that too are borderers. Like the horse, poetic language is neither alive nor dead, but somehow both at once. The point is that life *and* death are equally and constantly copresent in Wordsworth's theory, even as both are inextricably present in the Incarnation of the Word and the transubstantiation of the Last Supper, the biblical intertexts.

Despite the preoccupation of Wordsworth's poetry and poetics with both life and death, it has been usual in recent years to stress the predominance of death. Certainly there are good reasons why this should be so. It is difficult to think of another poet whose verse and prose present so many graves, corpses, spirits, eulogies, and epitaphs. Frances Ferguson has commented on the fact that Wordsworth's poetic theory receives one of its fullest developments in his *Essays upon Epitaphs,* noting that "Funeral monuments seem, in Wordsworth's discourse, almost to be the first poetry" (28–9). I want to suggest a slight shift in the approach to the epitaph: in Wordsworth's poetics, the epitaph is not precisely poetry; rather it is a *figure for poetry* in the form of poetic language embodied in the materiality and permanence of stone, occupying a borderland (and speaking) between the living (the writer of the epitaph or the traveler who reads it) and the dead (over whose body the stone is positioned and whose message is often spoken in the first person—as is, for example, Wordsworth's "A Poet's Epitaph"). Like Ferguson, Haney emphasizes the "close and complex link between poetic incarnational language and human mortality" (73). In his chapter "The History of Death," Alan Bewell argues that from 1798 onward, poems from "We Are Seven" to the *Excursion* "constitute a major philosophical project, that of a general history of death" (188). Andrzej Warminski, in his discussion of the drowned man, underscores the theme of death, asking rhetorically, "How [can one] get this linguistic, tropological machine . . . to produce a living spirit?" (30). The answer, implied in the question, is that it cannot be done. Part of the claim of this chapter and the succeeding chapter is that the answer is at the same time both right and wrong. In what follows I hope to correct what I believe is a critical overemphasis on death by arguing that Wordsworth's is a poetics which insists that poetry speaks in the borderland between life and death. My attention is chiefly focused on the language and rhetoric of Wordsworth's poetry—how he in fact practiced his theory—in the process attempting to understand his sophisticated and various interrogation of the relationships among thought, feeling, world, word, and body (and the mysteries to which these are referred) in an arena in which both words and bodies live and die.

THE BIBLICAL INTERTEXTS AND NATURE'S SENTENCES

Certain biblical texts must be considered in relationship to Wordsworth's poetics: The first chapter of Genesis; the important first chapter of the Gospel of John mentioned above; and the synoptic gospels' recording of Jesus' statements and acts at the Last Supper. The first of these demonstrates a reality-making power of (divine) language and the way in which words are things: "God said, 'Let there be light'; and there was light" (Gen. 1:3), whereby the word *light* spoken by the creator becomes the thing light; that is, it is incarnated, given physical presence, and thus is true and real. The second, more difficult text demonstrates a radically metaphorical process wherein words set in motion a figurative chain-reaction whereby one thing is said to be and therefore is another: "in the beginning was the Word, and the Word was with God, and the Word was God. He was in the beginning with God; all things were made through him, and without him was not anything made that was made" (Jn. 1:1–3). Thus far, these verses seem congruent with those of Genesis, claiming the transmutation of words into things or the reification of words and the reality-making, creative power of the Word. But the gospel adds another, deeper mystery by asserting further that "the Word became flesh and dwelt among us, full of grace and truth; we have beheld his glory, glory as the only Son from the Father" (Jn. 1:14). In rhetorical terms, the text presents a series of metaphoric transmutations: originary (in the beginning), creative (all things were made through him) Word is God and with God; God is Father; Word is "the true light" (that mentioned in Genesis?) (Jn. 1:9); Word is flesh, man "dwelling with us" (active and alive); man is God (the Father) *and* "the only Son from the Father."[19] In the Note to "The Thorn" cited above, Wordsworth speaks of words as "*things,* active and efficient" that are not merely "symbols" of passion, but are "part of the passion," in the sense indicated by the Greek *logos.*[20] Wordsworth might almost be describing not just words, but the Word, an originary first sentence, its words active and efficient things in the world and constituting the world, from which other words and realities follow, the mysterious and unique union of God as thought and Word and human flesh.

The Word-become-flesh provides its active and efficient life and thingness and its words as it embodies the thought and (pro)creative passion of God. Nevertheless, implicit in the Word's becoming flesh is the fact of mortality: "And being found in human form he [the Word, Son] humbled himself and became obedient unto death . . ." (Phil. 2:8). Both Word and words as flesh become subject to death—as things, as flesh. The last of the biblical intertexts is that spoken of earlier by Marin. It adds further links to the figurative chain that constitutes the rhetoric of incarnation, with its simultaneous assertions and denial of mortality. The Gospel of Matthew reports Jesus' action and words to his disciples at the Last Supper, when Jesus is already anticipating his own death: "Now as they were eating, Jesus took bread, and blessed, and broke it, and gave it to the disciples and said, 'Take, eat; this is my body'" (26:26). This utterance (language), like the creative word of Genesis, brings into being that which it says ("this [bread] is my body") by which metaphor both the Word, Jesus, and the words of Jesus are incarnated in the bread, which is his body and a sign of his body, in a present and future, ever-repeatable, -efficacious, and -living reality of the sacrament of the Eucharist. The bread as sign is, like Jesus' pronouncement, like language in general, repeatable, and with each repetition the renewed efficacy of the originary utterance. The body as bread is thus immortal. Like the first divine fiat, this second divine metaphor creates the reality that it enunciates. "This is my body" moreover signifies the paradoxical doubleness of the metaphor. It is both the living body of Jesus, which is the food of life and the promise (that is, performative words) of life present at the Last Supper and subsequently at every repetition of the Eucharist, *and* at the same time the mortal body of Jesus soon to be crucified and laid in a tomb. It also serves to add yet another link in the figurative chain, for now the originary Word that became flesh (body), and therefore subject to death, now becomes bread, called in John the "bread of life" (6:35), which is at the same time body, the flesh that is the soon-to-perish, but ever-repeatable and therefore ever-living Word, through which/whom "all things were made." This biblical figurative chaining associated with the Incarnation and its paradoxical linguistic encompassing of life and death offers a model for the complex tropology of Wordsworth's incarnational poetics.[21]

The *first* sentence or utterance (the Word) implicit in incarnational poetics is manifest (embodied) in both the world ("all things that were made") and in the flesh of the God-man, immortal-but-dying incarnation of the originary Word. In Wordsworth's theory, there is clear indication that the natural world of this originary utterance continues to speak, repeating messages to a human perceiver through its materiality, the "language of the ancient earth." In this respect, Wordsworth's poetics not only reveals a Kantian bent but anticipates certain recent ideas. Geoffrey Bennington, in his exposition of Jean-François Lyotard's theories, presents a secular but congruent (and, one wants to say, incarnational) view of this relationship between language and world (or "reality"—things in themselves—as perceived). Bennington's analysis might almost serve as a gloss on Wordsworthian poetics. He explains that for Lyotard "perception 'itself' (and not just reports of perception) can and must be analyzed in terms of sentences" (131). Further, Lyotard finds that there must be two kinds of sentences: "First a sentence (or quasi-sentence . . .) in a 'language' or idiom called 'matter' [what I have called a natural code]—of unknown sender, addressed to a receptive addressee. This is a sentence with no referent and an unclear meaning. . . ." There follows a second sentence, uttered by a human percipient, the "receptive addressee," which reverses the relationship between unknown sender and addressee: "The addressee [percipient] of the first [obscure, ambiguous] sentence becomes the sender of a sentence in a language or idiom called 'form.' This sentence does have a referent, called 'phenomenon,' and this referential function of the second sentence hangs on the capacity to apply criteria of space and time [the Kantian forms of sensible intuition] to the first sentence: The second sentence is what Kant calls 'intuition'" (Bennington 131–3).[22]

This second sentence in human language, corresponding to Wordsworth's poetic utterance, often constitutes a reading, interpretation, or translation of the first sentence conveyed to the senses under constraints of space and time by and through the idiom called matter or natural code. The human linguistic response to sensation is always problematic. Lyotard explores the special position of sensation in Kant's analysis, observing that sensation is the only exception to the normal situation in which a subject is both active and passive at once; in the case of sensation, the situation is one in which, "through matter, something which does not proceed from the subject seems to affect it" (Bennington 100). Sensation yields intuitions. This passivity with respect to sensation makes the human percipient the receiver of a "sentence" with whose sender he or she can then engage in a dialogue. But again, as Bennington puts it, "we shall never know if the sender (if there is a sender) of the first sentence understands in return, i.e., whether space and time are valid in themselves" (133). To put it in Wordsworthian terms, perceptions come as impressions or impulses, which (in an oddly undecidable figural-literal sense) speak their first sentence—e.g., "One impulse from a vernal wood / May teach you more of man; / Of moral evil and of good, / Than all the sages can"—to one who passively "watches and receives" ("The Tables Turned" 20–4; 32). The human percipient's production of a second sentence (which is of necessity both response and interpretation/translation) reveals an active-passive interaction—a dialogue conducted in two languages, two sign systems, the natural code and human language—in which the human percipient "half perceive[s] and half-create[s]" "all the mighty world / Of eye and ear" ("Tintern Abbey" 106–8). In other words, the originary Word conducts a monologue that creates the natural world ("all things"), whereas the human percipient conducts a dialogue with that originary Word, half-perceiving (hearing, seeing) and half-creating (speaking) the second, human sentence. Thus in incarnational poetics human poetry or "making" attempts to replicate the reality-producing efficacy of divine speaking, wherein thought becomes creative word and word becomes thing.

In the passage on incarnational poetics, Wordsworth makes several claims about language (all language, one assumes, but poetic language in particular); he is concerned about the relationship of that human language to the enduring truth of Nature's code—of second sentence to the first sentence—and the clumsy inadequacy of the vocabulary of the second sentence: words can control thought for good or evil; words properly used must be thought embodied (as the thought of God is embodied in the Word made flesh and the world); if words do not embody, but merely clothe (veil, conceal, disguise), they are counter-spirit (counter-breath, counter-speaking), working "to subvert, to lay waste, to vitiate, and to dissolve." The poet properly does not "trifle" with words, but seeks to employ this "awful instrument" like the forces of nature (gravity, air—natural embodiments of God's thought) to "uphold, and feed, and leave in quiet" (*Pr. W.* 2:84–5). Good words partake of life, sustaining and nourishing; bad words partake of death, wasting, vitiating, dissolving.

The concern with life and death integral to incarnational poetics is apparent in the poetic practice, wherein Wordsworth, recognizing a cocreative force in human language, uses words to transgress the binary relationship between life and death in order to construct an intermediacy or interstice in the deadly either/or of existence. Speaking of the *Essays upon Epitaphs*, but with relevance to Wordsworth's poetic practice in general, Paul de Man has proposed that what Wordsworth does is to ground his enterprise in "a consistent system of thought, of metaphors, and of diction," a

> system of mediations that converts the radical distance of an either/or opposition in a process allowing movement from one extreme to the other by a series of transformations that leave the negativity of the initial relationship (or lack of relationship) intact. One moves, without compromise, from death *or* life to life *and* death. (*Rhetoric of Romanticism* 74)

Through such a series of transformations, Wordsworth does not erase death, the negation, or transform it through Pauline maneuvers into its opposite, but rather acknowledges in it a power to give structure, meaning, and beauty to life. As de Man notices, "The existential poignancy of the [Wordsworthian] text stems from the full acquiescence to the power of mortality; no simplification in the form of a negation of the negation can be said to take place in Wordsworth" (74).[23] In his depictions of "life *and* death," the poet subtly but radically revises the received traditions, the "words" of Christian orthodoxy on the nature of life and death, the relationship of spiritual world and natural world, and the mysteries of eternity and time.

Nowhere is this revisionary effort clearer than in "We Are Seven," a dialogue between an orthodox, empirically minded adult and a "simple" child. The point of contention is, of course, the "status" of two of seven siblings. The narrator insists that something must be one thing or another, either here or there. He makes uncompromising distinctions between the living and the dead and between spirit and body; he keeps heaven separated from earth. By contrast the little girl lives in a borderland, which, as so often in Wordsworth, is also a place of graves, where the living and the dead form one society. The narrator, voicing a traditional Christian understanding of death, insists that the child's family consists of only five (the number of the senses, incidentally) because two are dead and "Their spirits are in heaven!"

The child, however, responds with an argument framed not in empirical, but in figurative terms: "Their graves are green; they may be seen." The graves containing the dead children are in a borderland, a place of communion where the child works and eats and even sings to them. The child's sense of the community of living and dead is shared in the *Excursion* by the Pastor. Speaking of the churchyard in which he and his visitors are talking, he says, "To a mysteriously-united pair / This place is consecrate; to Death and Life, / And to the best affections that proceed / From their conjunction . . ." (5:903–6). The child's siblings' graves are green, the color of living nature; moreover the ambiguity of "they may be seen" allows the dead children a continuing (visible) presence, similar to that of Lucy Gray. With his empirical eyes, however, the narrator cannot "see" them, and therefore they do not count. Bewell makes a good point when he distinguishes between empirical and poetic views of death:

> For Wordsworth, the notion of immortality, our first religious idea, is derived not from the grave, but from life; rather than providing us with the symbolic materials for an idea of afterlife, our empirical knowledge of the dead robs us of this belief, leaving poetry the task of finding a linguistic means for us to recover from this mortal theft. The history of death is thus a dialectic, built upon the conflict between ideas of immortality, drawn from the continuities of nature, and our empirical knowledge of the dead. (195)

Bewell's phrase, "finding a linguistic means for us to recover from this mortal theft" succinctly describes Wordsworth's project in the practice of incarnational poetics. Certain images and image clusters signal the effort. One is the green grave, the keystone of the child's argument in "We Are Seven," as are also related images of mossy caves and stones, things turning to stone, and engraved headstones, among others. Such images are of the borderland; they are Wordsworthian "intermediate images" existing, as he explained, where "two objects unite and coalesce in just comparison." As intermediate images constructed of words, they represent aspects of that "series of transformations" through which one moves from life *or* death to life *and* death. They are themselves borderers, dwelling "betwixt life and death," where the poet works to "recover from the mortal theft."[24]

The linguistic topography of the borderland is broad and diverse, permitting a number of expressions of incarnational poetics, as I hope to demonstrate in the next chapter, when I turn my attention specifically to Wordsworth's varied and variously focused practice of incarnational poetics in order to appreciate the complexities of the theory and its variations as they are manifest in the poems.

CHAPTER 3

The Word as Borderer

OF CLOTHING AND
INCARNATION—THE PRACTICE

Where tones of learned art and Nature mixed
May frame enduring language.

—*Prelude* 6:604–5

In an effort to keep this chapter to manageable length, I have selected for analysis four poems and one passage spanning the years 1797 to 1805, years in which various aspects of Wordsworth's incarnational poetics are prominent: "The Thorn," "Lucy Gray," "Three years she grew in sun and shower," "To H. C., Six Years Old," and the drowned-man episode of the *Prelude,* Book 5. These poems from the early period demonstrate the practice of a poetics that is given its fullest theoretical expression only several years later (in the "Preface to Poems" and in the *Essays upon Epitaphs*), by which time the poetic practice, but apparently not the theory, has shifted to reflect the poet's increasing religious orthodoxy. While the later poetry has its beauties, the particular artistry of incarnational poetics is of necessity compromised when the terrain on one side of it changes radically, as it must when a fairly well-defined afterworld crowds in upon nature and the natural man. Each of the selected poems demonstrates Wordsworth's concern with the power of words as things, his willingness to explore the implications of incarnational poetics in light of shifting or evolving premises concerning nature's sentences (signs), the human linguistic response—to incarnate or to clothe in words—and the relationship of that embodiment or clothing (the vital/fatal poet's work) to the originary utterance whereby Word becomes flesh and through whom all things are made.

THE THORN AS "FIRST SENTENCE" AND "THE THORN" AS TRANSLATION

Approach and read (for thou can'st read) the Lay,
Grav'd on the Stone beneath yon aged Thorn.

—Thomas Gray, "Elegy Written in
a Country Church-Yard" 115–6

"Approach and read"—Gray invites his addressee to read the human language (an epitaph that he calls a "lay") engraved on the headstone beneath the "aged thorn." In the two parts contributed by Wordsworth to "The Three Graves," visitors inquire of an old sexton why a churchyard thorn is "neither dry nor dead," but "blooms so sweet," above three "green and dark" graves, although surrounded by images of death—toads, dock, and nettle.[1] In the first of the Mathew elegies, "Could I the priest's consent have gained," the poet says that he would have buried Mathew "beneath this [thorn] tree we loved so well"; even so, he will "where trunk and branches blend" "engrave . . . [Mathew's] epitaph." In "Just as the blowing thorn began" the poet writes his elegy for Mathew, "this verse beneath the hawthorn bough." In "Carved, Mathew, with a master's skill," Wordsworth makes the thorn a sort of natural monument as he has the dead Mathew's name "Carved" on "the hawthorn tree," where "'Twill live." This same thorn appears in yet another of the Mathew elegies—in "Remembering how thou didst beguile"—as "this silly thorn / Which blooms as sweetly as before," an image evocative again of the life force of the thorn depicted in "The Three Graves." As such examples demonstrate, in Wordsworth's verse the thorn is complexly implicated with death, graveyards, epitaphs, and poetry, and, at the same time, with life. This two-sidedness of life and death in Wordsworth's thorns reflects aspects of popular lore, wherein the thorn (or hawthorn) was a tree of contradictions. By turns both lucky and unlucky, it was associated with life and its processes—sexuality (Maying), marriage ritual, and birth—but, at the same time, with enforced chastity; it could be both life-preserving and death-dealing.[2] In France and other parts of Europe, Jesus' crown of thorns was said to have been made of hawthorn, and hence to signify the suffering and death of Jesus, the Word become flesh (Cavendish 8:1134). In "The Thorn," therefore, even though the scene contains no churchyard, no graves, no gravestone, no epitaph, no engraved poem and no elegy, the tree brings with it not only intertextual associations from a poem like Gray's "Elegy" and Wordsworth's own works, but also pervasive cultural associations with both life and death. Aged like Gray's, Wordsworth's thorn itself is the antithesis of that which he depicted in "Just as the blowing thorn began" or "The Three Graves" for rather than flourishing with life—"spread[ing] again its vernal shade" or blooming "so sweet"—it is itself an image of death clinging to life; it has neither blossoms nor leaves and, paradoxically, not even any thorns. Wordsworth's aged thorn thus stands as a kind of metonymy, in its solitary isolation implicating churchyards, graves, sexuality and chastity, epitaphs and poetry, life and death. This is the thorn that presents itself to the poet's eyes, offering its "first sentence" (in Lyotard's sense), yet that "first sentence" is not merely an obscure message in a natural code originating from an unknown source; it constitutes an involuted and complex semiotics of natural, intertextual, and cultural signs.[3]

It is this "knotty" text that Wordsworth would approach and read, one of his two stated purposes in the poem. In the Fenwick note, Wordsworth explains that he had often passed a particular thorn without noticing it, until he came upon it in a storm. In the poem he wishes "by some invention" to make "this Thorn permanently [or prominently] an impressive object as the storm has made it to my eyes at this moment" (P. W. 2:511).[4] The thorn as first sentence is presented to the poet, the percipient-addressee, and couched in the idiom of matter, without specific referent, and with an "unclear meaning." The poet's task, as he sees it, is to "read" the natural sign (along with the intertextual and cultural signs implicit in it) and translate it into a second sentence—a poem—whose referent is the meaning-laden phenomenon. Stephen Maxfield Parrish argues cogently that the poem has consistently been misread as a poem about a woman. Rather, he says, it is about "a man (and a tree); not a tale of horror but a psychological study; not a ballad but a dramatic monologue" (101). I agree that the poem is about a man and a tree (although I would reverse the emphasis and say that it is about a tree and a man, and argue that these might be called as well a text and a reader); I also want to add that the apparent "monologue" in this situation is really a submerged dialogue between the tree and the man and that in this dialogic relationship language is the driving force and ultimate reality. The narrator's deictic "There is a thorn" is only the beginning. It names a phenomenon but is inadequate to convey the import of the object, the "unclear meaning" encoded in the "matter" of the first sentence—that stormy, thorny impression, the unknown source, and the message worthy of permanence, which the poet strives to embody by encoding it in human language.

Given this purpose, it is puzzling that the task of the poet in "The Thorn" is delegated to what seems an unreliable narrator, a poet manqué. Again in the Note, Wordsworth tells us that the narrator is a type, perhaps a retired sea captain, talkative, credulous, and superstitious, a man whose words probably cannot be taken at face value. Thus between the poet and the thorn stands a narrator with his suspect, superstitious language and (to complicate matters further) his reports of the (superstitious) language of the townspeople. The poet has chosen to convey the message of the storm and the thorn by filtering it through other "texts"—custom and tradition, intertextual and cultural echoes in the thorn itself and the "readings" of the captain and the villagers, themselves linguistic artifacts. This seeming aporia between the avowed purpose of the poet and his appointed spokesman can be resolved if one assumes that the narrator is just that "invention" needed to convey the poet's translation of the thorn's semiosis, in which case the captain's language must be doubly significant: It will simultaneously mean what the captain "reads" in the natural scene (conveyed largely in simile) and at the same time what the poet "reads" (conveyed in the denser figuration of metonymy and metaphor). The entire complex will indicate something of the linguistic accretions through which and by which a percipient must "approach and read" the natural code, translate it, and thus create it.

Much of what we know of the captain comes not through the poem, but through the description offered in the Note, which, as Ferguson notices, constitutes a "fiction supplementary to the poem" (11). Wordsworth says in the Note that in addition to being "credulous, talkative" and "prone to superstition" (which a reader might have surmised from the poem), the captain is a man suitable "to exhibit some of the general laws by which superstition acts upon the mind" (P. W. 2:512). As such, he represents not a curious oddity, but *human beings in general,* who attempt to interpret the world, its phenomena, and events through a screen of language, custom, and belief that largely constitutes their "knowledge" of nature, supernature, life and death; a legacy through which they approach and read what is presented by the senses.[5] The captain is the sort of man of whom Wordsworth speaks in the *Essays upon Epitaphs,* whose thoughts are dominated by language. Words themselves skew his readings of things and events. What the captain "knows" is borne in language, his own and that of others. Epistemology and language are therefore primary concerns, as the captain's refrains demonstrate: "I cannot tell; I wish I could," "I'll tell you all I know," and "No more I know, I wish I did, / And I would tell it all to you" (89, 114, 155–6). The captain speaks all that he knows, but what he knows *is* what he and others have spoken. Wordsworth says that it was his intention in the poem to "shew the manner in which such men cleave to the same ideas; and to follow the turns of passion, always different, yet not palpably different, by which their conversation is swayed" (P. W. 2:512). Ideas and passions "sway" conversation; conversation feeds ideas and passions. Ideas, passion, conversation—thoughts, feelings, words: these are the matter of poetry, to be sure, but something is amiss with the captain's "poetry," that failure residing in the relationships among his words, his ideas, his passions, and his "reality." His words do not incarnate, it seems, but clothe. As clothing, his words tend to obscure the natural code, its signs, and significance. A sort of linguistic fabric conceals the messages he might otherwise read in the natural code. As percipient, he finds that the little hill is clothed in a "mossy network" as if "woven" like cloth; the thorn, like a stone, is clothed in lichens and moss, perhaps red moss; Martha, who looks like (and may well be) a crag,[6] is imperceptible behind her red cloak (which may be moss and which, like Hester Prynn's scarlet letter or Jack the Giant-Killer's coat of darkness labeled "Invisible," represents her/it, hides her/it in language). Unable to see beyond his own words, the narrator is devoid of what Wordsworth calls in the Note "fancy," meaning "the power by which pleasure and surprise are excited by sudden varieties of situation and an accumulated imagery" (P. W. 2:512). Thus the narrator may be said to become a victim of language as he produces and listens to words that clothe, hide, deceive—like those "possessed vestments" from "superstitious times" that "alienate from his right mind the victim who put[s] them on" (Essays upon Epitaphs, Pr. W. 2:84–5).

Wordsworth does not say explicitly just where the pathology lies, but the poem provides certain kinds of evidence. The narrator's language and "reality" are dominated by simile and personification. It is largely through such tropes that he creates as gloomy and sinister the thorn and surrounding scene on the mountain ridge. The thorn is, the narrator says, "old," "grey," "Not higher than a two-years' child," yet it "stands erect," a "mass of knotted joints," "wretched" ("attended by misery and woe") and "poor" (1–22). The cumulative effect of this language is to "read" the person in the thorn and thus to animate and ascribe to it an order of human suffering. The moss that grows on the thorn is likewise figuratively invested with human emotion and will: It is a "melancholy crop" that seems "bent / With plain and manifest intent" to drag it down and "bury this poor thorn for ever" (20–3). Death and burial are already edging into this reality. The object, clothed in the narrator's language, is not a mossy thorn, but a suffering participant in a mortal agon, in a scene that includes a muddy, haunted pond and a "beauteous" hill of moss that, the narrator finds, "Is like an infant's grave in size." This simile also becomes a part of the captain's reality (he cannot perceive the hill except through the figure, which might have been called up through association with the earlier similes of "murder" and burial), and he reacts through his simile not as to a hill of moss, but an infant's grave. The rhetorical crafting of the scene, with which the poem opens, then appears to draw to itself like a magnet an imagined human drama whose actors perform the acts and assume the figurative meanings read by the captain in the natural scene.[7] The wretched, stony, transplanted churchyard thorn is figured in the miserable Martha; the hill then must be a grave, and like an "infant's grave" must enfold a phantom baby who may or may not have been born, murdered, and buried in the little mound of moss, but whose shadowy face, the narrator assures us, may be seen in the little pond looking back at the observer. That a little face may be "seen," that is, perceived (a curiously empirical claim), is evidence that the captain's words as human code or "second sentence" are in effect clothing the "first sentence" of the natural code. As a result, the world shows the narrator what he says about it in a kind of verbal mirroring. Yet it is not just the pond that acts as a mirror, but the entire scene that, couched in the language of simile, personification, and gossipy superstition, reflects the narrator's thoughts, and as his words attach to the thorn, the pond, and the mound, they dominate the narrator's mind and sway his conversation: What he thinks and feels, he says; what he says, he perceives; what he perceives constitutes his world and dominates his thought, in a recursive cycle creating the narrator's reality and reinforcing superstitious thought and feeling.

To reiterate, the poem is about a sort of Everyman reader and his text, about language and its relationship to epistemology. What can we know, and how can we know it? To what extent is knowledge a matter of language? How is it related to the world conveyed in the natural code, the incarnate word? Running through the captain's speech like a leitmotif is the theme not of knowledge, but of ignorance: "I cannot tell; I wish I could; / For the true reason no one knows" (89–90), an admission that does not, however, keep him from "telling." Bolstering the theme of ignorance is the constant questioning by an auditor (or even in some readings by the captain himself): "Wherefore to the mountain-top / Can this unhappy woman go . . . ?" (100–01). Or, "But what's the thorn? and what's the pond? / And what's the hill of moss to her?" (210–11). The framing of the questions is an indication of the questioner's thought, for it expresses a taken-for-granted knowledge—for example that the thorn, the pond, and the hill have some sort of human significance; what does the thorn "mean" to Martha Ray? What the narrator claims he can say for certain is what he can observe empirically, and although he makes a show of being an empiricist (with his measurements and telescope), what he knows empirically is little and does not seem to constitute a reading of the thorn's message: the pond is three feet long and two feet wide; the hill is half a foot high; he has "seen" a wretched woman named Martha, who wears a scarlet cloak and sits by the thorn. It is with such "empirical" knowledge that the poem ends: "And this I know, full many a time, / When she was on the mountain high . . . / That I have heard her cry, / 'Oh misery!'" As suggested above, such information concerning Martha is empirically suspect, not so much a matter of perception but of the narrator's language-made "knowledge" of an abandoned lover, a dead baby, a haunted pond, and eerily moving ground; of the thorn as wretched, child-sized, and poor; and melancholy moss of evil intent. Yet when the poem closes, these matters too have become a part of the narrator's reality. In the lines that immediately precede the "this-I-know" passage, the narrator denies knowledge of whether the "little babe is buried there," but claims that he can know about the thorn: "But plain it is, the thorn is bound / With heavy tufts of moss, that strive / To drag it to the ground" (244–6). In other words, he "knows" what he has said and felt about it and the mortal combat in which it is engaged. This linguistic or figurative knowledge (what he has said), combined with stories of the townsfolk (what they have said), the narrator's few empirical observations of the scene, and his "perception" of the woman constitute the entirety of the narrator's knowledge. In all crucial respects, the captain's knowledge is linguistic, a word-made reality attached to an object and a place, to which he can direct readers and where they too may participate in this reality, approach and read, and "something of [Martha's] tale may trace" (110).

Wordsworth's comment on the relationship of thought to language mentioned earlier makes explicit the connection of words with passion, the status of words as things, and their potency in the world. He takes care, he says, "that words which in . . . [superstitious] minds are impregnated with passion, should likewise convey passion to Readers" (P. W. 2:512). The mind is interested in words as things, which are at the same time constituted of perception, thought, and passion. These comments seem to include both good words and bad words, those that feed and those that vitiate. Although words take form as things in the narrator's world (the staring face in the pond and the trembling earth bear testimony to this), they are of the nature of clothing, or "counter-spirit," rather than incarnation. What one knows, Wordsworth shows, is a function of what one says and the way one says it. Words (that "awful instrument for good and evil") can be, like the Christian Incarnation of the Word or like poisoned vestments, not only mediators between mental and physical, spiritual and bodily, but also reifiers of the mental and spiritual—providing a "life" (as does the body of Christ), a thingness, for thought and passion. A case in point is the beautiful hill that, the captain says, is like an infant's grave. In so saying, he "knows" it (and probably readers know it) in this way. Neither he nor they could then "know" it as, for example, nature's window box or as a cradle. The captain's words and those he has borrowed from the townsfolk, repeated again and again, become vehicles for the passion that at first produced them and now invests the scene of thorn, hill, and pond. Those who read his words may even look for the thorn and, finding it, may "see" it through the screen of the narrator's language so as to "trace" Martha's tale there, to "read" the evil intent of the moss, and to observe the face in the pond.

"The Thorn" thus expresses aspects of Wordsworthian poetics through the instrument of the Everyman narrator and his words. The sea captain, like the poet, is faced with the problem of making breathings for incommunicable powers apprehended in the thorn and its setting, a natural system of signs entangled with intertextual and cultural meanings. Nevertheless, behind the narrator stands the poet with his poetic project. Wordsworth's comment that he wanted to make the thorn "an impressive object" as the storm had made it *to his eyes* strongly suggests that the gossipy and superstitious narrator and his tale are indeed poetic devices for achieving this end, for presenting, interpreting, translating into human language, and hence embodying, the message of nature as the poet heard it in the storm and saw it in the thorn. The question is, then, are the narrator and his language designed figuratively to "incarnate" the thought of the poet as regards the thorn? To find an answer requires a shift in perspective and another look at the language of the scene and its central image. First, it may be posited that whereas "The Thorn" is a poem spoken in the words of the sea captain, the aged thorn he describes is interpreted by one in thrall to his own words. What *he* cannot see is, nevertheless, glimpsed through his words—that the thorn and its significance are not separable from language—the "first sentence" of the natural code, the intertextual echoes, the cultural accretions, and the translation and figurative pronouncements of the captain. It is an artifact made of words. Seen through or beyond the captain's words, the thorn is revealed, finally, as metaphor. It is one of those Wordsworthian borderers between life and death, tenaciously clinging and speaking to life even as it is turning to stone: "like a stone / With lichens it is overgrown." A flowering of human suffering and commiseration, it is a natural graveyard growth; it is leafless (without texts?), knotty (entangled, complicated, difficult to read). In its enigmatic, stony endurance it is, as mentioned, like the old leech gatherer or like the horse with its "statued life." And though removed from the churchyard, it *is* in a way a grave marker, as the captain suggests, although not the sort he imagines. The quite sensitive and apparently well-intentioned sea captain, faced with the poet's problem of hearing the ghostly language of the ancient earth and embodying it in human language, is not quite up to the task, but in his failure he ironically fulfills the poet's task by demonstrating aspects of Wordsworthian poetics mentioned in the Note—the principle of repetition and its aesthetics, the relationship between language and passion, the verbal nature of knowledge, the "general laws by which superstition acts upon the mind," and imaginative assessment, by which Wordsworth means "the faculty which produces impressive effects out of simple elements" (P. W. 2:512). It is with imaginative and passionate credulity or superstition that the narrator calls to his aid Martha and her tale to specify the significance of the thorn. Moreover the narrator says more than he knows, providing language through which the poet can express his own reading of the thorn and, like the storm, render it impressive in human language (P. W. 2:511).

To the narrator, the thorn appears as a grave marker for a dead infant who no one can say was ever born. To the poet, it is both a natural sign and an intertextual artifact, transplanted from Gray's country churchyard, where it has formed a scene with gravestone and epitaph. It represents that scene metonymically. It is thus a natural monument,[8] its obscure message a poem, "heard in a storm" (the knotty branches speaking in the wind in an unknown tongue), an epitaph spoken by all the dead to all the living, encrypted in a stony suffering that is the "permanent, obscure and dark"[9] condition of humanity as it hovers between life and death, a suffering reified in a thing figured in "a mass of knotted joints." "The Thorn" is thus a poem about poetry, a verse essay upon epitaphs. As its focus and center, the aged thorn stands in the borderland between the living and the dead, an incarnation permanently impressive as poetry itself.

"THREE YEARS SHE GREW IN SUN AND SHOWER"

An Author of Nature being supposed, it is not so much a deduction of reason as a matter of experience, that we are thus under his government; under his government in the same sense as we are under the government of civil magistrates.
                        —Joseph Butler, *Analogy of Religion* 110

In "The Thorn," the sea captain clothed nature in language, a possessed vestment that first disguised and then constituted the "reality" to which he, under the dominion of his own and others' language and "alienate[d] from his right mind," of necessity responded. In "Three years she grew" an intriguing reversal of this situation is depicted. Here it is not the human who imposes linguistically on nature, but Nature who imposes on the human. The difference is telling. Wordsworth has created two personae—one in thrall to language, and another a master of language, with godlike linguistic power to create (in fact, rather than in superstition) that which his language dictates, a being whose words become flesh and dwell among us. In "Three years she grew," a fiction is created that Nature's code is clear and accessible, that the "first sentence" and the "second sentence" are and must be congruent, and even that Nature speaks human language. The thorn and its dark enigma, embodying Nature's first sentence, is here replaced by Lucy, who constitutes the flesh in which Nature's words become incarnate. Nature as the primary speaker of the poem is not, as Ferguson observes, a benevolent mother; rather the voice is "preemptive," that of a "Plutonic male," even a "child molester," a lover who competes with and bests the human poet-lover (188–9). Susan Eilenberg likewise sees in Nature a Pluto or a Hades figure associated with the underworld.[10] Each lover claims Lucy as his own. Nature says, "She shall be mine, and I will make / A Lady of *my own*," whereas the poet-persona says, "How soon *my Lucy's* race was run!" (emphasis supplied). Ferguson observes:

> Through most of thirty-five lines, Nature dwells lovingly on his plans for Lucy, with the prurience of an aged lover contemplating a young girl forced to be his bride. If Lucy is a flower, she has been sown to be reaped, in Nature's view; Nature's reaping and raping have moved so close to one another that human laments on the death of virgins become inevitable rather than extraordinary. (189)

Probably the most original rendering in poetry, the Nature of "Three years she grew" evokes a range of responses. Again, Ferguson's reading is perceptive: "Even though Nature speaks like a reaper who considers himself more gay than grim, his tone of noblesse oblige has a sinister edge" (189). Ferguson contrasts the situation of "Three years she grew" with that of Milton's God, Adam, and Eve, wherein there is no competition between the divine and the human for the love of the woman (188).

While comparisons of Nature with Pluto or Hades and the contrast with Milton's God are pertinent to a poem that seems to act as an intertextual echo chamber, they are, I believe, less instructive than an unmistakable biblical intertextuality. Wordsworth's extraordinary Nature and Nature's language find their prototypes in God and his language. Nature's words carry the same kind of potency as those of God.[11] "Thus Nature spake—The work was done" suggests the linguistic efficacy of the first creative fiat: "God said, 'Let there be light' and there was light." In both cases, to say is to accomplish as words become

things in the world. Another biblical text, however, is of particular interest. In Ezekiel 16, God appears in his role of lover and husband to
Jerusalem. He finds Jerusalem as an exposed baby girl, sown, as it were,
in "an open field," unwashed, naked, "polluted in [her] own blood"
(Ez. 16:3–5). God commands the child to live and grow, to flourish as
"the bud of the field." As Jerusalem grows, God observes with clear appreciation for the sexually maturing girl, "thou art come to excellent
ornaments: thy breasts are fashioned, and thine hair is grown" (Ez.
16:6–7). As is Nature's interest in Lucy, God's interest in Jerusalem
can be described as prurient: "Now when I passed by thee, and looked
upon thee, behold thy time was the time of love; and I spread my skirt
over thee, and covered thy nakedness: yea I sware unto thee, and en-
tered into a covenant with thee, saith the Lord God, and thou be-
camest mine" (Ez. 16:8). Like Nature's transformation of Lucy, God's
transformation of Jerusalem is that of the aesthete concerned with
making her beautiful: "Then washed I thee with water; . . . I anointed
thee with oil." God adorns Jerusalem with fine cloth and jewels, gold
and silver, and he observes that she is "exceeding beautiful"; indeed
Jerusalem is renowned for her beauty, "*for it was perfect through my comeli-
ness,* which I had put upon thee, saith the Lord God" (Ez. 16:9–14; emphasis mine).

Both Wordsworth's Nature and Ezekiel's God are types of Pyg-
malionesque artists, fashioning the beloved artifact whose beauty's
source is the artist himself. God invests Jerusalem with his own "comeli-
ness"; Nature likewise bestows upon Lucy his own beauty—the playfulness and joy of the fawn, the state of the floating clouds, the form of the
willow, the beauty of the storm, and the murmuring sound of the rivulets.
Both God and Nature are artist-lovers who fashion from girl children
sexually mature beloveds. Both are proprietary. Jerusalem, claimed as
God's own, will for her infidelity suffer shame, pain, and death: "They
shall stone thee with stones, and thrust thee through with their swords"
(Ez. 16:40). Similarly, Nature is intent to take possession of the child
("She shall be mine") and make of her "a Lady of [his] own." The human
speaker may even suggest that Lucy has been faithless to Nature in becoming, as he says, "my Lucy."

Both Nature and Ezekiel's God tell their own tales of the beloved and act
through their words; both use language to bring about that which they say;
both "women" are passive, lacking both choice and language. God commands Jerusalem, "Live," and she lives and grows, like Lucy, as a "bud of the
field." He dictates both her demise and her apparent reanimation. Ultimately he silences her permanently: "I will establish my covenant with thee;
and thou shalt know that I am the Lord: That thou mayest remember, and

be confounded, and never open thy mouth any more because of thy shame, when I am pacified toward thee for all that thou hast done" (Ez. 16:63). Like Jerusalem, Lucy is wholly passive and malleable, subject to Nature's "law and impulse," the "overseeing power / To kindle or restrain." Nature calls her too a flower, and she is as passive as a flower. Nature uses the passive voice to describe everything that occurs to Lucy: she *has been sown* on the earth and then *is rendered* calm and silent as "mute insensate things"; her form *is moulded* by the beauty of the storm; her face *is made* beautiful as the sounds of the rivulets "pass into her face"; her form is "rear[ed]"; her bosom is "swell[ed]" by "vital feelings of delight." Not only does Nature speak of Lucy in the passive voice, but his linguistic formula is the emphatic pronouncement or decree: "Myself *will*," or "She *shall*," or it or they "*shall*."[12] In both Ezekiel 16 and "Three years she grew," situations are presented in which a powerful being (God or Nature) claims a human girl-child, causes her to grow into a sexually mature woman, fashions her with his own beauty, responds to her sexually, and, explicitly or implicitly, precipitates her "death." In both cases, the language of the supernatural speaker is incarnational, linguistically determining everything that happens to the girl-woman.

Both Jerusalem's and Lucy's deaths present problems. After Jerusalem is seemingly killed with stones and swords, she apparently "survives" to endure further verbal abuse, against which she is unable to respond: Like the mute Lucy, she can "never open [her] mouth any more." But, as her name suggests, she is not only beloved bride, but chosen people, and holy land, and therefore has an apparently renewable existence. Likewise, although Lucy's one act is to die (whether *to die* is an active verb is moot), she cannot really be said to die so much as to be transformed into, or appropriated to, Nature. She becomes in a sense a form of "first sentence," a "natural artifact"—a message spoken by Nature—as she is embodied in Nature's aspects; she is then translated ("read") in the poet's "second sentence," although, as noted, there is an eerie congruity between Nature's language and the poet's, suggesting the privilege of the prophet to reproduce divine messages verbatim. It is one of the great ironies that the divine Word can speak clearly only through human language and human flesh. The prophet, while claiming absolute fidelity to the divine message, is always vulnerable to the accusation of false prophecy. The present case offers at least the fiction that the poet's voice has been usurped; that he does nothing more than record faithfully and completely Nature's words. Critics have at times accepted the "reality" of that fiction, and at times debated whether Nature speaks for the poet, or the poet speaks for Nature.[13]

When the text is read against Ezekiel 16, however, the situation resolves itself in other terms. The human poet-persona who speaks the opening line-and-a-half of "Three years she grew" is like the prophet

Ezekiel, whose words open his chapter 16, and whose task is simply to repeat God's words verbatim: "Again the word of the Lord came unto me,
saying, Son of man, cause Jerusalem to know her abominations . . ." (Ez.
16:1–2). Wordsworth's speaker says, in effect, "Again the word of Nature
came unto me, saying. . . ." As prophet of Nature, his job is to repeat verbatim what Nature says and, in effect, to *realize* the message he receives. A
question in each case concerns whether the poet-prophet must "translate"
the language he hears. Ezekiel's God seems to speak Hebrew, but what
language does Nature speak? Again Lyotard's notion of a "first sentence"
in the idiom of matter with obscure meaning and without referent is pertinent. Wordsworth makes clear in other contexts that he must read,
translate, and interpret nature's language in order to make breathings for
incommunicable powers. Ferguson suggests that the appropriation of
Lucy's voice and spirit or breath "constitutes a suppression of the poet's
voice" (189). While it is safe to say that the biblical poet-prophet's voice
is always appropriated as he is compelled to speak not his own words, but
faithfully to repeat the divine message, the "natural" language reported in
"Three years she grew" must either be Nature's English, or the poet's
"reading" of a natural code. Unlike Ezekiel, who remains silent as his
chapter 16 ends, Wordsworth's poet-persona offers a coda in his own
voice and, as Eilenberg points out, in a style quite distinct from Nature's
(132). First he affirms the linguistic incarnational legitimacy of Nature:
"Thus Nature spake—the work was done." *Work* suggests the poet's or
artist's product, but it also suggests the efficacious power of Nature's
speaking and its necessary accomplishments. (The *work* of creation in
Genesis 1 is likewise accomplished by speech.) As he continues, the
speaker's tone is curiously uninflected as he accepts Lucy's loss (unless one
reads "How soon my Lucy's race was run!" as a cry of anguish and regret
or as an implied criticism of Nature).

The speaker shares, however, Nature's habit of speaking of Lucy in the
passive voice: Lucy doesn't run her race; it is run for her. Finally the poet-
persona receives Lucy's legacy of land—the natural scene to which, as it
seems, she has been assimilated. He makes no judgment of Nature, ac-
quiesces apparently in Lucy's fate, and appears placid as he contemplates
his "calm and quiet scene." He ratifies Nature's poem and even seems to
benefit through the legacy from Lucy's death-that-is-not-a-death. As
Ferguson observes, "in imperious tones" Nature has created "an eternal
Lucy." If, as I believe, Jerusalem is Lucy's precursor, the "eternal" and
"natural" form of Lucy may well be not only as Nature's bride, but as
land—a land that is also a chosen people. In Lucy's case, the "holy land"
she has become is the poet's England, the heath, the "calm and quiet
scene," which he celebrates and for which he confesses his love as Lucy's

home in the last of the Lucy poems, "I travelled among unknown Men": "Nor England! did I know till then / What love I bore to thee."[14] Who controls whose language is, I believe, a problem only within certain language-made "realities." The fiction of prophecy, that the prophet merely repeats (or acts as a conduit for) the words of the divine message, carries as well the fiction of the appropriated voice. But Wordsworth creates the fiction, creates the voice, creates Lucy as the incarnation of Nature's speaking. Wordsworth's poem presents a figurative form of incarnational poetics, a demonstration at two levels (the poet's and Nature's) of words that incarnate thought. Whatever fiction the poem presents, Nature's language is not Nature's own. It is the poet's "translation" of the natural code, the second sentence in this difficult dialogue. Nature did not write Wordsworth's poetry for him; rather Wordsworth wrote Nature's poetry. And the question is, why this prophetic intertext, this figure, this language, this depiction of Nature's hostile takeover?

The sea captain of "The Thorn" and Nature of "Three years she grew" can be said to illustrate opposite poles of language use. In one, the poet assumes the mode of the linguistic inept, in thrall to language; in the other, he assumes the mode of divine decree. In both instances the language has great power. In the captain's case it dominates his thought as clothing or "counter-spirit"; in Nature's case, it is language as incarnation, creating the reality it enunciates. In both instances the poet is the translator; in both the product is the poem, whose subject—the eternal Lucy or the ever-suffering thorn—remains an incarnate denizen of the borderland between life and death.

"LUCY GRAY" AND THE BRIDGE
OF TIME, OR WHAT'S IN A NAME?

> *Eternity is a self-sustaining temporal structure built by language over the abyss of death.*
> —J. Hillis Miller, *The Linguistic Moment* 104

In his early "Letter to the Bishop of Llandaff," Wordsworth mentions the "sublime allegory of Addison" in which the author "represents us as crossing an immense bridge, from whose surface from a variety of causes we disappear one after another, and are seen no more" (*Pr. W.* 1:32). Wordsworth's reference is to Addison's "The first Vision of Mirzah," a text that Wordsworth knew well, admired, and remembered. In that "first Vision," Addison represents the bridge as life, containing many concealed trapdoors. When those crossing the bridge step on the trapdoors, they fall through them "into the Tide" and immediately disappear. Beneath the bridge is "Part of the great Tide of Eternity" or *"that Portion of Eternity which is called Time"* (*Pr. W.* 1:60–1; emphasis supplied). Wordsworth seems to have recalled this allegory again when he wrote of the enigmatic and solitary Lucy Gray. Another denizen of the border-land, Lucy Gray is neither of this world nor completely out of it ("some maintain that to this day / She is a living Child," and the narrator has seen her at break of day); unaccountably inhabiting both timeless and timed dimensions, she is neither living nor dead. She disappears into the blowing snow of a winter storm. The next day her parents follow her small footprints onto a bridge, where they mysteriously stop: "They fol-lowed from the snowy bank / The footmarks, one by one, / Into the middle of the plank, / And further there were none." Lucy seems to have found her way out of the mundane world of rural England, into a text, and onto that allegorical bridge of life where she stepped onto one of the trapdoors and slipped into a borderland, "that Portion of Eternity which is called Time."[15]

Although Lucy Gray shares several characteristics with the child of "Three years she grew" (both are solitary; both live on the moors like flowers and "die" young and quickly), there are telling differences. As dis-cussed, Lucy of "Three years she grew" takes on the silence of "mute in-sensate things" as she is absorbed into Nature, whereas Lucy Gray is never deprived of speech. Lucy Gray's very name suggests the aspect of Nature to which she is appropriated: "gray light." She disappears into the gray light of blowing snow, and reappears, to be seen by the narrator, in the gray light of dawn. Solitary and singing as she moves through the twi-light between time and eternity, life and death, she and her song are fig-ures for the poet and poetry. And, as Wordsworth often suggests, the poet is not dead until he is silenced, for poetry acts as a medium wherein the living spirit may abide; embodied in language it can continue to live, or at least, like Lucy Gray, will "not wholly perish," as Wordsworth claims in this passage from *Home at Grasmere:*

> I would not *wholly perish* even in this,
> Lie down, and be forgotten in the dust,
> I and the modest partners of my days
> *Making a silent company in death.*
> It must not be, if I divinely taught
> Am privileged to speak as I have felt
> Of what in man is human or divine. (903–9; emphasis supplied)

Death, the lines suggest, is "silent," without speech. Life speaks, and the living spirit through that language does not "wholly perish." It moves into the language-crafted borderland where the old leech gatherer dwells, "not all alive nor dead."

As a spirit of dawn and twilight, Lucy Gray sings in solitude, a poetic sibling of the Danish boy, another solitary singer, a "Spirit of noon-day" ("The Danish Boy" 23), who sings in a "forgotten tongue" (36). In "The Danish Boy" (called merely "A Fragment" through the early years of its publication history), Wordsworth has taken care to disclose in rather evocative terms something of the features of the borderland of which I have been speaking. It is a "sacred" dell, now separate from profane space and time yet bearing enduring signs of both: former human habitation and natural devastation and the ruins of time—"a tempest-stricken tree" and a "corner-stone by lightning cut, / The last stone of a lonely hut" (3–8).[16] A temporal representative of a forgotten people and sole resident of the dell (a place devoid of wholly natural beings—birds, bees, sheep, and horses), the boy continues to sing "Beside the tree and corner-stone" (43–4), an image evocative of Wordsworth's own poetic occupation in *Michael*. The sacred dell is apparently inhospitable to things that die, but not the boy, who is like the eternal, self-renewing wild flowers that flourish there (12–20). The dell of the Danish boy has been marked by time (as evidenced by the ruined hut, the boy's ancient attire, and forgotten language), but is not in time (as evidenced by the continued existence of the boy—he is a "thing no storm can e'er destroy" [10]—and his apparently eternal singing). Like Lucy Gray, the boy is a borderer; he inhabits that portion of eternity that is called time, and like her he can be seen and heard:

> The lovely Danish Boy is blest
> And happy in his flowery cove:
> From bloody deeds his thoughts are far;
> And yet he warbles songs of war,
> That seem like songs of love,
> For calm and gentle is his mien:
> Like a dead Boy he is serene. (50–5)

Although the boy is called a "shadow" (11) and a "spirit" (23) and is, "*Like* a dead Boy," serene, he is clearly not dead—not all alive, perhaps, but not dead. Like Lucy Gray, he and his songs are figures for the poet and poetry, a poet who will not "wholly perish" so long as he is "privileged to speak"; his language may be unknown, but, like that of the solitary reaper, is nevertheless significant in the borderland where things are not governed by the either/or of ordinary existence, where one may be not "all alive or dead," and where "songs of war" may seem like "songs of love." It is the place where Lucy Gray exists in an eternally present moment, never look-ing behind; where she sings her song, her poem, a sort of epitaph spoken to the living by the dead-but-living child; and where souls evade the ter-rors of the "silent company" of death and, incarnated in word-things, not only do not "perish wholly," but endure and prevail.

"TO H. C., SIX YEARS OLD"—
INCARNATION AND REINCARNATION

H. C., like Lucy Gray and the Danish boy, is a borderer, and like them he sings a solitary song, his "self-born carol." So isolated is H. C. that he ex-ists in a dimension separate from but adjacent to that of ordinary earth-lings. As with Lucy Gray, the space of this child touches on or overlaps with common space and time. H. C. is a "Faery Voyager," a traveler through realms where earth and heaven are not separated, but are per-ceived in "one imagery." There is even some question as to whether H. C. is wholly embodied—incarnated—as his "boat" (or body) is "afloat in such clear water" that it seems rather to "brood on air than on an earthly stream"; he exists between heaven and earth, "suspended in a stream as clear as sky." Parallels between H. C. and the child-philosopher of the "Intimations Ode" add support to the implicit theme of reincarnation associated with this child of the border—he is, like Jesus, associated with the lamb, the word become flesh. He has brought his fancies "from afar," and, like the Danish boy, he knows a forgotten tongue, but he must of ne-cessity use inadequate human language. His border vision is such that he can only make of his words "a mock apparel, / And fittest to unutterable thought." As a percipient of heaven and earth in "one imagery," he must find nature's code absolutely mysterious; superimposed upon that code brought "from afar," it is implicated in and intermixed with thoughts for which there simply are no human words; they are "unutterable," untrans-latable. As a result, the child's response in this dialogue cannot incarnate the language of nature because of interference from the signs of that other realm from which he has traveled. He can only *clothe* or conceal those unspeakable thoughts, the fancies brought from afar, in the words of humans and the signs of nature; that is, he can only disguise or conceal them as he dresses them in "mock apparel."

Situated in the borderland between eternity and time, between air and earth, and between life and death—quite clearly on an "Isthmus of a Middle State"—H. C. lives precariously, both figuratively and literally. Human misery will probably destroy the blessed vision and the self-born carol; nature may well kill him ("end [him] quite"). A "Dew-drop," the child is both air and water, ill suited to life on "the soiling earth" and, "at the touch of wrong," able to "Slip[] in a moment out of life." The phrase, *to slip out of life,* does not appear to mean "to die" but rather to move from the borderland—a blessed state between heaven and earth where vision is enhanced by celestial light and language proves nearly adequate to its task (is "fittest to unutterable thought")—into "the light of common day," or the "universe of death," where words can dominate thought and one is always conscious "of the inadequateness of . . . [one's] own powers, or the deficiencies of language" (*P. W.* 2:513).

As a kind of Wordsworthian precursor of Shelley's Sky-Lark, H. C. is a figure for the ideal poet, the joyous visionary at home between heaven and earth and untouched by human suffering: "I thought of times when Pain might be thy guest, / Lord of thy house and hospitality; / And grief, uneasy Lover!" To exist beyond pain and grief may be a condition to be envied but for the human poet is not only impossible but probably undesirable to sustain. H. C., like the Sky-Lark, lives joyously, a blithe spirit unacquainted with suffering; his condition is, Wordsworth suggests, a phase in the life of the poet, but not one in which he may remain. For the poet's task, intimately keyed to "the still sad music of humanity," is to find words not to clothe but to incarnate the dialogue between the human and the natural, ephemeral man and the "soiling earth" in which he lives and dies, the world breathed by God into a dense, material system of signs that the poet must read and translate.

THE DROWNED MAN

But some man will say, How are the dead raised up? and with what body do they come? Thou fool, that which thou sowest is not quickened, except it die.

—1 Cor. 15:35–36

Not surprisingly, Book 5 of the *Prelude,* entitled "Books," is marked more heavily than other parts by what Genette calls "transtextuality" and "textual transcendence" (discussed in the introduction), which he defines as "everything that brings [the text] into relation (manifest or hidden) with other texts" (81–2). Book 5 thus offers the best example of Wordsworth's practice of incarnational poetics, its biblical underpinnings, and its intertextual dimensions—the society of mighty poets, living and dead, whose "visionary power" is "embodied in the mystery of words" (*Prelude* 5:620–2). Questions that haunt both the poetics and the indeterminacy of the borderland between life and death are those that St. Paul says "some man" will ask. The questions are Wordsworth's: "How are the dead raised up? and With what body do they come?" Wordsworth's text (Book 5 as a whole, and particularly the drowned-man episode) takes these questions seriously and poses additional questions: What does it mean to be dead, or to be "raised up"? and What does "body" (raised or not) mean in human terms or in the context of incarnational poetics? A rich array of background texts is brought to bear on the questions and provides a density of texture in which meanings proliferate, equivocate, and echo not only intertextually, but intratextually—between texts but also within Book 5 itself.

Therefore, while my chief concern is the significance of the drowned-man episode (5:450–81) for an understanding of Wordsworth's incarnational poetics and the phenomena of the borderland, I must come to this episode through the wider context of Book 5 and its intertextuality. Focusing on the dream of the Arab-Quixote, J. Hillis Miller in *The Linguistic Moment* provides a fine analysis of Book 5 and many aspects of its intertextuality, and in what follows I shall draw on his insights. I shall also draw on those of Andrzej Warminski, whose discussion of the drowned man is extensive, thoughtful, and informed. Given my intertextual interests, I must also keep in mind Cynthia Chase's intriguing reading of the episode and her claims that it is essentially nonfigurative, one in which the figures of preceding episodes are "divest[ed] of figurative meaning," and that it therefore "resists figurative interpretation" (16–7). An implication of this analysis is that the episode breaks free of intertextual and intratextual significations. Although in some ways Chase's own reading negates her claims for the literal, I will want to stress the role of intertextuality and intratextuality in rendering the episode inevitably figural and equivocal. My intention, for the most part, is to supplement the work of these and other critics, and to argue—in response to Miller's observation that "The poem on the page is a dead body" (105) or Warminski's implication that it is impossible to get this "linguistic, tropological machine," this poetry, "to produce a living spirit" (30)—that it is desirable to restore a critical balance in Wordsworth's poetics, tipping the scales back toward that point where the theory demonstrates the power of words to hold life and death in precarious and equivocal balance. Certainly Wordsworth knew, as do his critics, that death is inevitable and universal, although what *death* means is for Wordsworth an elusive idea to be tracked through a linguistic and intertextual labyrinth. It takes a poet of Wordsworth's stature to reveal that language itself is the birthplace, the homeland, and the only milieu in which the abstractions *life* and *death* can be represented, engaged, and confronted. It is testimony to his genius that, armed only with words, the poet is able to demonstrate for moments (or years or centuries) at a time both the truth and the lie of *life* and *death*. In other words, I want to show that

Wordsworth recognizes the textual nature of human reality and is able to create a verbal space that proves hospitable to the dying or dead body and the living spirit, the vital breath, the Word made flesh in the "linguistic, tropological machine" that constitutes Book 5 and, in particular, the drowned-man episode.

Nevertheless, on the side of death is that unforgettable image of the dead body rising from the lake "bolt upright" (5:471–2), a most ironic-seeming resurrection. The risen body of the drowned man appears, in one sense, as a dismissive answer to St. Paul's questions: How are the dead raised up? With "grappling irons and long poles." With what body do they come? A *dead* body, a "spectral shape / Of terror" with "ghastly face." Despite all this, there are other possibilities to consider as the intertexts exert their claims. The episode appears as a last reiteration of a theme running through episodes of Book 5 (the intratexts) and a common thread to be traced in the intertexts—drowning or destruction by water, followed by recovery. The theme is central to the dream at the beginning of the book, a text that is probably "borrowed from one of the three famous dreams of Descartes described in Baillet's *Life of Descartes*" (Miller 92). The dream episode makes reference to Cervantes' *Don Quixote,* transforming its ironic hero into a type of Noah (afloat on a "ship of the desert") and transporting this figure to the scene of an impending universal flood. He seeks to rescue not people and animals but "books" from the flood, the stone and the shell, a pair that evoke the traditional topos of the two books—the Bible and nature (Miller 93)—the shell representing prophecy or revealed scripture, and the stone, nature. At the same time, the stone is a human text, "Euclid's Elements," and the shell is a trumpet—a prophetic trumpet, like Gabriel's, that would be blown to announce the resurrection of the dead (1 Thess. 4:16), but also like the trumpet whose sounds St. Paul compares to words. Taking up the subject of speaking in tongues, St. Paul asks, "For if the trumpet give an uncertain sound, who shall prepare himself to the battle?" (1 Cor. 14:8). Miller points out that key terms in St. Paul's discourse—*prophesy, unknown tongue, interpretation,* and *understanding*—"all reappear in Wordsworth," along with the trumpet (97n). An intriguing prototype of the speaking and prophetic trumpet appears in Revelation: "the first voice I heard was as it were of a trumpet talking with me; which said, come up hither, and I will shew thee things which must be hereafter" (4:1). The apocalyptic flood of Book 5 suggests, of course, the biblical flood as well as Milton's version of it. Destruction by water is thematic as well in Shakespeare's Sonnet 64 (a direct quotation from which appears at line 25). The sonnet's speaker declares, "I have seen the hungry ocean gain / Advantage on the kingdom of the shore." Another thus far unrecognized but equally pertinent intertext is Ovid's account of a universal flood in his *Metamorphoses,* for Ovid, like Wordsworth after him, explored the linguistic borderland, and his text intriguingly provides many of the echoes and images that pervade Book 5 and illuminate the episode of the drowned man. Taken together, these and other intertexts demonstrate the complexity of figuration and involuted layers of significance among the drowned man, a universal flood, books, bodies, stones, shells, life and death, and incarnational poetics.

Parallels between Ovid's flood and the biblical flood are several, but the postdiluvial events are of greatest interest here.[17] Following the biblical flood, Yahweh facilitates the regeneration of earth and humankind, blessing Noah and his sons, saying, "Be fruitful and multiply, and replenish the earth" (Gen. 9:1). Survivors of Ovid's flood, Deucalion and Pyrrha, however, must offer thanks and praise "the fortunate / Will of God" (40) before Jove, observing "this gentle innocent / And his bride," sweeps away the clouds and lets the sun shine once more on earth. At that time, Triton blows his "curved sea shell" trumpet to recall the flood waters from the land. Through an oracle, Deucalion and Pyrrha then learn that they are to restore the race of humankind not by being fruitful and multiplying, but by scattering the "mother's bones," the "guiltless stones" of mother earth (42). Following instructions, the pair drop pebbles, which "grew into rocks, rocks into statues / That looked like men; the darker parts still wet / With earth were flesh, dry elements were bones, / And veins began to stir with human blood" (42). Thus in Ovid's text are found key images to be reinterpreted in Book 5—the killing flood, postdiluvial regeneration, and the "books" of the dream: the sea shell trumpet and the vital stones.

Through Ovid's intertext Wordsworth's stone and shell assume another layer of significance. As bones of mother earth, the stones still in a sense represent nature (as does the stone-book "Euclid's Elements"), but not so much the book of nature as the creative, regenerative artistry of nature, an artistry that Wordsworth acknowledges as the power of nature's "living presence" to "subsist / Victorious" through apocalyptic disaster and restore itself (5:29–36). Like Wordsworth, Ovid presents nonhuman nature as self-regenerating, providing an intertextual model of the borderland in the form of an indeterminate stage between death and life revealed when a postdiluvian peasant turns the saturated soil and

> finds under it a world
> Of things that live, half-live, or creep or run
> As though one body of earth were alive,
> *Half dead, so in all things*

And in a single body, half motionless,
Inert, yet half alive. (42; emphasis supplied)

The passage is evocative of Wordsworth's old leech gatherer and other borderers between death and life. Ovid reveals nature (earth) in its myriad parts, half alive and half dead, as though of "one body." Ovid's stones are human seeds "raised up" from this body, who on their way to becoming living beings likewise achieve an indeterminate not-all-alive-or-dead stage, passing through a type of Wordsworthian condition of "living statue" or "statued life," as "rocks [grow] into statues / That look[] like men," in which "veins beg[in] to stir with human blood." The whole of this half-dead, half-living indeterminacy and intermediacy exists "in all things / And in a single body," each "body" a metonymy *in se.*

Wordsworth's sea shell trumpet is closer akin to Triton's horn than to the ram's horn trumpets of the Bible, yet its function is radically different from Triton's. One might even say that Wordsworth's shell is Triton's, but one altered to announce death by calling forth the flood waters, rather than announcing life by recalling the waters and preparing the way if not for a universal resurrection (as does Gabriel's), at least for a universal regeneration. Through intertextual association, then, Wordsworth's sea shell trumpet is implicated in both life and death. The fact that Wordsworth's shell is associated with language generally (having "voices more than all the winds" [108]), speaking in tongues (its message is in an "unknown tongue" [94]), prophecy (the true speaking of the impending flood), and poetry (it is an "ode in passion uttered" [97]) requires not only that it reveal something of Wordsworth's incarnational poetics, but that in the process it implicate both life and death: impending universal destruction and, through the intertexts, regeneration (Triton's shell) and resurrection (Gabriel's trumpet). It is an appropriately paradoxical instrument for this text about the relationships among poetry, life, and death. It speaks in unknown but intelligible tongue, giving its "uncertain sound" in the poetic space where language can render life and death oxymoronic partners and mutually implicating processes; it is the shell of a dead sea creature, yet it speaks with the voice of a living god, and of "many gods," voices more "than all the winds"; it announces universal destruction "by deluge now at hand" and *at the same time,* like Triton's and Gabriel's trumpets, it provides "a joy, a consolation, and a hope" (5:94–109).

Once the intertextual signs are recognized, the drowned-man episode and its relationship with other episodes of Book 5 reveal additional, if more intricately equivocal, possibilities of meanings. Water as the destructive element, concentrated in this episode in Esthwaite's Lake, acts as a metaphor for human mortality and is related to the water that flows beneath the bridge of life through which Lucy Gray has fallen, water that is "Part of the great Tide of Eternity" or "that Portion of Eternity which is called Time" (Pr. W. 1:60–1). As the inexorable movement of time, it has appeared in conjunction with death several times in Book 5. It is the sea on which the dreamer gazes while contemplating the mortality of humans and their works before "passing into a dream" (63, 70). In the dream itself, the destructive element takes the form of the apocalyptic flood, the "waters of the deep / Gathering upon us" (130–1), the "fleet waters of the drowning world" (136) from which the Arab-Quixote madman flees to bury (or to sow) his books, the stone and shell. In the Boy of Winander passage, the destructive waters take the form of mountain torrents and lake, which may be seen to invade the boy's heart and mind—the "voice of mountain torrents" is "carried far into his heart"; the scene "enter[s] unaware" into his mind with its "solemn imagery, its rocks, / Its woods, and that uncertain heaven, received into the bosom of the steady lake" (409–13). The visible scene, reflected in the lake, seems to ambush the boy, for in the stanza break following these lines the boy dies. Although no cause is mentioned, he has apparently drowned in internalized waters that appear as the sort of "intermediate image" assimilating potential life (suggested in "that uncertain heaven") to inevitable death (the destructive element of water that invades him).[18]

The drowned man as a metonymy for "the drowning world" comes to represent every mortal human being, including the poet, and provides Wordsworth a focus not only for enunciating in verse his incarnational poetics, but for consolidating and turning (troping) once again the several images, themes, intertextual echoes, and interrogations of Book 5 as a whole. Central images in the drowned-man episode suggest Wordsworth's exploration in this passage of books (poetry) as written language in two common metaphors for language: clothing and incarnation, those same metaphors that Wordsworth will later employ to enunciate his incarnational poetics in the Essays upon Epitaphs quoted earlier. The former is figured in the abandoned "heap of garments"; the latter, in the risen body of the drowned man.

A version of the episode was recorded in the 1799 Prelude as one of the "accidents in flood and field," that, Wordsworth says,

> impressed . . . [his] mind
> *With images* to which in following years
> Far other feelings were attached—*with forms*
> That yet exist with independent life,
> And, like their archetypes, know no decay.
> (First Part 283–7; emphasis supplied)[19]

The claim is that an incident such as the drowned-man episode is impressed on the mind as image (like the thorn) and form, almost a Platonic form, an archetype, enduring, changeless, existing with "independent life." The initial experience is presented as a kind of "first sentence," a hieroglyph that the speaker will learn over time to read as it draws to itself feelings and significance. Such an image or form is endlessly interpretable. Given the claim of permanence in the image or form, it is not surprising to find that the actual details of the passage remain virtually unchanged between 1799 and the 1805 *Prelude*. Aside from some careful rewordings or reorderings that seem intended to shift focus slightly or adjust the meter, the changes of 1805 consist largely of the addition of interpretations made possible as the poet-persona learns to "read" the incident, its attendant feelings, and its meanings. The first of Wordsworth's interpretations of the incident is implicit in his placement of the episode in the 1805 *Prelude*. The poet transports the passage from a context in the 1799 *Prelude* related to "spots of time" to the climactic 1805 position in a context dealing with books (texts and intertexts) and human mortality (death by water). The poet, now having learned to decode its images, focuses on the metaphoric implications of clothing and body to the themes of Book 5—poetry and human mortality.

The first explicit interpretation consists of the addition of a single line. The 1799 version reads, "The succeeding day / There came a company" (274–5), whereas the 1805 version inserts within dashes between the lines (now slightly altered), a "reading": "Those unclaimed garments telling a plain tale" (468). This addition not only recognizes the garments as sign and sentence, "telling a plain tale," but also language quite obviously figured *as clothing,* a metaphor the poet is now able to recognize. Language as clothing is contrasted in the *Essays upon Epitaphs* with embodiments, those expressions "which are not what the garb is to the body but what the body is to the soul," which latter sort is able to express "energy, stillness, grandeur, tenderness, those feelings which are the pure emanations of nature, those thoughts which have the infinitude of truth" because the words themselves are "a constituent part and power or function in the thought" (*Pr. W.* 2:84). Yet at the same time this metaphor of abandoned garments echoes intratextually another instance occurring early in Book 5 when Wordsworth refers to books "worthy of inconquerable life" but inevitably to perish, as garments, of which humans may have no need when they are dead: that is, books as garments are separable from the body-soul incarnation that might achieve immortality and "survive," but, without books, in a condition "Abject, depressed, forlorn, disconsolate" (5: 23–7). Thus the garments lying by the lake are a complex figure, representing, on the one hand, suspect language, language as clothing, *and,* on the other, poetry itself. As garments, books are to verse what bodies are to souls: "Poor earthly caskets" covering, containing "immortal verse"—the language that incarnates the thought of a "Shakespeare or Milton, labourers divine" (5:163–5). In this latter sense, the garments may be seen as a version of the shell-book, the abandoned "garment" of a sea creature long dead, which *is* poetry, prophecy, and revealed scripture, from which in unknown but intelligible tongue immortal voices are heard.

The garments, then, as complex image representing language, both suspect and legitimate, tell a plain tale. At first reading, "plain tale" has a clear meaning, for in two of its senses *plain* means "evident, obvious, manifest," and "full, plenary, entire, or perfect" (OED at *plain*). The unclaimed clothing *tells* that its owner has drowned in the lake. The plain tale (the story all poetry tells, according to Miller [98]) is an obvious, unambiguous, perfect story of death. The dead schoolmaster has no further need of his garments-books-poetry, all of which reiterate the message of the shell: "Destruction to the children of the earth / By deluge now at hand" (98–9). Other meanings of *plain*, however, add possibilities. *Plain* can mean also "of simple composition," "without embellishment or decoration" and "guileless, free from ambiguity" (OED at *plain*). These meanings contrast the plain tale of the garments-as-book with the story of the shell-as-book, for the shell's message is anything but simple, unadorned, and unambiguous.[20] As the dreamer puts the shell to his ear he seems to hear the fatal tale of the garments, but it is spoken as prophecy and poetry, passionately in an unknown tongue that he nevertheless understands; it is articulate, but at the same time inarticulate as the blast of a trumpet. He hears

> that instant in an unknown tongue,
> Which yet I understood, articulate sounds,
> A loud prophetic blast of harmony,
> An ode in passion uttered, which foretold
> Destruction to the children of the earth
> By deluge now at hand. (5:94–9)

Although the shell's tale may seem plain enough, it is complicated not only by being spoken in tongues, but by a cacophony of voices. The shell's voice or voices are those of a god or many gods, "more than all the winds," and while telling of impending disaster nevertheless constitute "A joy, a consolation, and a hope." It is no plain tale that prophesies universal destruction and at the same time brings joy, consolation, and hope. The archetype of such tales is found in the difficult and mysterious Book of Revelation.

In a similar way, the plain, unambiguous tale of the garments is to be contrasted with and its message equivocated by the tale of the body. The episode recounts that the poet-persona as a child, having just come to Esthwaite, wanders with "half-infant ['half-wordless'] thoughts," and, seeking he knows not what, crosses one of the fields "which, shaped like ears, / Make green peninsulas" on the lake, from which point he sees on the opposite shore the "heap of garments," left, he assumes, by someone bathing in the lake. As he watches,

> the calm lake
> Grew Dark, with all the shadows on its breast,
> And now and then a fish up-leaping snapped
> The breathless stillness. The succeeding day—
> Those unclaimed garments telling a plain tale—
> Went there a company, and in their boat
> Sounded with grappling-irons and long poles:
> At length, the dead man, 'mid that beauteous scene
> Of trees and hills and water, bolt upright
> Rose with his ghastly face. . . . (5:463–72)

The remarkable lake with ears (ears that may hear the horns of Triton recalling the flood waters and Gabriel announcing the Resurrection) tells in many ways of death. It is calm, dark, and shadowed in "breathless stillness," a condition that suggests absence of life (the dead man is breathless and still), absence of spirit (breath), and absence of language (the stillness of the "silent company in death" [*Home at Grasmere* 906]), a stillness snapped by the fish up-leaping. The fish is a sign, a part of the natural code, evocative of Jesus, and the rising of the fish from the lake offers an image of restored life in Jesus' resurrection, which constitutes the defeat of death and its engulfing waters through the breaking of the awful breathless stillness.[21] Jesus' own resurrection, suggested in the rising of the fish, is said to be the necessary first resurrection from death to life, making possible the second, universal resurrection (which Gabriel's horn announces). The subsequent rising of the dead man "bolt upright" with his "ghastly [terrifying, yet ghostly or spiritual] face" amid the "beauteous scene" reiterates the import of the fish rising, a restoration to life, a breaking of the breathless stillness.

Pausing to retrace the steps, the scene and events surrounding the rising of the dead man have been "impressed" on the youthful mind of the poet, where they remained, "know[ing] no decay." Many years later the images and their implications, now inextricable from thought—that of the poet and that of the sages and bards he has obtained from books (those intertexts) about death and resurrection—become flesh as they attain thingness, materiality in the *verbal* images of the garments, the scene, and the naked body. The tale of the body constitutes a sort of ironic incarnational punning on the notion of the Word become flesh, because here it is the naturally encrypted, nonreferential, imagistic perception of the naked rising body (flesh) which becomes word, as it is experienced by the boy with his "half-infant" thoughts, in response to which he later learns to speak the "second sentence" in human language, translating the "plain" tale of the garments and the complex tale of the body into human language. Wordsworth has established a situation in which a "real" drowned and risen body, its verbal representation, the interpretation of that representation, and its figurative significance are ironically made to cooperate in an interrogation and demonstration not only of death and life but of words as things, as "body"—all mutually implicated in his incarnational poetics. It is difficult to discern any boundary lines here, either between the literal and the figural, or among the material, the mental, and the verbal. As with the originating metaphor, thing, thought, and word are one: "This is my body."

The second interpretive addition to the archetype of the drowned man comes in conjunction with this risen body and demonstrates yet further that the tale of the body is not a plain tale. The body is interpreted as "a spectre shape—/ Of terror even," and yet this shape of death and terror is paradoxically not frightening: "And yet no vulgar fear, / Young as I was, a child not nine years old, / Possessed me." The reason offered for the lack of fear is an intertextual one: that fairy tales and romances (the texts that had driven Don Quixote mad) had presented "such sights" to the "inner eye," so that the "reality" of death and the image of terror presented by the drowned man are read through a palimpsest of texts; they are intertextualized—textually transformed and adorned—and are "known" through the word-made-flesh, the vision of authors "Embodied in the mystery of words" (5:621).[22] Thus the body rises from the lake with the character of a "spectral shape" or spirit (ambiguously meaning breath, life, and words) invested with decoration and grace to become art:

> Thence [from those texts] came a spirit hallowing what I saw
> With decoration and ideal grace,
> A dignity, a smoothness, like the works
> Of Grecian art and purest poesy. (5:472–82).

Equally interesting are the suggestions that the dead man rises of his own volition ("bolt upright") and that the risen body is moving toward the condition of stone, the opposite process from that which Ovid describes when the bones of mother earth move toward the condition of flesh, as pebbles become rocks, become statues, and "veins began to stir with human blood" (42). The drowned man rises from the lake like a work of art, his human nature adorned with "decoration and ideal grace"; rather than a statue that looks like a man, he is a man who looks like a statue, a Greek statue, characterized by "dignity" and "smoothness." He has attained the status of flesh made art, word in "purest poesy." In all this, he has achieved an incarnation, or reincarnation, a life like stone, the "statued life" or the "living statue," a condition not all alive or dead. His flesh is made stone and word. His is a growing back toward living stone, the condition of the borderland between life and death and the abode of poetry. In Book 5 stones are books, and books are caskets containing not dead bodies, but "immortal" verse.

Whereas the plain tale of the garments is in some ways like the stone-book called "Euclid's Elements," the story of the body is like that of the shell. It is not plain, but, like the drowned man himself, invested with "decoration and ideal grace," not at all simple and free from ambiguity, but highly complex and equivocal. It is a tale of life and death, life that is not life, and death that is not death. Here words have the sort of power that Wallace Stevens ascribes to them when played by the man with the blue guitar, where "things are as I think they are and say they are on the blue guitar" (xxviii), for the story of the body is about the process of moving about in a world in which life and death are what we say they are, having been created in and understood through texts. The episode places the drowned man and, through him, all humanity in a space constituted of the "mystery of words," that realm discussed in the grand finale of this book on books—a place where "darkness makes abode, and all the host / Of shadowy things do work their changes there / As in a mansion like their proper home." The drowned man, like other "forms and substances," is transformed in this mystery, "circumfused"

> By that transparent veil with light divine,
> And through the turnings intricate of verse
> Present themselves as objects recognized
> In flashes, and with a glory scarce their own. (5: 622–9)

The intricate "turnings" (tropings) of verse are "real" artifacts that embody the stony, wordy facts of life and death, of word made flesh and flesh made word, where mortality encroaches as watery destruction, from which a fish rises with an intertextual promise of life; from which a body rises to a new existence in words; from which a man emerges on his way to achieving immortality in "immortal verse," becoming art, a statued life. The destructive, apocalyptic waters of the drowning world, "the waters of the deep / Gathering upon us," appear as "glittering light" (5:129–31) reflected at last in the "glittering verse" whose complex, paradoxical tropings make their home in the borderland of life and death. In the drowned-man episode, the plain tale of the garments is, of course, not as plain as it may at first seem, for the clothes themselves are not (only) what they seem; they are as well a metaphor for language, and this not-so-plain tale forms a part of Wordsworth's complex poetics, which is completed by the story of the dead-and-risen body—clothing and incarnation: "If words be not (recurring to a metaphor before used) an incarnation of the thought, but only a clothing for it, then surely will they prove an ill gift; such a one as those possessed vestments, read of in the stories of superstitious times, which had power to consume and to alienate from his right mind the victim who put them on" (*Pr. W.* 2:85). Wordsworth saw that human lives transpire in a world created by texts, the works of "sage and bard," the mighty poets who incarnate their thought and their visionary power in words. It is through such texts (the Bible, Ovid, Shakespeare, Milton, even the romances of "superstitious times") that the realities of life and death are encountered and shaped; there that the word is made flesh; there that the resurrection becomes word-thing. And it is there in that poetic borderland that one can witness the transformation of death to life and life to death, of stone into flesh, and flesh into stone; there that one can observe the rising of the fish and the metamorphosis of the drowned man into living stone and verse.

SUMMING UP

In the course of this discussion I have argued that Wordsworth's incarnational poetics is a nonrepresentational, nondualistic theory whose implications pervade his poetic practice. I have examined only a few of numerous texts in which the theory is apparent, showing that Wordsworth explored the theory and its implications for life and death from various perspectives, using language to hollow out a space where life and death are held in suspension, often taking on a stony permanence like a grave marker, as do the old man, the horse, the thorn, and the drowned man, or singing in a twilight between time and eternity, as does Lucy Gray or the Danish boy. Lucy of "Three years she grew" is assimilated to land, rendered eternal through, and embodied in, Nature's and the poet's linguistic artistry. The drowned man is revealed to be spiritual (ghastly), through his resurrection to be progressing ambiguously toward an aesthetic condition, the condition of poetry and sculpture, of word and stone—the vital stone of the *Metamorphosis,* or the marble of a Greek statue—a state in which he may inhabit like the leech gatherer and the thorn the word-crafted borderland between life and death.

The point is not that Wordsworth proposes an aesthetic surrogate for spirituality or "life" as a way of evading death, but that his incarnational poetics leaves open a breathing space, as it were, a place of breath things, that holds in perpetual suspension the implications of the Word made flesh and flesh made word, speech and silence, cloud and stone, life and death. To see into this space is to enjoy the mental torsion of perfect paradox: the "pleasure" resulting from the sight of a horse glimpsed in the moonlight with one foot raised, standing absolutely still, "Like an amphibious work of Nature's hand, / A borderer dwelling betwixt life and death, / A living statue or a statued life" (*Prelude* 498).

CHAPTER 4

How Awesome Is This Place!
WORDSWORTH'S *POEMS ON THE NAMING OF PLACES*

[Some minds] find tales and endless allegories
By river margins, and green woods among.

—P. W. 2:486

Wordsworth's intense and quite idiosyncratic interest in the relationship of language to land, while evident throughout his works, is focused in the *Poems on the Naming of Places*,[1] written in his first year of residence at Grasmere. The epigraph to this chapter is found in MS. M as *Motto for Poems on the Naming of Places* (P. W. 2:486). It appears to issue a caution against reading these poems as personal history and invites close attention to their poetic devices. The phrase "endless allegories" is particularly suggestive, for, as in Robert Lowth's *Lectures on the Sacred Poetry of the Hebrews,* the term *allegory* at this time suggested a master trope of resemblance—often a created rather than an intrinsic resemblance, and especially evocative of biblical models, encompassing metaphor, continued metaphor, parable, and mystical allegory.[2] Yet Wordsworth, in the "Advertisement" to these poems, purports to claim the status of personal history for them, and even to trivialize their subject matter—"little incidents." This apparent discrepancy in authorial claims provides only one dimension of the poems' difficulties. Are the poems found tales and endless allegories, or are they exercises in recording the "*private and peculiar* interest" attendant on certain unnamed sites near Grasmere? Here is Wordsworth's "Advertisement":

> By persons resident in the country, and attached to rural objects, many places will be found unnamed or of unknown names, where little Incidents must have occurred, or feelings been experienced, which will have given to such places a private and peculiar interest. From a wish to give some sort of record to such Incidents, and renew the gratification of such feelings, Names have been given to Places by the Author and some of his Friends, and the following Poems written in consequence. (*P. W.* 2:111)

One reason the poems have not received much critical attention may be traced to this curious understatement (or misstatement) of the poems' nature and the author's purpose. That the motto and advertisement offer very different perspectives on the poems is appropriate, for I believe that this discrepancy is only one of many indications that the *Poems on the Naming of Places* are not exactly what they seem, and why they tend to produce conflicting responses. "It was an April morning," a poem to which I shall return later, illustrates the conflict. At first reading, the poet/speaker appears ingenuous, artless, "natural." His language is simple; his images are concrete, apparently descriptive of no more than the natural scene in which the poem is set; and the poem's meaning is, so it seems, transparent: The poet discovers a pleasant, "wild nook," dedicates it to his sister, and names it "Emma's Dell." In a brief discussion of these poems, Stephen Gill, in his fine biography of Wordsworth, remarks, in line with the claims of the advertisement, that "Most of [the *Poems on the Naming of Places*] relate some new pleasure found locally . . ." (181). Further consideration, however, undermines one's sense of an artless narrator who tells a simple tale. Indeed he begins to sound not ingenuous, but ingenious, or, more intriguingly, actually disingenuous.

A certain disingenuousness may be seen even in the language of the advertisement. Its difficulties are several, but chief among them is the ambiguity of the phrase, "some sort of record." If Wordsworth had said, "From a wish to record such incidents," the names and the poems would more clearly have an objective, historical relationship to the incidents of "private and peculiar interest." The actual wording, however, makes it reasonable to assume that "some sort of record" might be quite different from a history: it might be a fiction, for example, a found tale, or an allegory, or a figurative rendering (such as a mythological etymology) whose relationship to the incident, real or imagined, need be neither objective nor historical. I want to accept the challenge of the motto and argue that the *Poems on the Naming of Places* are imaginative, complex works ("tales and

endless allegories") that reward careful study and, indeed, express concerns and develop theories central to Wordsworth's poetry and poetics. I
will argue further that in these poems, as so often elsewhere,
Wordsworth mines sacred poetry, finding in the biblical etymological tale
his narrative model, and finding in biblical language, tropes, and images
his own language, tropes, and images. In appropriating and adapting
these to his purposes, Wordsworth establishes powerful intertextual
echoes and effects radical revisions of the precursor texts.

Certainly human beings have always named places important to them
and told stories about the naming, but the great textual precedent for
Wordsworth's poems is to be found in the etymological tales of the Old
Testament. There the tale and its effects, as in the story of Jacob's dream
(Gen. 28:10–19), are powerful and enduring. No matter how barren, isolated, or undistinguished, if a place has a name like Bethel, "house of
God," and a story to explain the name, it gains "significance." Or a story
about the naming of a ruined tower may haunt Western humanity in per-
petuity. Bethel, Babel—both sites are textualized by being inscribed, as it
were, with human signs. More than that, they are spiritualized, taking on
the character of sanctuary and named so as to acknowledge a spirituality
or uncanniness that invests the place now and that, perhaps, was always
already there, but unknown, unspeakable because unnamed.[3] At the same
time, the human actors and acts take on a form of permanence or immortality. In Jacob's naming of Bethel, he remarks, "How awesome is this
place! This is none other than the house of God, and this is the gate of
heaven" (Gen. 28:17). Not only does the name single out for attention an
apparently unremarkable space by bestowing an extraordinary name, but
the act of naming itself appropriates the permanence of land to the
human awareness of the uncanny, to a mystery of spiritual space, to
human deeds and human feelings. Hence through the millennia, Jacob,
his uncanny dream vision, and his dialogue and covenant with God hover
about a place named Bethel, "house of God."

The biblical etymological tale appears to require three elements: a
perhaps fictional event or deed occurs or is said to have occurred at a particular place; the place is named to suggest the nature of the event, deed,
outcome, or its participants; and, finally, the story of the event or deed is
told and recorded so as to assign a meaning to the place name that then
encapsulates, calls up, or verifies (by its objective site in the world) the
narrative of events. In the process, a merging of the human actor or actors, the name of the place, and the language of the narrative occurs,
often producing a curious blend of empirical and imaginative "facts."
Without the place name that might be shown on a map, the narrative and
its characters have the status not of history, but of fiction; without the

narrative, the name of the place is essentially meaningless; without the named place and narrative, the human actors pass away like most things human, without a trace. Only in the coincidence of both place name and narrative are the person or persons and human acts protected from oblivion. Only in the coincidence of both are the significance and spirituality of place established and preserved.[4]

Each element must endure for the etymological tale to perform its functions, but those are achieved only through language, ephemeral in its oral form and even in its written form subject to change and decay. As discussed, in his advertisement, recognizing the fate that most human acts and feelings suffer, Wordsworth announces the linguistic defense he has erected against oblivion—naming places and writing poems about those acts of naming.

Although focused in the *Poems on the Naming of Places*, the philosophical and artistic concerns of these poems are evident throughout Wordsworth's works. Therefore, before turning my attention to the individual poems in the group, I want to draw into this discussion some suggestive passages from "The Ruined Cottage" and the *Prelude* (1799, 1805), which prove helpful in understanding the *Poems on the Naming of Places*. In "The Ruined Cottage," with allusion to Psalm 103, Armytage says, speaking of the effects of a drought, "And of the poor did many cease to be, / And their place knew them not" (143–4). Psalm 103, invoked in Armytage's allusion, offers two metaphors for human life—grass and wild flowers: "As for man, *his days are like grass; / he flourishes like a flower of the field;* / for the wind passes over it, and it is gone, / and its place knows it no more" (my emphasis). In the *Prelude* (1805), as the poet is looking about for "time, place, and manners," a theme for his work, images of wild flowers and place recur. The poet suggests that he might select "some old / Romantic tale" neglected by Milton, for example a tale of Wallace:

> How Wallace fought for Scotland, *left the name*
> *Of Wallace to be found like a wild flower,*
> *All over his dear Country,* left the deeds
> Of Wallace, like a family of Ghosts,
> To people the steep rocks and river banks,
> Her natural sanctuaries, with a local soul
> Of independence and stern liberty. (I: 177–219; emphasis supplied)

These passages reveal a cluster of associations among ideas of mortality, names, places, and vegetal images of grass and wild flowers. A human being as grass or flower is fragile, short-lived, and doomed to oblivion. By contrast, Wallace's name, planted like a wild flower "All over his dear Country," endures, suggesting a kind of self-perpetuating power *as name,* to be endlessly repeatable, self-regenerating like the wild flowers. Moreover, the suggestion in the Wallace passage is that the naming of place substitutes a "clonable" name for the person, permitting the place to "know" the human, ephemeral flower of the field, after it is gone, because person and place have become one in the name. With the name or the naming, a kind of numinosity adheres to place, through which the human being achieves a place-bound immortality, an uncanniness as a sort of local spirit: "the deeds / Of Wallace, like a family of Ghosts, / [are left] to people the steep rocks and river banks, / [his country's] natural sanctuaries," that is, her sacred places. The name of Wallace as a place name is thus a metonymy not only for the man, but for his "deeds" and the accounts of deeds, all of which are rendered sacred, immortal, in and through the permanence of place.[5]

This same cluster of associations is found in the "spots of time" passage, which recurs in all three versions of the *Prelude.* The lines in question immediately precede the account of the murderer's grave, a passage that undergoes intriguing revision between the 1799 version and the 1805 and 1850 versions. In its earliest form, the passage reads as follows:

> . . . I led my horse, and stumbling on, at length
> Came to a bottom where in former times
> A man, the murderer of his wife, was hung
> In irons. Mouldered was the gibbet-mast;
> The bones were gone, the iron and the wood;
> Only a long green ridge of turf remained
> Whose shape was like a grave. (First Part, 307–15)

The sight of the hanging place, with its grave-shaped "ridge of turf," triggers within the narrator, then a child, a preternatural awareness of "visionary dreariness" in ordinary sights—a pool, a beacon, a woman walking against the wind (315–27). Here human mortality and grass are virtually one. Nothing survives of the long-dead man, his crime, his execution, or even his body ("the bones were gone"), and certainly not his name; grass only remains, a sign of the brevity of human life: "his days are like grass . . . for the wind passes over it, and it is gone, and its place knows it no more." Indeed it is difficult to see how the child "knows" about the murder and execution, unless he is sensitive to some ghostly investment. In the 1805 revision, however, the source of the child's knowledge is explicit, as emphasis shifts from that which passes to that which remains. Now the turf in the shape of a grave is gone, and in its place is monumental writing, text, epitaph—a name carved in the turf:

> ... I led my horse, and stumbling on, at length
> Came to a bottom where in former times
> A murderer had been hung in iron chains. ....
> *Some unknown hand had carved the murderer's name.*
> *The monumental writing was engraven*
> *In times long past, ... and to this hour*
> *The letters are all fresh and visible.*
> *Faltering, and ignorant where I was, at length*
> *I chanced to espy those characters inscribed*
> *On the green sod.* ... (1805, XI, 287–301; emphasis supplied)

Through such repeated images Wordsworth smudges the boundaries between death and immortality, between fame and oblivion. When a person is like a wild flower or grass, he or she perishes quickly and is unremembered; when that person's name is planted like a wild flower in a particular place—rendered as text, written on a map, or engraved in grass—it endures. Wallace and the murderer perish like flowers of the field or like Bible grass; yet they are rescued from oblivion through language—names—planted like a wild flower, in the case of Wallace, and carved in turf, in the case of the murderer. In this way, Wordsworth has made the biblical metaphors for the brevity and oblivion of human life become names, and then to serve an opposite purpose—to preserve, lengthen, immortalize. Both men have become names; their places know them because place and man have become textualized and, bearing a common name, are essentially one.

If the place name, actors, and events are coincident with an oral narrative, they can "live" and retain their significance and spirit only so long as they survive in the memories of the living. When memory fails, as Wordsworth suggests, it is necessary to create a text, to give "some sort of record," to such names and incidents. Certainly the incidents recounted in the biblical etymological tales survive because they have been recorded, and it therefore appears that implicit in the cluster of ideas surrounding the etymological narrative is the notion of text. To endure, the narrative must be written; the name of the place must be inscribed on a map, perhaps mental. Wordsworth's faith in the saving, rescuing powers of language is thematic in *Home at Grasmere,* which he composed during the same period as the *Poems on the Naming of Places.* In *Home at Grasmere,* the poet says that he has been given an "internal Brightness ... / That must not die, that must not pass away." This gift, he says, he would impart, "Immortal in the world which is to come":

> I would not wholly perish even in this,
> Lie down, and be forgotten in the dust,

I and the modest partners of my days
Making a silent company in death.
It must not be, if I divinely taught
Am privileged to speak as I have felt
Of what in man is human or divine. (886–909)

To "speak" clearly implies to write. A recurring idea of this period (one might even say an obsession of this period), evident in both the *Poems on the Naming of Places* and *Home at Grasmere,* is of the powers of language to rescue from oblivion, to avert an unthinkable membership in a "silent company," so as to prolong, to save, or to render "immortal." Such linguistic powers reside in the processes of speaking, naming, and composing. Wordsworth asserts that he will not "wholly perish" if he is "privileged to speak."

"IT WAS AN APRIL MORNING: FRESH AND CLEAR"

This capacity of language to rescue one from death and oblivion is thematic in the *Poems on the Naming of Places*. At the end of "It was an April morning," Wordsworth speculates that some of the local shepherds, years after he and his sister "are gone and in [their] graves," will call the place by the name he has given it, "Emma's Dell." This briefer, oral mode of endurance is dependent on human memory and inclination. But Wordsworth hedges his bets. While purporting to depend on the humble remembrance of the local folk and their oral tradition, he nevertheless writes the poem, merging name, place, and person in the more permanent mode of text.[6] A deeper mystery inheres in the fact that the poet permits Dorothy (if, in fact, Emma is Dorothy) to "live" through the record of his own observations, experiences, and dedication, but paradoxically under a pseudonym, Emma, which may be only a metrical equivalent for "Dolly," a childhood nickname for Dorothy (*P. W.* 2:486), making hers a twice-deferred sort of immortality: The place is "Emma's Dell," not "Dorothy's Dell" or even "Dolly's Dell." The name on the poem is, however, William Wordsworth, one privileged to speak.

Another example of the sort of language that leads to a perception of artful complexity and misdirection in this poem may be found in the phrase, "The voice / Of waters," a "connective" in Riffaterre's sense. The function of the connective is to serve as a "signpost" (operating at the level of word or phrase). It presents a difficulty or a mystery or an obscurity in the text that "only an intertext can remedy." At the same time that the connective poses a problem, it will also "[point] the way to where the solution must be sought" (58). The phrase in question, when traced to its source, is found in the book of Ezekiel: "And behold, the glory of the God of Israel came from the way of the east: and his voice was like a noise of many waters: and the earth shined with his glory" (43:2).[7] For Ezekiel, God's voice sounds like "many waters." At the opening of his book, Ezekiel says that he saw "visions of God," the visions occurring "in the thirtieth year, in the fourth month, in the fifth day of the month, as [he] was among the captives by the river of Chebar" (Ez. 1:1). Ezekiel's vision includes a detailed description of the cherubim surrounding the divine throne, and the observation that when they moved he "heard the noise of their wings, like the noise of great waters, as the voice of the Almighty, the voice of speech, as the noise of an host" (Ez. 1:24).[8] As the water in the Chebar canals flows by him, Ezekiel hears in its sound the voice of God, which, taking visual form, appears before him as the remarkable vision of the Merkabah, with its cherubim, wheels, throne, and God. Both the wings of the cherubim and the voice of God sound like waters.

The opening of Wordsworth's poem reveals intriguing parallels: Wordsworth is writing also of a time in the fourth month—April, in 1800, his thirtieth year (perhaps even on his birthday; he would have been 30 on April 7)—beside a rivulet, whose "voice" he hears.[9] Like Ezekiel's vision, Wordsworth's is full of sounds suggested by the waters; like Ezekiel's vision of wheels within wheels associated with the living creatures, whose movement is also like the sound of waters, Wordsworth's narrator hears a "circling," as "The spirit of enjoyment and desire, / And hopes and wishes, from all living things / Went circling, like a multitude of sounds." Ezekiel remarks twice within successive verses that "the spirit of the living creatures was in the wheels" (Ez. 1:20–1); Wordsworth's "spirit" goes "circling," like wheels. By contrast to Ezekiel, Wordsworth's vision or imagining remains auditory, rather than visual. Ezekiel transposes the experience of the voice of waters into a visual image of the divine; Wordsworth's perception of the numinous remains that of audition—indeed that of language, or almost language, as he hears the voice of waters, the "circling" of spirit, like the wheels of the divine chariot "seen" by Ezekiel, the voice of uncommon pleasure, and the remarkable antiphonal chant between the voice of waters and the "song" of nature that appears not only natural, but eternal. It is a song that "seemed like the wild growth, / Or like some natural produce of the air, / That could not cease to be." In tone, Wordsworth's account is altogether different from that in Ezekiel. In Ezekiel, the dark passions prevail. The watery voice of God is angry, threatening destruction; in Wordsworth's poem, the voice of waters has been "softened down into a vernal tone." The song of the "living things" (Wordsworth's counterpart of Ezekiel's "living creatures")[10] is characterized by "the spirit of enjoyment and desire, / And hopes and wishes." In effect, Wordsworth calls Ezekiel into his text to transform the apprehension of a mysterious "perception," the relationships between natural and numinous, and the character of the visionary experience.

Despite the strong revisionary impulse, the oblique invocation of the theophany in Ezekiel and the common prophetic experience of hearing the voice of waters have the effect of "raising the stakes" in the poetic transaction, for they alter the status of the narrator, whose voice is authorized by the prophetic experience and amplified to that of bard; it creates a numinous dimension for the scene and the perception of the scene; it discloses a divine accent and cadence in the sound of the rivulet; and, all in all, it implies a denser significance in each word of the poem. This place, this "wild nook," like Jacob's desert, is awesome. Like Jacob's desert and like Ezekiel's riverbank, Wordsworth's place has been textualized and intertextualized; the experience of the poet-prophet has been given, to say the least, "some sort of record," and rescued from oblivion.

The poet's dedication of this remarkable, haunted, spirit-filled place to "Emma" is difficult. It succeeds the ecstatic experience just described and calls the ownership, if not the reality, of the poet's experience into question. The poet actually quotes himself, including his formal performative language uttered on that occasion, commenting, "to myself I said, / Our thoughts at least are ours; and this wild nook, / My EMMA, I will dedicate to thee." How is one to understand "Our thoughts at least are ours"? Does "thoughts" simply mean something like, I own the right to think of this place as Emma's, although it really is not hers? Or does "thoughts" encompass the entire visionary experience just recounted? If so, does this imply that though the poet may not own the site personally, the visionary experience of the place and his record of it constitute a kind of quitclaim deed, transferring textual ownership of the site? Or have they transformed it, in the process creating an internalized mind place, an imaginative mirror of the place over which the poet has all rights? These are possibilities, since the next lines continue the narrative, after a typographical hiatus in the form of a dash, to insist through the repetition of "my" a kind of ownership: "Soon did the spot become my other home, / My dwelling, and my out-of-doors abode." "Owning" the place—the place itself or the imaginative replication—clearly bestows a kind of immortality upon the poet, his experience, and his thoughts, and upon the sister (whose name does not appear), because they abide while place abides:

> And of the Shepherds who have seen me there,
> To whom I sometimes in our idle talk
> Have told this fancy, two or three, perhaps,
> Years after we are gone and in our graves,

When they have cause to speak of this wild place,
May call it by the name of EMMA'S DELL.

The voicing of this modest hope for a paradoxical and brief immortality
contradicts the more ambitious motives implicit in the making of the
"record"—the poem that encompasses by allusion and "re-vision" all of
time from Ezekiel to Wordsworth and inscribes itself on the place, this
bit of earth, which, as the author of Ecclesiastes says, "abideth forever."

"TO JOANNA"

Wordsworth did not write the "Poems on the Naming of Places" in the
order in which he arranged them. That he presented "It was an April
morning" (actually the third poem written [*Oxford P. W.* 697]) as the first
of the series indicates that it introduces the intricacy and complexity to
be found in the poems as a group.[11] The second poem, "To Joanna," was
written as the fifth in the group. This poem further undermines the apparent claim in the advertisement that the poems record "little incidents"
of personal history. As de Selincourt remarks, "the poem must not be
taken literally," for Joanna's personal history is misrepresented (she did
not grow up "amid the smoke of cities"), and she could not have visited
Grasmere in summer, the season depicted in the poem (*P. W.* 2:487). To
complicate matters, according to Wordsworth's note on the poem, the
account given to the vicar of the carving of Joanna's name in the rock begins apparently as a fiction, a kind of joke, whose curious transformation
to "truth" emerges as the narration proceeds (*P. W.* 2:487). From such
clues, it is clear that "To Joanna" is one of those found tales and endless
allegories of the motto; to understand the poem, therefore, it is necessary
to sort out the allegories.

Taking *allegory* to encompass a range of rhetorical figures, I find that
the major trope operating in the poem is that of endless figurative reduplication. The poem is a structure of repetitions, reflections, refractions,
and echoes, and of a kind of infection—an infectious passing of imaginative visual and auditory impressions, encompassing both the natural and
the human, and resulting in an awesome recognition of something within
or beyond the natural and human released by and participating in a peculiar sequence of reduplicating processes.

In one sense, the poem seems like a conversation poem between the
narrator and the Vicar, but it may be more aptly styled a catechism, a system of question and answer, for the topic under consideration is apparently religious belief and act, and, concerning the Vicar's questions, the
narrator says that he was "not loth to be so catechised." The vicar wants

to know why the narrator has, "like a Runic Priest" chiseled "Some uncouth name upon the native rock," in the process "Reviving obsolete
idolatry." Paradoxically, the "uncouth" ("rude, foreign, unknown,
strange") name engraved in the rock is "Joanna," a replication of the
name of the woman after whom the vicar has just inquired, referring to
her as "that wild-hearted maid!" In response to the vicar's question, the
narrator replies with a tale of a curious occurrence: On a morning walk,
the narrator and Joanna have come upon a great rock, a barrier:

> [W]hen we came in front of that tall rock
> That eastward looks, I there stopped short—and stood
> Tracing the lofty barrier with my eye
> From base to summit. . . .

From its very introduction, the rock appears to be not quite a rock, for it
"looks" eastward, and later in the poem the narrator will refer to it as "living stone." As J. Hillis Miller notices, "Stones play an important role in
Wordsworth's poetry," citing with approval Charles Du Bos's claim that
"a living stone . . . is Wordsworth's best symbol for his inmost being"
(81–2).[12] This insight offers a starting place, but rocks are very rich in
other figurative connotations for Wordsworth. Often in his poetry, as
Miller notices, the rock is a metaphor as well for the poem or book,
human or divine; or it may suggest an altar or a covenant, or a site marker,
center, monument, or gravestone instinct with memory and spirit; or, as
in biblical literature, the rock or stone may figure forth the divine—God
as rock. In this case, a complex of associations attaches to the rock and
requires interpretation of several layers of signification.

A cluster of associations links this rock both with the self and with
something more than self. The narrator stresses first of all the size of the
rock, insisting upon its height in the words *tall* and *lofty*. This tall rock is
reminiscent of the language of the Psalm addressed to God: "Lead thou
me to the rock that is higher than I; / for thou art my refuge" (61:2–3).
Moreover this rock is paradoxically both a kind of refuge and at the same
time a "barrier" in the path, the combination of attributes recalling Isaiah's "[The Lord] will become a sanctuary . . . and a stone of stumbling . . . a trap and a snare" (8:14; and see Rom. 9:33, 1 Pet. 2:8). The
narrator having been brought up short, trapped in a sense, by the rock,
stumbling over the rock, the processes of reduplicating and refraction are
set in motion through "*tracing* the lofty barrier" with his eye:

> . . . such delight I found
> To note in shrub and tree, in stone and flower,

> That intermixture of delicious hues,
> Along so vast a surface, all at once,
> In one impression, by connecting force
> Of their own beauty, imaged in the heart.

This second reduplication is one wherein the stunning beauty of the visual impression images itself or is imaged, "traced," first in the eye and
then in the heart. The refraction implicit in beauty's passing from the
medium of the rock to the human heart, or making visible, like a mirror,
something already in the heart, is refracted once again to the eyes of the
narrator:

> —When I had gazed perhaps two minutes' space,
> Joanna, looking in my eyes, beheld
> That ravishment of mine, and laughed aloud.

The response of the narrator to the "ravishment," having been seized, delighted, and enraptured by the rock, is reflected in his eyes, which is then
communicated to Joanna and refracted once more, this time from a visual to an auditory medium—Joanna's laugh. Having assumed the auditory form, the beauty, spirit, and psychic being of the rock and the man
are liberated, scattered like a virus in the surrounding air: "The Rock, like
something starting from a sleep, / Took up the Lady's voice, and laughed
again." The surrounding rocks, hills, and mountains, affected by and in-
fected with the sound, laugh in their turns, creating a system of tumul-
tuous echoes and reverberations throughout the valley, an auditory
refraction of the earlier images and reflections: beauty and spirit transformed to sound are laughter. The laughter of the hills settles back into
visual image in the vicar's smile of astonishment at hearing the tale.

The mystery of the occurrence remains. The narrator says he does not
know whether this was simply a "work accomplished" by the mountains,
or whether his "ear was touched / With dreams and visionary impulses /
To [him] alone imparted." Of one thing he is sure, "That there was a loud
uproar in the hills" (whether physical or metaphysical is uncertain), and
he reports Joanna's response as an attempt to "shelter from some object
of her fear." Part trick, part trance, as Wordsworth claims in his note (*P.
W.* 2:487), the narrative turns on its teller, transforming "extravagance,"
or "wandering beyond" in the telling to a "wandering beyond" of the
imagination, a genuine glimpse of a normally concealed reality in himself
or in nature, or in an echoing symbiosis between them, so that the narrator cannot tell inside from outside, image and echo from dreams and visionary impulses. As Wordsworth says in the note, "caught in the trap of

[his] own imagination," he could not tell what "did really" take place from what "might have taken place" (*P. W.* 2:487).[13]

Here fiction, lie, and trick provide the unlikely high road to metaphysical truth, a visionary encounter of self with self—Zoroaster walking in his garden; of human with divine—the man with the living rock, the tall rock of refuge, barrier, and stumbling; of physical with metaphysical, through the medium of beauty, and an elaborate sequence of reflection, imaging, refraction, and echo. There remains only the naming of the place to fix image and echo, the man, his vision and imagination, in the permanence of rock. With the telling of the tale, the vicar's question has been answered. Or has it? A logical connection between narrator's experience and his naming of the place, if one exists, is difficult to find. Visitors to the rock may read "Joanna" chiseled "deep in the living stone," the engraved image of a spoken name for a once-living woman, and may still hear echoing from the surrounding hills a ghostly laughter, an auditory mutation of a poet's encounter with beauty, with the uncanny, with self and more than self, and his own awesome vision.

"THERE IS AN EMINENCE"

Why is it "Joanna's Rock" and not "William's Rock"? Again, as with "Emma's Dell," the place is strangely named. Dorothy (if Emma) does not appear in any incident of the first poem; in the second, a fictionalized Joanna appears chiefly as an instrument through which the narrator's vision is refracted. It is only in the third poem of the group, "There is an Eminence," that we come to a place named for William, and here the causal connection between incident (if indeed there is one) and naming is equally as tenuous and obscure as in the first two poems. Part of the difficulty in this third poem arises because the speaker does not name William's Summit; someone else, whose motives are wholly mysterious, does. The only view of the mountain presented is that of the speaker.

On its surface, "There is an Eminence" is about a mountain named for a man; less superficially, it is about a man who is like a mountain. The mountain itself is an "Eminence," the word, applied to landscape, suggesting a height, but, applied to a man, a position of distinction or achievement. The poem's theme is the metaphoric identity of man and mountain, explored through the mountain's paradoxical conjunctions of isolation and communion, silence and speech, the somber and the joyful, the near and the far, the accessible and the inaccessible. William's Summit, like Joanna's Rock, is animate and instinct with spirit, attributes permitting it to commune with both the heavens and the earth, whose two spheres appear to meet as in traditional symbolism at the mountain's apex: It "parleys with the setting sun," it is the "haunt" of meteors, and rests under the influence of the "star of Jove" (Jupiter), the happy god, the jovial one (whose traditional abode, of course, is Mt. Olympus, holiest of Greek mountains). This peak "so high above," and "so distant in its height" is apparently inaccessible, and yet the speaker says that he and his companion "can behold it" from their orchard seat, and he repeats that it "is visible" on their evening walk. Moreover, it communicates with the inhabitants of earth, seeming "to send / Its own deep quiet" to restore the hearts of the speaker and his companion. Nevertheless, for all its communion with the heavens and the earth, it is the "loneliest place we have among the clouds."

If this is the place where heaven and earth meet, if the mountain communes with both the supernatural and the natural, spirit and matter, if it is, despite such communion, the loneliest place, is it aptly named for the poet? The poem's rhetoric implies that the characteristics of the mountain are those of the man. Just as the mountain is an "Eminence," so is the poet, standing apart by virtue of his sensibility. Like the mountain, the mind of the poet communes with the heavens and with the earth; it is the place where eternity and time, the spiritual and the physical, overlap; it is the place of both visions, or imaginative perceptions, and sense perceptions. As Wordsworth acknowledges in *Home at Grasmere*, as a poet he would sing of "the individual mind" that, like the mountain, is inaccessible, "keep[ing] its own / Inviolate retirement" (969–70). In his vocation, the poet is isolated, seeking merely "fit audience . . . though few" (972). The poet, like the mountain, ascends "aloft" but also must "sink deep"; he is a man of two worlds, and of none, a lonely man whose name will be given to this "loneliest" place.

The closing lines of the poem reiterate the paradoxical situation in which solitude and communion, the attributes of both man and mountain, are transformed, distilled, and held in suspension in the alembic of the sentence:

> And She who dwells with me, whom I have loved
> With such communion that no place on earth
> Can ever be a solitude to me,
> Hath to this lonely Summit given my Name.

At first glance, the conjunction *and*, which begins this passage, implies logical connections among the first 13 lines describing the mountain, the introduction of "She who dwells" with the poet, the curious jostling of loving "communion" and loneliness,[14] and the act of naming. The connections, however, are not logical in the usual sense, but forged—created—by the power of language to bring some new mystery into being: the identity of man and mountain implied in the naming. In the course of the poem through a type of rhetorical sleight-of-hand, an exchange of particles has occurred between mountain and poet: the mountain is a poet, and the poet is a mountain—William's Summit.

"A Narrow Girdle of Rough Stones and Crags"

The fourth poem in the series breaks a pattern established in the first three. In each of these, a place is named by a single person and given a personal name—Emma, Joanna, William. Moreover, through each of the first three runs a theme, overt or muted, of uncanny exuberance, gradually toned down from the "glad sound" of the stream, to the echoing laughter of the rocks, to the jovial serenity and isolation prevailing on the mountain. By contrast, the fourth poem shifts to an autumn season and an autumnal tone; its place is named by the poet and two companions not for a person, but in "self-reproach" for a thoughtless act—"Point Rash-Judgment." Here the "happy idleness" of the walkers and the "busy mirth" of the harvesters are sobered down by a recognition of the plight of the ailing fisherman struggling to "gain / A pittance from the dead un-feeling lake." Having initially misjudged the man as "Improvident and reckless" to be fishing during harvest season, the three idle walkers receive a lesson in charity and memorialize their initial rash judgment in the place name.

Recognizing this fourth poem as a moral tale permits the further understanding of its kinship not simply with biblical etymological tales, but with a range of moral narratives, including fable, parable, allegory, and myth (*allegory,* as included in this list, is akin to Wordsworth's use of the term in his motto). Discussing these narrative forms, Colin Murray Turbayne points out that each of them may be seen as "extended or sustained metaphors," which present "the facts which belong to one sort as if they belonged to another," and whose audience may or may not be told that metaphor is involved. Each of these forms is "offered and meant to be understood in the spirit of serious make-believe": "The vehicle for them all is usually a fictitious narrative which we make believe is true." Each of these forms presents a story plus a moral lesson (Turbayne 19–20).

Wordsworth's tale of naming Point Rash-Judgment is an allegorical moral tale, or, to use his phrase, an "endless allegory." Like the others in the group it is not necessary or even very useful to take it literally, as personal history. Rather it should be read, in Turbayne's phrase, in the "spirit of serious make-believe." In Wordsworth's allegory, a delicate web of suggestion and allusion creates a narrative that wavers between apparently factual and figurative accounts. One of the best kinds of evidence for its allegorical nature lies in the wealth of detail devoted to the journey and the landscape, which, along with the allusive language employed, creates a sense of a pilgrim's progress or a knight-errant's journey toward the bit of moral enlightenment obtained at the end.

The three travelers begin a journey one September morning by crossing a sort of Bridge Perilous, "A narrow girdle of rough stones and crags, / A rude and natural causeway," on the way to enlightenment. As is usual with the path of the pilgrim, it is a "difficult way," which leads them, once past the bridge, into a "privacy," an enchanted place by a dead lake (18, 65). It is ruled by the fairy presence of Queen Osmunda, royal moonwort, who is associated in the poem with the Grecian Naiad and the Lady of the Lake, "Sole-sitting by the shores of old romance," in whose realm the "*figure* of a Man" presents "through a thin veil of glittering haze" an image of Man as fisher. Both the fisherman and the act of fishing are rich in associations. The Man is clearly evocative of the Fisher King of Arthurian legend. Like the Fisher King, the Man is ill, wasted, and weak. He is engaging in the apparently hopeless enterprise of fishing a dead lake (a most surprising description of Grasmere Lake), which like the Fisher King's wasteland realm, reflects the moribund condition of the fisher. Fishing suggests a search of the depths—of the world or the soul—for treasure or wisdom. Alongside the Arthurian symbolism is that of the Christian tradition, wherein the fish is associated with Christ and the fisherman is suggestive of both Christ and his disciples, whom he made "fishers of men" (Mt. 4:19).

Beyond the Arthurian and Christian suggestions, an even more interesting dimension of this "figure of a Man" may be seen in his kinship with others of Wordsworth's solitaries—the hermit or the blind man of "Tintern Abbey," the discharged soldier of the *Prelude,* or the leech gatherer of "Resolution and Independence." Like them, this figure is a shadow cast by the poet, a distorted and therefore unrecognized image of himself, who he is or what he may become. As a result of this "meeting," the narrator says that he and his companions have given a "memorial name" to the point from which the ailing man fishes—as uncouth a name as ever a mariner gave to a site on "a new-discovered coast." "Point Rash-Judgment" does indeed designate a place on a new-discovered coast, a bit of enchanted interior topography, where wisdom may be gained. It is named in a manner similar to Jacob's naming of Peniel, "face of God," after a mysterious struggle with a night caller who appears as the figure of a man, but whom Jacob recognizes as God (Gen. 34:22–30).

"To M. H."

The last of the five *Poems on the Naming of Places* was probably the first composed, and like the first three examined above tells of the naming of a place with a personal name. "To M. H." is a sort of prothalamion, naming for the bride-to-be (Mary Hutchison) a place called "Mary's Nook," a garden spot with a mythical aura, which proves to be a sort of revised biblical-Miltonic paradise. Wordsworth's paradise is located appropriately "among the ancient trees," a phrase which suggests that first garden and those most ancient trees of life and death. And as with Milton's Paradise, there is "no road, nor any wood-man's path" leading to this enclosure. In Milton's poem, the traveler can find no way through an overgrown thicket that guards Paradise:

> But further way [Satan] found none, so thick entwin'd
> As one continu'd brake, the undergrowth
> Of shrubs and tangling bushes had perplext
> All path of Man or Beast that past that way. (*Paradise Lost* 4:174–7)

Milton's Satan chooses to leap over the trees and wall, rather than try the gate on the far side of the garden. In the Wordsworthian revision, while road and path may be missing, the trees themselves have created a "track, that [brings the travelers] to a slip of lawn, / And a small bed of water in the woods."

The privileged speaker and his companion are, like Milton's Adam and Eve, "brought to" this place. The sense is that one cannot simply travel to this primordial site and gain easy access, for it is not so much a place as a feminine space in which the speaker has a proprietary interest: it is, after all, "Mary's Nook," and she, as the speaker says, is "[his] sweet Mary." In truth, Mary's Nook is a Wordsworthian spot of time. Getting there requires an imaginative time travel: it is hidden, barred, unknown, a spot "made by Nature for herself: / The travellers know it not, and 'twill remain / Unknown to them; but it is beautiful. . . ." No rival traveler, no fallen and wayward angel, it is implied, will find his way here. The Nook, oddly enough, will remain "unknown," despite the fact that the speaker knows it, and tells about it, and names it. This business of *knowing* or *not knowing*, in conjunction with paradise imagery, raises the specter of the Fall and, in a poem dedicated to the bride-to-be, delicately raises the issue of conjugal love: Mary, the beloved, and this hidden garden are one: "A garden inclosed is my sister, my spouse" (S. of S. 4:12). She is beautiful; it is beautiful.

Is the speaker's knowledge a sort of forbidden knowledge? The poem's closing lines lapse into a subjunctive mode and remove the speaker a short distance from the garden. The lines sound an elegiac note in the fore-knowledge of loss:

> And if a man should plant his cottage near,
> Should sleep beneath the shelter of its trees,
> And blend its waters with his daily meal,
> He would so love it, that in his death-hour
> Its image would survive among his thoughts. . . .

The speaker, a mere mortal, a son of Adam,[15] like Adam lives outside the garden under sentence of death, lives with the inexpugnable image deep in his memory of a perfect garden and inviolable beauty once known, and, though closely guarded, inevitably to be lost. The image of the place survives in the thoughts of the man. Does the place have something like thoughts in which the image of the man and woman can survive? This possibility may be found here and there in Wordsworthian places. "The Thorn" suggests in its details a spot transformed, shaped, and animated by something like thought and memory of human action and feeling that inhere in the place and may be communicated to the perceptive visitor, as does the murderer's grave passage from the earliest version of the *Prelude* (First Part 315–27, discussed above, pp. 83–4). Speaking of Sarnum Plain in the *Prelude,* the poet raises the possibility of reading such memories, of catching from such places "a tone, / An image, and a character"; in this experience, the poet undergoes "an ennobling interchange . . . / Both of the object seen, and eye that sees" (*Prelude,* 1805 12:363–79). A knowing place may be able to serve as a medium between the past and present, the living and the dead. And yet, to receive that communication, the visitor must read ("view" or "fancy") in the place "monumental hints" (*Prelude,* 1850 13:350–2). Such hints include, one supposes, a mound of turf in the shape of a grave, a child-sized and knotted thorn, a stone circle, a name chiseled in stone, a name, like "Mary's Nook," recorded in a poem by William Wordsworth. In the case of "To M. H.," the poet "in his death hour" will know the place, and, one feels, the place, named and inscribed by the poet, will know him too, and will be subtly altered by that "knowledge," the alteration noticeable to some, if only as monumental hints, a tone, image, and character that "like a family of Ghosts" abide in the place.

Taken individually, each of the five poems is an artifact whose subtle intricacy becomes apparent on close study. Like a Japanese paper flower dropped into water, each "little incident," dropped into the medium of language, expands into an endless allegory. In the process, the private, local, and trivial become universal and profound; the ephemeral becomes enduring and nearly timeless. Taken as a group, the *Poems on the Naming of Places* participate in the mythologizing of the poet's beloved landscape. Like Wallace, the poet has left names "like wild flowers / All over his dear Country"; left his thoughts and visions inscribed in the land "like a family of Ghosts / To people the steep rocks and river banks, / Her natural sanctuaries, with a local soul." Unwilling to make one of a "silent company" of the dead, to be without words, speech, language, the poet textualizes with names and poems his Edenic Grasmere, the place he calls "my home" and "my World" (*Home at Grasmere* 42), his enduring possession assured through language. As a result, at Grasmere place and life have become one; the site has been made a bit of Wordsworthian autobiography, identical now with its author who, having achieved a dense, material permanence and ultra-signification through and in this land, might with some justification declare, "Grasmere—*c'est moi!*" How awesome is this place!

CHAPTER 5

Wordsworth's Prodigal Son

MICHAEL AS PARABLE
AND AS METAPARABLE

A shadow, a delusion, ye who pore
On the dead letter, miss the spirit of things

—*Prelude* 1850 8:296–7

ordsworth's *Michael* is a poem both enriched and complicated by its web of biblical allusions, echoes, and evocations. Behind the poem's protagonist stand such Old Testament figures as Jacob and Abraham, and in Michael's situation are parallels to such narratives as "The Sacrifice of Isaac," "Jacob and Esau," and "Joseph and his Brothers" (Bloom, *Visionary Company* 182–3; Bushnell 246; Levinson 20; Collings 163). Beyond these specific figures and pre-texts, biblical language, themes, and tropes are pervasive. Roston, for example, says that *Michael* "has a patently biblical substructure" (182), by which he suggests a dependence on biblical names (Michael, Luke), figures (shepherd, patriarch), phrases ("mess of pottage," "helpmate"), and images ("unhewn stones"). From such examples he is led to claim that the "language of the Bible . . . is . . . more than a linguistic device," for "the entire poem is permeated with biblical morality . . ." (183). Analysis of the poem's biblical characteristics and allusions supports an array of critical conclusions. Bushnell, for example, argues for an intriguing Wordsworthian irony in the poet's revision of the "Sacrifice of Isaac" narrative (250). Levinson discusses Wordsworth's poem as a structure of "sustained biblical allusion," examining Abraham's and Michael's sacrifices so as to foreground a sociopolitical agenda of the poem, finding that biblical elements are introduced to permit Wordsworth not only to make an economic point, but to "slip in from below a substitute subject: poetry" (68–9; 72).

Much of the critical focus thus far has been on Old Testament pretexts, a focus that the poem itself clearly invites and justifies. In this study, I would like to take the poem's invitation a step further, however, to argue that the very form of the poem is a biblical form—that of the parable, which is primarily a New Testament narrative structure. When seen as parable, Wordsworth's poem is placed against a background of New Testament texts that address a universe that is radically dualistic (of the letter, the literal, and of the spirit, the figurative). While parabolic allusions and structures are in evidence here and there throughout Wordsworth's poetry, they come to the fore in *Michael,* where the devices of parable reveal their kinship to those of dream explored in Book 5 of the *Prelude,* and the visionary spots of time recorded here and throughout Wordsworth's poetry, all serving an evolving Wordsworthian poetics. As Allen Bewell shows, "Wordsworth's interest in biblical narrative should not be seen as separate from his reflection on the origin and ends of poetry"; the anthropological and biblical paradigms serve as "major keystones" of Wordsworth's aesthetics (120–2).[1] Thus recognizing *Michael* as parable is to my mind helpful in understanding not only this poem, but something of Wordsworth's method elsewhere, for it is here that Wordsworth joins the lyrical and the narrative in a complex mode that permits him to create his own form of poetic narrative and explore its heuristic and aesthetic potential.

Echoes of Wordsworth's theoretical concern with parable are discernible even in the Preface to the *Lyrical Ballads* (1800) (in which *Michael* first appeared), where metaphors of New Testament parables weave their designs in Wordsworth's first articulation of critical theory. Here Wordsworth says that his "principal object" in these poems was

> to make the incidents of common life interesting by tracing in them, truly though not ostentatiously, the primary laws of our nature: chiefly as far as regards the manner in which we associate ideas in a state of excitement. Low and rustic life was generally chosen because in that situation the essential passions of the heart find a better soil in which they can attain their maturity, are less under restraint, and speak a plainer and more emphatic language. . . . (*Pr. W.* 1:122–4).

Wordsworth here invokes through a planting metaphor the parable of the sower (Matt. 13:3–9), a tale interpreted by Jesus as equating the sower's seeds with Jesus' words. The "low and rustic life" of which Wordsworth speaks is exactly the scene of the biblical parables, whose various soils are those in which the seeds fall, some finding the "good soil" and bringing forth grain. In Wordsworth's revision, it is not words per se, but "essential passions" that are sown, yet they are passions balancing on the verge of language, struggling to speak a "plainer and more emphatic language." They are passion-seeds from which words may grow, once they have found a better soil in which to flourish; they are the speaking passions not only of those whose life is low and rustic, but, ideally, of the poet as well, ur forms, at once feeling and language.

The remainder of the paragraph from which these lines are cited continues in this vein, stressing, on the one hand, the "primary," "essential," and "elementary" "laws of our nature," "passions of the heart" and "feelings," and, on the other, their protolinguistic nature, seeking a language in which these human universals may be expressed by the poet and comprehended by his readers. Wordsworth says that the appropriate language for these purposes is, in fact, the very "language . . . of these men"—men of "common life" and "rural occupations" because their language is the language of the affections, because it grows out of a communication with "the best objects," because it consists of "simple and unelaborated expressions," and because it is "more permanent" and "far more philosophical" (Pr. W. 1:124).

His advocacy of the simple, essential, universal, permanent, and philosophical language of these men, in preference to the poets' more usual "arbitrary and capricious habits of expression" (Pr. W. 1:124) is, of course, at the heart of Wordsworth's poetic radicalism. It is the matter that he stresses in the letter to Charles James Fox (January 14, 1801) recommending Michael to the member of Parliament as one of two poems demonstrating the "constant predominance of sensibility of heart" (Letters 260) among a class of "small independent proprietors of land" (261). The great tragedy in the recent social and economic revolutions, Wordsworth asserts, is a "decay of the domestic affections among the lower orders of society" (260), those very classes in whom elemental feelings and poetic language, or as poetic language, have been vested. On this point Wordsworth cites Quintilian: "For it is strength of feeling that makes eloquence, and energy of intellect. And even to the illiterate, if only they be moved by deep passion, words are not wanting" (tr. in Zall 36n). For Wordsworth, what is at stake in the social and economic changes is language itself, or, more specifically, poetic language, that essential, primary code that is emotion, which, as he says elsewhere, though "lost beyond the reach of thought / And human knowledge" and "to the human eye / Invisible," yet "liveth to the heart" (*Prelude* 2:422–4).

My claim, then, is that Wordsworth's form is that of the New Testament parable, a form that he renders more complex than traditional parable by a network of wider biblical and Miltonic intertextuality. While Old Testament stories offer their material—their persons, acts, and images—to the processes of intertextual figuration (and, as has been shown, Wordsworth employed them in this way), their form is that of history, for they claim to be literally true—of the law, the letter. As sacred history, Old Testament narratives purport to be accounts of real people and events in the world. In this sense—as history—they cannot serve as models for Wordsworth's narrative. By contrast, the New Testament parables' claim is to "spiritual truth." That is, they are not about real people and events at all, but about something, as Jesus says, "hidden since the foundation of the world" (Mt. 13:35). In Wordsworth's phrase, cited above, they speak of things "beyond the reach of . . . human knowledge," things "to the human eye / Invisible." They oppose to law and letter such notions as grace and spirit, introducing a radical poetics that pushes language to its outer reaches. The parables' emphasis on language, its complexities, its powers, and its failures mirrors Wordsworth's chief and enduring concerns. It is the sort of poetics to which he refers when, in a passage of the *Prelude* linked thematically to *Michael*, he cautions against "pour[ing] over the dead letter" and "miss[ing] the spirit of things" (*Prelude* 1850 8:296–7). The concern with the New Testament's parabolic or metaphoric "spirit of things," as opposed to the "dead letter," dominates the poetics of *Michael*. An effect is that the parabolic form and functions make the poem more difficult, equivocal, and, I believe, darker than has usually been seen.

I argue that the poem itself is parable, and that its art and its difficulty grow out of the nature of parable, a paradoxical form that conceals its complexity beneath a seemingly simple, narrative surface. Its everyday, often domestic subjects, its straightforward narrative line, and its transparent language attempt the paradoxical task of articulating the ultimately unspeakable. When Wordsworth's poem is seen as parable, certain facts about it become understandable. For instance, this unassuming "history / Homely and rude" (34–5) is written in blank verse, a form Fox complained was too grand for such a simple subject (Moorman 504–5), but the verse form and meter are not inappropriate for the poem's linguistic task, and in its dignified prosody, the poem's language remains true to the spirit of parable, which is rhetorical rather than poetic (Jeffrey 581), and which of necessity treats grand universal mysteries in the simple language of common domestic persons and acts.[2] Unlike that of the better-read poems of the same period, the language of *Michael* may strike readers as unambiguous, "unpoetic." In true parabolic form, it is at once clear and obscure, inanely simple and impossibly difficult.

I have said that *Michael* is parable, but I want to go further and claim that the poem is more properly understood as metaparable; it is a parable about parable, as a metapoem is a poem about poetry. The poem's primary pre-text is Luke 15, a chapter that contains in rapid succession the parables of The Lost Sheep, The Lost Coin, and The Prodigal Son. *Michael* constitutes a re-vision of the chapter, one that pays particular attention to the parable of The Prodigal Son, and, in the process, incorporates all of parable's difficulties and paradoxes, all its demand for, and at the same time resistance to, interpretation. Behind Wordsworth's parable is the attempt to articulate the inarticulable relationship between letter and spirit; between language and that to which language refers; between the human poet, text, and existence and those grand, obscure precursors—the divine author and his "books," scripture and nature.

THE PARADOXICAL PARABLE

I will open my mouth in parable,
I will utter what has been hidden since the foundation of the world. (Mt. 13:35)

In order to appreciate the complexities of parables and their literary forms, some review of current theory is helpful. J. D. Crossan defines parable as "paradox formed into story" (cited in Jeffrey 582), a notion echoed explicitly or implicitly by most other critics. David Tracy, following Paul Ricoeur, defines parable as "the conjunction of a narrative form and a metaphorical process," a definition that draws both metaphor theory and narratology into a consideration of the parable. Tracy insists that an interaction theory of metaphor is crucial to an understanding of religious metaphor in general and parable in particular. Such a theory acknowledges its relation to scientific heuristic models, as "heuristic fictions," and suggests that parable "is a *mythos* (a heuristic fiction) that has the *mimetic* power of redescribing human existence" through the metaphorical process, "which transfers the meaning of the story from fiction to redescribed reality" (97–8). Tracy's view recognizes in parable the sort of world-changing power accorded certain reality-defining or redefining metaphors. The language of parables, Tracy says, is "limit language," metaphor operating at its own outer edges, test-ing its ability (or inability) to draw into the linguistic domain (and hence "reality") what has been unknown, absent, unspoken, or unspeak-able—as Wordsworth says, "beyond the reach of thought," or, as Jesus says, "hidden since the foundation of the world." J. Hillis Miller empha-sizes this aspect of parable, pointing out that etymologically "the word means 'thrown beside,'" that a parabolic trajectory is like that of the comets, which "come once, sweep round the sun, and disappear forever": "When this is taken as a parable of the working of parable in literature or in scripture, it suggests that parable is a mode of figurative language which is *the indirect indication, at a distance, of something that cannot be described di-rectly, in literal language*" ("Parable and performative" 135–6, emphasis sup-plied). Ricoeur, Tracy, and Miller are alike in their understanding that parable is a language of last resort; language attempting, through metaphor pushed into narrative motion, to speak the heretofore unspo-ken or the unspeakable.

Beyond the recognition of the metaphorical nature of parable and its impossible task is the biblical view that the parables are mysterious speech. Not only must they employ human language to express that which cannot be expressed in human speech (that which has always been hidden, especially the nature of the kingdom of God), but also they are actually couched in a form designed to conceal their "real" meaning; that is, they are *intended to be misunderstood* by their audience, the very people to whom they are addressed, the multitudes outside the small group of dis-ciples, to whom Jesus speaks in parables, "so that they may indeed see but not perceive, and may indeed hear but not understand" (Mk 4:12). Yet ironically, the disciples (insiders, to whom has been given "the secret of the kingdom of God" [Mk. 4:11] and who, therefore, should understand) do not, in fact, understand at all and must have the parables explained to them (Mk. 4:13–20, 34). Paradoxically, the explanation, like the parables themselves, must employ inadequate human speech. Thus an intention behind Jesus' use of parables is, through figurative language, to prevent outsiders, with their "hardness of heart," from understanding, "lest they should turn again and be forgiven" (Mk. 4:12). This effect is apparently achieved, along with a second, ironic effect—to prevent the disciples, in-siders, from understanding. As Miller puts it, "The parables are posited on their own inevitable misreading or nonreading" (141). Behind the parables, therefore, is the idea that if they are to be understood at all (which they inevitably will not be), they will be understood "spiritually." There are those who find only shadows and delusions, rather than true understanding, those who, as Wordsworth says, "pore / On the dead let-ter" and "miss the spirit of things."[3] Jesus' disciples, despite their obtuseness, will, it is at once both affirmed and denied, understand "spiritually." Miller says that Jesus "has said [the disciples] understand, but he goes on to speak as if they could not possibly understand" (141). If these insiders, the disciples as privileged audience, ironically uncomprehending despite their privilege, have their counterparts in the audience Wordsworth identified for *Michael*, of "a few natural hearts" (36), and of that he identified in *Home at Grasmere* as "fit audience . . . though few" (972), this paradox raises interesting questions about the possibility that perhaps no comprehending audience exists, and about Wordsworth's apparently ironic appropriation of Milton's "fit audience . . . though few" (*Paradise Lost* 7:31), behind which stands Jesus' audience of insiders, the informed but ironically uncomprehending disciples.

The paradoxes of significance and audience are compounded by the paradoxical position of a parable's narrator. As John Drury notices, the biblical parables are said to be spoken by Jesus, the Word, "who alone knows about the start and finish of things," and who, as prophet and speaker of the parables, "stands over and above the midtime narrative he is in. At the same time, and as a historical character within it, he can only be paradoxical and parabolical in his revelation" (431–2). Miller, taking up this point, notices that "Christ as the Logos is in the awkward position of not being able to speak the Logos directly but of being forced to translate it into a form suitable for profane ears. The Word cannot speak the Word as such" (139–40). The parables, although spoken by the Word, "are not logical"; they rest on a "failure of analogy between anything human, including human languages . . . , and the divine Logos, the Word of the kingdom of heaven"; in other words, human language, the language Jesus must use, "is already irremediably parabolic" (141–3).

The result of all these paradoxes is that parable explicitly invites— demands—interpretation, while resisting it through all the means at its disposal: the mystery of its message (what has been "hidden from the foundation of the world"); the complex relationship between the narrator and his text (at once both omniscient teller and limited character immersed in his own narrative); the medium of its message (the equivocal, and parabolic, system of signs in which it is necessarily rendered); and the implied nonequivalence between anything human (of "the dead letter") and anything divine (of "the spirit of things," "the kingdom of heaven"). The everyday domestic scenes and events depicted in the parables, their unassuming language, and their simplicity of plot form only the horizontal plane of the narrative; beneath, abysses of meanings and equivocations stretch into the unnamed and unnamable, the unspoken and unspeakable.

POETICS OF PARABLE—NAMING

[U]nto them that are without, all these things are done in parables: That seeing they
may see, and not perceive; *and hearing they may hear, and not understand; lest . . .*
they should be converted. . . .

(Mk. 4:11–12; emphasis supplied)

Nor should I have made mention of this Dell
But for one object which you might pass by,
Might see and notice not.

(*Michael* 14–16; emphasis supplied)

Michael is not Wordsworth's only parable, nor even his only re-vision of
The Prodigal Son, but it is one of the most intriguing and in some ways
paradigmatic. It not only raises the questions inherent in the genre, and
the literary appropriation of the genre, but relates them to matters with
which Wordsworth typically struggled: the nature and role of the poet; his
own and his text's relationship to nature and scripture, God's texts; the relationship of both human and divine texts to the "whence" and "whither"
of human life (*Pr. W., Essays upon Epitaphs* I 2:51); and language, its essential
forms, its equivocations, its fragile and suspect referential powers, and its
functions in the ongoing struggle against personal annihilation.

Attempting to specify the differences between sacred and literary
parables, Miller almost admits the impossibility of the task when he runs
into the double paradox that, whereas sacred parables are spoken by the
divine in his human incarnation, using of necessity human language in
which the divine message by its nature cannot be uttered, secular parables are spoken by a human narrator who cannot avoid "the temerity of
at least tentatively, implicitly, or hypothetically putting himself in
Christ's place and claiming to serve as an intermediary between this
everyday world and the kingdom of heaven on the other side of the
frontier of which all parables bring word" ("Parable and performative"
149). But there is a difference, if only in degree, that may make all the
difference, especially when the human parable-maker specifically invokes and then respeaks sacred parable, issuing in the process the generous and sinister intertextual invitation of which Miller speaks in "The
Critic as Host." For while Jesus' parables clearly carry intertextual
echoes and allusions, and while they are re-visionary of Old Testament
realities, they lack the self-consciousness of Wordsworth's parable. They
do not constitute narratives that are themselves at once parables, revi-

sions of other parables, and explorations of the very nature of parable and its language. Wordsworth's poem is such a narrative. This fact produces what I have called metaparable, a parable exploring the nature of parable as poetic paradigm, its power and paradox, and its complex processes of metaphor and narrative, of naming and plotting—processes that are foregrounded within the poem.

Indeed, one of the first and primary transactions of parable is that of naming, wherein something "hidden" or "beyond the reach of thought" is given an ordinary, this-worldly name, the appropriateness of which cannot be challenged. Naming is the first powerful act by which some airy no-thing[4] is brought into the realm of language, so as to constitute a part of a linguistic system of "being" or "reality" within whose grammar the previously unknown becomes speakable, in some ways defined, subject to predication, exploration, interpretation, control: "What woman, having ten silver coins, if she loses one coin, does not light a lamp and sweep the house and seek diligently until she finds it?" Or, "There was a man who had two sons" (Lk. 15:8, 11). Who/what is this "woman," or this "man"? Who/what are the "silver coins," or the "elder" and "younger" sons? What "lamp" does the woman light? What light can these named details of their "low and rustic life" possibly shed on things "hidden since the foundation of the world"? And yet something mysterious has been named "a man," a "woman," "sons," "a coin," "a lamp," and the parabolic narrative has issued a challenge to those who have ears to hear. Something "lost beyond the reach of thought," something invisible "to the human eye," has been brought into the realm of language, where it may be assigned significance, and made subject to interpretation.

In Wordsworth's *Michael*, ordinary persons and objects (Michael, Luke, Isabel, an oak tree, a lamp, a scattering of stones) participate in the parabolic enterprise, as does the grain in the parable of The Sower or the coin in the parable of The Lost Coin, being at the level of the "dead letter" simply what they are (things which one "might see and notice not"). At the same time they are made subject to the powerful parabolic processes of naming and plotting, by which they become figurative, "of the spirit," pointing to persons, objects, and events in that inaccessible realm beyond the limits of language, of which the parable brings word.

A case in point is the cottage lamp, a reprise of the lamp used to find a "lost coin"—however that naming is understood. It is an "aged utensil," having performed service "beyond all others of its kind" through "uncounted hours." Thirty-four lines (112–46) are devoted to a description of the lamp and its light, of which the narrator speaks "minutely" (134), insisting that his description is not "a waste of words" (131). Certainly such emphasis invites attention to the lamp and its significance within the parabolic frame, beyond the level of the letter. It is from the constancy and antiquity of the lamp that the cottage itself is named "the Evening Star" (146), establishing a metonymic relationship between cottage and lamp, and the "eternal" nature of both, pointing to a metaphoric identity between things earthly—cottage, lamp—and things hidden, mysterious, heavenly—the star suggesting the presence of the divine, the eternal, the undying (J. C. Cooper 159), or in the language of Jesus, "what has been hidden since the foundation of the world." Yet Wordsworth's Evening Star is not eternal, but a human artifact existing in the world of time. Literally, the cottage sits squarely on English soil; figuratively, it draws into the flow of time the distant, mysterious, meaning-laden star. The "Evening Star" thus invites the gaze upward along a disappearing parabola toward a metaphoric, other-worldly light shining in the darkness. The lamp's uncounted hours extend into eternity. It must be older than the cottage or the hill on which the cottage sits, older than anyone who can "see and notice not."

From this perspective, the light it sheds is not only lamplight, but "spiritual light," akin to the "holy Light, offspring of Heaven first-born," which Milton invokes at the opening of Book 3 of *Paradise Lost,* where he requests that the light

> Shine inward, and the mind through all her powers
> Irradiate; there plant eyes; all mist from thence
> Purge and disperse, that I may see and tell
> Of things invisible to mortal sight. (51–5)

The invocation of the holy light is to enable one to "see and tell / Of things invisible to mortal sight"—the parable-maker's task as well as the poet's. Others, those with mere "mortal sight," might, in Wordsworth's phrase, see "and notice not"; the parable-maker and poet see and tell. Moreover, both Milton and Wordsworth knew of "things invisible to mortal sight" and they knew also that the "offspring" of Heaven (Uranos, "Heaven"), his "first-born," was Aphrodite, or Venus, the Evening Star.[5] The curious allusion implicit in Wordsworth's naming of the cottage the Evening Star connects the aged lamp that illuminates Michael's cottage with Milton's inward-shining holy light by which one may "see and tell" of "things invisible to mortal sight." The aged lamp sheds a form of that light which, in Wordsworth's phrase, shines when the "light of sense / Goes out," whose flashes reveal "the invisible world" (*Prelude* 6:534–6), the world of the imagination, the spirit, rather than of the dead letter. The parabolic functions of naming the lamp-house of Michael, Isabel, and Luke the Evening Star places this scene and these figures and all their acts not in a literal, but a figurative, light, an inward-shining light, and all the poet's language, while functioning literally, is prevented from remaining in that mode. Each dead letter or word becomes Word, alive with potential, pointing always beyond itself, inviting readers to see, understand, interpret by this light.

As the gaze is directed upward along the parabola of parable, the literal falls away. All must appear "spiritual" and "inward" in the glow of the primordial child-light, which as "offspring of Heaven first-born" has burned, in Jesus' phrase, since "the foundation of the world," and in Wordsworth's, "through uncounted Hours" (120). In its glow the mysterious "House-wife" performs "her own peculiar work, / Making the cottage thro' the silent hours / Murmur as with the sound of summer flies" (127–30). In the spiritual light of the Evening Star, this spinner may be associated with the spinner of the heavens, the moon, who like the Greek Clotho, is archetypal spinner of lives and destinies. The sound of spinning is language, or almost language, "murmur[ing]" an almost comprehensible, albeit sinister, message of the ephemeral, of "summer flies," their swarming offspring, and death. The sound of flies suggests that, in fact, Wordsworth's star is not Milton's, although the name is the same. For muse Milton has his Venus, his evening star, offspring of Heaven; Wordsworth has his aged utensil and the cottage named for it, and a spinner who makes a noise like flies.

But how does this knowledge serve the reader? The paradoxical parable both invites interpretation and resists it. Nevertheless, one can say that if knowledge of the lamp does nothing else, it fosters an awareness that everything seen in this remarkable light is both what it is and something else, like the lost sheep, the lost coin, and the prodigal son of Luke's parables. Moreover, it is clear that the lamp is only one such parabolic naming. Wordsworth's metaparabolic enterprise, its difficulties, and its devices are well delineated in another curious naming in the poem—the "large old Oak" known as the "CLIPPING TREE," a name that calls special attention to itself by being printed entirely in capital letters (the only phrase in the poem so printed), and further distinguishes itself *as a name* by enduring into the present—it is "a name which yet it bears" (179)—long after its literal, if not its spiritual, appropriateness has passed. For a tree to "bear" a name suggests that the fruit of this tree is language itself, a notion reinforced by the word *clipping*. Etymologically, *clipping* is related to "clasping," "embracing," "gripping," "shearing," "ringing" (a bell), and "eclipsing"—a tree whose branches embrace, and whose shade eclipses, the process of shearing sheep; but also, through the form *clipian* (a variant of *clepe*), *clipping* suggests "crying," "calling to," "inviting," "speaking," and "naming" (OED under *clip* and *clepe*). If Milton's phrase for the poetic enterprise, "see and tell," echoes in Wordsworth's poem (and I believe it does), seeing is figured in the unearthly light of the aged lamp; telling, in the ancient named and naming tree.

Merely by being named, the old oak tree is placed into the category of mythological trees. Like Yggdrasil, or the tree of life, or the tree of the knowledge of good and evil, the CLIPPING TREE has roots that appear to reach into primeval soil and branches that sway well above the winds of time. Named at some unspecified moment in the past, the word *clipping*, according to Wordsworth's note of 1800, "is the word used in the North of England for shearing" (*Oxford P. W.* 701), suggesting merely a tree where sheep are sheared. However, when one considers that Wordsworth used a "northern" word, an archaic word, to name this tree, then put it all in capitals, and further underscored the name by writing an apparently unnecessary note, one is left with no option but to pay close attention to this tree.

I have already suggested that this is a tree of language, but, more than that, it is a tree whose very name suggests the difficulties of language through time. There may be language (*logos*) that is true, accurate, and unchangeable—capable of speaking what has been "hidden since the foundation of the world"—but that is not the language of the human poet, nor even of Jesus when he "open[s] [his] mouth in parables." This tree, apparently named for a literal activity said to have taken place beneath it—shearing, "clipping" sheep—endures with its name intact. In the present of the poem the *literal* meaning of the name is wholly inappropriate; it is no longer a tree in whose shade sheep are sheared. The cottage is gone, the sheep are gone, even the pastures are gone ("the ploughshare has been through the ground" [486]). The oak stands alone in the field of time, a text from the eternal realms. It is reminiscent of that single tree that dominates "The Thorn," ancient beyond knowing, all "knots." It is also like that "Tree, of many one"; its ground, like that "single Field" of "Intimations Ode": "Both of them *speak* of something that is gone" (51–3; emphasis supplied). The CLIPPING TREE speaks too of something that is gone; it bears a name once meaning "shearing," but now meaning "speaking," "telling," "naming." It is a tree whose insistent name itself demonstrates the processes of language in time. Its equivocal message is intended for insiders, "a few natural hearts," disciples who might be able to hear the speaking tree and understand its message.

Sometimes a tree that appears to speak is a tree with a talking serpent coiled around it, or a tree like Yggdrasil inscribed with runes, for whose ancient wisdom a god may hang himself on that tree. In either case, it is a tree of language or word wisdom issuing a costly invitation to knowledge. To encounter the tree and receive its wisdom is to experience a fall, to plunge into the world of words, of rhetoric, of names, and naming—

and things that are and are not (only) what their names imply. Milton's serpent, for example, tells Eve that he is able to speak *because* he has eaten the fruit of the tree of knowledge (*Paradise Lost* 9:598–601). The poetic enterprise in the fallen world, like the House-wife's toil beneath the aged lamp, the Evening Star made to shine in the humble cottage of time, is a diminished one, resulting in a tale spoken in fallen language—"homely and rude"—murmuring "through the silent hours" of mysteries, of things so changed (a single tree, a scattered heap of unhewn stones) that the poet must of necessity murmur too, resort to the devices of parable in order to speak of the invisible world.

POETICS OF PARABLE—PLOTTING

> *Beside the brook*
> *There is a straggling heap of unhewn stones!*
> *And to that place a story appertains.* . . .

Michael 16–8

If naming is a crucial process of parable, so too is plotting, narrative structure. Critical opinion has been curiously divided on *Michael* as narrative. For example, its progress has been described, on the one hand, as straight forward and, on the other, as having no plot. The difficulties presented by the plot of *Michael* are in some instances typical of parable, whose events and acts at the literal level are often surprising and inexplicable, or arbitrary, or illogical. A case in point is the parable of the false steward (Luke 16). That is, the plot of parable tends like its other aspects to be suggestive, allusive, mysterious or uncanny, qualities which clearly adhere to the story of *Michael*.

Assuming that parable is, as David Tracy says, the conjunction of a narrative form with a metaphorical process, the metaphors, e.g., the lamp and the tree, or the "straggling heap of unhewn stones," and all their burden of significance must participate in plot. As the epigraph from Wordsworth implies, the straggling heap, which one might see and notice not, is, in fact, already partly plot; it is an object to which a story appertains. When turning attention from naming (Tracy's "metaphorical process") to the story, the narrative form, with which it is conjoined in parable, it is instructive to consider the plots of Wordsworth's pre-text in contrast to Wordsworth's own plot of stones and a lost son.

In Luke 15, as mentioned, Jesus recounts three parallel and apparently synonymous parables: the narratives of The Lost Sheep, The Lost Coin, and The Prodigal Son. The plot of each might be stated thus: Something

valued is lost and then found, and the finding occasions joy and celebration; a metaphoric equivalence, stated or implied, obtains between the
literal, domestic situation and a spiritual situation in heaven. Jesus comments on the lost sheep and the lost coin in parallel fashion: "[L]ikewise
joy shall be in heaven over one sinner that repenteth" (15:7) and "Likewise . . . there is joy in the presence of the angels of God over one sinner
that repenteth" (15:10). No such interpretation by Jesus, as narrator, is
included for the third parable of The Lost Son. Instead the father, a character within the tale, rather than Jesus, explains, "It was meet that we
should make merry, and be glad: for this thy brother was dead, and is alive
again; and was lost; and is found" (15:32). In this third case, Jesus, as narrator, attributes to the father, a character in the tale, his own function of
interpretation, implying an equivalence between Jesus-narrator and fa-
ther-character. Further, the parallel interpretations in their turn imply a
metaphoric equivalence among the lost sheep, the lost coin, and the
prodigal son. In each, the process of loss and recovery is metaphoric for
some other-worldly process mirrored in sorrow followed by rejoicing (in
heaven or within the domestic scene of the tale). Among the three parables, the sheep, the coin, and the son (all of which, along with their
"plots") are figures for something that cannot be spoken of directly. In
the father's interpretation of his son's loss and return is a further
metaphoric equivalence between loss and death, return (finding) and
life. Death (loss) and life (return) refer again to letter and spirit and the
relationship to which Wordsworth has called attention. Here is
Wordsworth's comment on the letter and spirit:

> Call ye these appearances
> Which I beheld of Shepherds in my youth,
> This sanctity of Nature given to man,
> A shadow, a delusion?—ye who are fed
> By the dead letter, not the spirit of things,
> Whose truth is not a motion or a shape
> Instinct with vital functions, but a block
> Or waxen image which yourselves have made
> And ye adore. (*Prelude* 8:429–36; cf. *Prelude*, 1850 8:294–301)

Wordsworth's allusion is to Second Corrinthians: "[God] . . . hath made
us able ministers of the new testament; not of the letter, but of the spirit;
for the letter killeth, but the spirit giveth life" (3:6), implying that he
himself is such a minister of the spirit. Within this series of overlapping
metaphors, certain identities are established: Lost (coin, sheep, son) =
dead = letter (the literal) = block or waxen image; found = alive = spirit

(the parabolic, figurative) = a motion or a shape instinct with vital functions. But here the paradoxical enters in, the demand for and resistance to interpretation. Surely Wordsworth's readers do not want to "adore" their own waxen images, and yet the thing of which the waxen image (the letter, the word) is representative is elusive, unspeakable.

In his revision of Luke 15, Wordsworth is keenly aware of the distinction between the dead letter and the spirit of things. Wordsworth's poet-persona narrates a tale whose plot might be stated thus: things valued—Sheep-fold, land, and son—are lost irrevocably, resulting in unavailing grief. But Sheep-fold, land, and son cannot be understood at the level of the letter: They are, in Wordsworth's language, motions or shapes instinct with vital functions. Wordsworth's single, rather than triple, plot not only reverses the plots of the pre-text, but conflates lost sheep (sheep/Sheep-fold), lost coin (payment required to save the land), and lost son, all of which might be subsumed under the name *Luke*. Unlike the pre-text (Luke 15), Wordsworth's poem names the Son (a word that, along with *Father* and other key names, Wordsworth capitalizes throughout his text, suggesting the generic rather than the specific). He calls the Son "Luke," a name that multiplies meanings and echoes at different levels of interpretation, for it is the name of the supposed author of the third gospel *and* the name of that text itself. Likewise complex is the appellation *Son,* with or without a capital, for the word designates not only Michael's son Luke, but, in the biblical context, Jesus, Son of Man, the Logos, the Word, the narrator of Luke's parables; but in addition it designates the prodigal himself—the lost and found son of Luke 15. Thus within the intricate web of metaphor and allusion—at the level of the spirit—A is B, but also C and D, and all participate in the story. Wordsworth's Luke is literally Michael and Isabel's son, but parabolically he is also Son, identified with Jesus, and he is Luke, author, and Luke, text, and, through analogy, prodigal son, understood from the biblical parable as equivalent to lost sheep and lost coin. Such multiplicity of parabolic reference has the effect of destabilizing each sign that exists in this multi-leveled system of seemingly endless self-referentiality. As mentioned, Wordsworth's single plot of loss without subsequent recovery (in the case of the lost son) appears to reverse the plots of Luke 15. However, Wordsworth's conflation in *Michael* of Son and land, land and Sheep-fold (and sheep), and all with lost coin, and lost text renders this reversal problematic.

THE LOST SHEEP-FOLD

When Wordsworth was composing *Michael,* his working title was apparently "The Sheepfold."[6] In the poem, the Sheep-fold is a "simple object [to which] appertains / A story," a story whose parabolic plot is "unenriched with strange events" (18–9). Wordsworth's text is in this way identified with the dominant image, the image that hovers over the entire poem as well as focusing both the beginning and ending. That is, Wordsworth's poem, like Michael's heap of stones, is called *Sheep-fold,* thus creating a metaphoric identity of Sheep-fold and text. The Sheep-fold, the narrator claims, is "an object," which a traveler "might see and notice not" (15–6). This language is a paraphrase of that of Jesus, explaining his use of parables so that those "without," the multitudes, "may see, and not perceive" (Mk. 4:12). The Sheep-fold is thus an "object," a "straggling heap of unhewn stones," or altar, a poem-text, and parable—all of these, but, ironically, not a sheepfold. Readers stumble on the image, return, as Luke (Son, text) never will, to "see / A work which *is not here:* a covenant . . ." (413–4, emphasis supplied). Michael tells Luke that the nonexistent Sheep-fold, of which Luke will lay the first stone, "'Twill be [a covenant] between us," and he might have added the succeeding words in Laban's pronouncement to Jacob concerning the stone/pillar Mizpah. Laban says, "'This heap is a witness between you and me today.' Therefore he named . . . the pillar Mizpah. 'The Lord watch between you and me, when we are absent one from the other'" (Gen. 31:48). With ironic implication for Michael and Luke, once the heap is made, Laban, father-in-law, and Jacob, son-in-law, will not see each other again. In *Michael,* the first stone that Luke lays is to be identified with the Mizpah pillar, a *heap* of stones, like Michael's "straggling heap," the name *Mizpah* meaning "watchpost." It is at this watchpost-heap that Michael will wait and watch year after year for Luke's return. Thus the sheepfold is a "work," a "covenant" with intertextual echoes. A covenant is an agreement in one sense, but also a text—God's text, as in the Old and New Covenants. The Sheep-fold that never was is a lost, fragmentary, meaningless text, but also a parable whose significance the reader might miss, or that the traveler might see and notice not. The site of the there/not-there Sheep-fold is an "utter solitude," where one is "alone / With a few sheep, with rocks and stones" (10–13). The few sheep are lost, without fold or shepherd.

THE LOST LAND

Wordsworth's site is a specifically situated and named one in the mountainous regions of northern England. This is Michael's ancestral land. Michael's name, however, and his designation as Shepherd and Father (with capital letters) suggest that whatever place he inhabits is difficult to locate on a map. His spiritual namesake, the archangel

Michael, is heavenly "poet" (Yeats' "singing master"), leader of the divine choir. He is said to have purified Isaiah's lips to make them fit to speak the divine message of confusion, "see ye indeed, but perceive not" (Is. 6–9), the message echoed in the New Testament by Jesus in his explanation of why he speaks in parables, and paraphrased by Wordsworth's "Might see and notice not." Michael is patron saint and protector of high places. His name means "Who is like God?" or, ambiguously, "Who is like God" (Jeffrey 504–5).[7] His other designations, Father and Shepherd, suggest biblical antecedents—the Old Testament patriarchs (Abraham, Jacob, Moses), all of whom were tribal fathers and shepherds—but also Yahweh, metaphorically named both *Father* and *Shepherd*.

Michael's land, therefore, is at the literal level simply a plot of English soil, but through the devices of parable it is a spiritual elsewhere—Land (with a capital letter), and a "plot" or story of Land, hidden since the foundation of the world. Michael's mountains, like other holy mountains, are animate—in Wordsworth's phrase, "instinct with vital functions." The winds that blow through them are numinous, significant, invested with "meaning" and "music" (48–51). There is a close identity between Michael, both the character and the poem, and this land:

> . . . These fields, these hills
> Which were his living Being, even more
> Than his own Blood—what could they less? had laid
> Strong hold on his affections, were to him
> A pleasurable feeling of blind love,
> The pleasure which there is in life itself. (74–9)

The mountains themselves are agents. They have "all opened out themselves / And made a hidden valley of their own," a place beyond the frontier of parable of "utter solitude" (7–8, 13), where the Shepherd/Father/Michael labors on land as text, the fields and hills that, "like a book" (70), not only present their own text, but preserve that original text as another is superimposed upon them—the record of Michael's labor, life, and love. As Michael lives and labors on the land/Land, he makes a text, leaves an imprint. One object of his labor and love is the "straggling heap of unhewn stones," a text of obscure meaning and intent, the Sheep-fold that never was. Scrawled across the land-of-hidden-significance, it is a fragment. The result is a mysterious palimpsest of text superimposed on text—human text on land and Land, an obscure, fragmentary text, homely and rude, a story of a land and a Land beyond the reach of words.[8]

Wordsworth's concern with the notion of human and divine texts and their relationship is elaborated in the important Book 5 of the *Prelude,* entitled "Books," composed in the spring of 1804. Miller has shown that in Book 5 Wordsworth was working with "the Biblical, medieval, and Renaissance topos of the two divine books, the book of nature and the book of revealed Scripture" (*The Linguistic Moment* 93). These divine texts are represented in Book 5 by human texts figured in the forms of stone and shell—one of science (corresponding to Nature) and one of poetry (corresponding to Scripture), which together are metonymic of all of human texts, humanity's "adamantine holds of truth . . . / The consecrated works of bard and sage" (39–42). Unlike divine texts, such human books, like their authors, are fragile and transitory: a volume is a "Poor earthly casket of immortal Verse" (164). Books die; humans die; but the earth (nature, God's text, with its "plot of Land") abides. Wordsworth's narrator asks, "Oh, why hath not the mind / Some element to stamp her image on / In nature somewhat nearer to her own?" (5:45–7).

Some four years earlier, in *Michael,* Wordsworth was already addressing this subject, attempting not only to understand the human dilemma, and the relationship—and incommensurability—of human and divine texts, but also to find some linguistic point of join or, more accurately, some linguistic escape hatch, through the paradoxical devices of parable.[9] For Wordsworth, Michael's Sheep-fold text, while not exactly adamantine, is, like "Euclid's Elements" in the dream, represented in stone, and while its meaning is obscure (it requires the poet-interpreter), it does endure. It is a sign for endurance, figured as well in Michael's life and work. If the human world has access to eternity, it is through such texts, such signs wherein eternity is fashioned, as Miller says in another context, as "a self-sustaining temporal structure built by language over the abyss of death" (*The Linguistic Moment* 104). The parabolic form, like the dream in Book 5, permits a blurring of boundaries and a merging of identities. The land is finite, a small piece of England, and, *at the same time,* an eternal, unnamed "hidden" Land that cannot be spoken of directly; it is pastoral valley, but also Nature, human text, and divine text. Like the dream's stone and shell that *are* books, like the Arab who *is* Don Quixote, things, acts, and persons of parables are always what they seem (the letter) and something else (the spirit); they are, inexplicably, "neither, and [are] both at once" (*Prelude* 5:126). Unlike the shifting gestalt of the often-encountered Rubin vase, parable demands that vase and profiles be "seen" and apprehended simultaneously; and, further, that the depiction is neither vase nor profiles, and yet both at once. Michael's land is neither Nature nor text, and yet both at once; it is neither of England nor

Elsewhere, and yet it is both; his straggling heap of unhewn stones is neither Sheep-fold nor text, and yet both at once.

According to the letter of the tale, in danger of losing the land, Michael sends away his son—loses him ("Our Luke shall leave us, Isabel; the land / Shall not go from us" [244–5])—keeps the land until he dies, loses it when he dies (sold to a stranger), yet at the same time becomes a part of the land and the ancestral mould, thus keeping it. The hidden Land, the spiritual Land, is typical of place in parabolic speech, which, Miller says, refers to "a place out of the world," one "that cannot be designated more precisely than in topographical terms drawn from the real world and applied figuratively to the place out of the real world." As with others of parable's spiritual referents, the language of the world is pressed into service to perform that which it cannot do, but attempts anyway. "There are no literal terms for the places in parable" ("Parable and performative" 145). What does it mean to the dead (and the "lost," the "dead letter") either to keep or lose this Land? What does keeping or losing mean to the living (the "found," the "spirit")? What does it mean in either case to exchange son (Son, Luke, text) for land (Land, a land "like a book," text)? Does the exchange (or "sacrifice") merely substitute one text for another? That is, is the Son lost?

THE LOST SON

As examination of Wordsworth's parable proceeds, words and names, like rolling snowballs, gain weight and momentum. The son/Son in Wordsworth's parable, as in Luke's, achieves a metaphoric representation in other key elements. In Luke's narrative, the son is a figurative equivalent (although the equivalency is paradoxical) for lost sheep and lost coin. The identity is achieved through the rapid serial narration of parallel plots. Something similar, but exponentially more elaborate, happens in Wordsworth's parable, where the metaphoric identity is achieved not through plot, but through names, words, each of which gains a cubed and snarled complexity through intertextual echoes that, in the pre-text, Luke 15, are either muted or find no counterpart.

Wordsworth's Son (and its synonyms, Boy, Child, Lad, with his occupation—Shepherd) is named Luke. As mentioned, Luke, as the name of the pre-text, forges a figurative identity not only of parabolic text and Wordsworth's Son, but of Wordsworth's Son and the lost-and-found (dead-and-living), prodigal son of Luke 15. In that tale the boy's father interprets the action in terms parallel with Jesus' interpretations of the first two tales—of the sheep and the coin—and hence identifies son, sheep, and coin, and all three first with sinner, loss, and death, and then with repentance, recovery, and life. At the same time, the father (and hence Wordsworth's Michael), through his functions as both forgiver and interpreter, is identified with Jesus, who is mysteriously both God and Son of God, and yet man and Son of Man, "neither, and both at once," or in this case, more accurately, none and yet all at once.

Yet *Son* (with a capital) also immediately suggests Jesus; and so Wordsworth's Luke, like Michael, is figuratively identified with Jesus, the Word, the Logos, the parable's "poet-narrator," and, in terms of Wordsworth's poem, most difficult of all, with Jesus as Stone. The Hebrew *ben* "son" and *'eben* "stone" became the basis of wordplay by New Testament authors using Psalm 118:22 to refer to Christ, "Son," as the corner/head stone of the temple (Jeffrey 737): "The stone which the builders refused is become the head stone of the corner." Hence Christ, Son, stone, corner-stone, and head stone (with more grim echoes) all enter Wordsworth's poem as invited guests, to become associated with the fragmentary Sheep-fold-text, and its narrator, and invest the crucial image of "a straggling heap of unhewn stones" with unfathomable depths of signification. As Luke sets the corner-stone for the never-to-be-completed structure, he makes himself a part of this text. He is both son (*ben*) and stone (*'eben*).

As mentioned, the sheepfold image dominates the poem, is identified with the poem through Wordsworth's working title, and focuses both its beginning and end. Two intriguing passages toward the end of *Michael* concentrate the parable's shifting and equivocal meanings in the Sheep-fold, for which the single stone—corner stone, head stone—is a metonym. The first of these is when, just before Luke's departure, Michael takes his Son to the intended site of the sheepfold, asks him to "Lay now the corner-stone" (403), and, when confronted with evil, to re-member the moment: "hither turn thy thoughts, / And God will strengthen thee" (406–7). At that time too Michael makes the curious pledge: "When thou return'st, thou in this place will see / A work which is not here: a covenant / 'Twill be between us" (413–5). To see that "which is not here" is to see beyond the letter to the spirit, to see *and* perceive. Luke does lay the "head stone of the corner," departs, falls into dissolute ways, and flees to some parabolic place "beyond the seas" (447). Then there is the secondhand report that after Luke's failure "'tis believed by all / That many and many a day [Michael went to the Sheep-fold] / And never lifted up a single stone" (464–6). However, the Sheep-fold is a phantom conjured out of language; it is a text, and a name, but not a stone structure. It is "that which is not here." In a way, Michael's presence so often and for so long at the site textualizes it, provides it with "plot"— the story that appertains to the straggling heap. At last the closing comments of the narrator move the reader into a future in which Michael and

Isabel are dead and all signs of human habitation are gone from the land, with the sole exception of "the remains / Of the unfinished Sheep-fold" (481), that curious text, literary "remains," that object that is not there, and will, at least literally, never be there, the heap/covenant/watchpost that one "might see and notice not."

THE WORD AND THE WORD

What of the poem's meaning? What of its "morality"? What poetics does it offer? At a literal level the poem is a story of deep affection, heroic labor, and irreparable loss. It has moments when these essential human matters become so compelling that letter overwhelms "spirit," as in this remarkable passage from the closing lines of the poem, as Michael watches and waits year after year for his lost son, laboring at times on the Sheep-fold:

> ... 'Tis believed by all
> That many and many a day he thither went
> And never lifted up a single stone.
> There, by the Sheep-fold, sometimes was he seen
> Sitting alone, with that his faithful Dog,
> Then old, beside him, lying at his feet. (473–8)

The strange idleness of this old man, proverbial for "endless industry" (96–7), whose life is and always has been ceaseless work, speaks poignantly of his literal, human condition, of his grief and loss. For a moment the site is just a bit of English landscape, Michael is just an old English shepherd, and a stone is just a stone. But the effects of parable are here too, and will not be denied. Michael's suffering is not just personal, his stones are not just stones. This fact may be what Harold Bloom has in mind when he speaks of "the majestic, covenantal suffering of the old shepherd in 'Michael'" (*The Western Canon* 247). Michael's suffering is figuratively all human and divine suffering for loss. Insisting on the "spirit of things" and on the poem's parabolic functioning, the last three lines of the poem bring the reader back to that enigmatic stone heap/text: "[A]nd the remains / Of the unfinished Sheep-fold may be seen / Beside the boisterous brook of Green-head Gill." Green-head Gill is where the poem ends and where it has begun. It is mentioned initially only because of that "object" that the traveler "might pass by, / Might see and notice not" (15–6). At the end of the poem this "object" is still there, "may be seen," but whether it will be "perceived" or "noticed" either by disciples or the multitudes is problematic.

It is easier to be convinced about what the poem does not mean than to attempt to specify among its complexities and equivocations what it does mean. Despite the letter to Fox, one can be fairly certain that the poem is not primarily a call for socioeconomic reform. If that were the case, a political tract might have been a more effective instrument for achieving that end. The narrative of *Michael* proposes neither social cause nor social cure for the situation of the old shepherd; for whatever the turnings of plot, Michael is not driven from his land, but dies on it and is buried in it. Moreover, if the poem is not chiefly a call for social reform, neither can one say that it is about the corrupting influences of the city, for Luke's failure is recounted almost casually in six lines.[10] It is likewise probably not chiefly about the endurance and universality of Old Testament attitudes and behaviors, for a New Testament poetics threatens to overwhelm the Old Testament allusions. Looking hard at the final image, and keeping in mind the poem's parabolic method and pre-text (Luke 15), one can say tentatively that the poem invites its pre-text in to imitate its method, but to destroy it by reversing its hopeful message. Wordsworth's parable ends not with joy, but with grief; not with community—either human or heavenly—but with deep isolation, "utter solitude." *Michael* is not about repenting (finding) and living, but about loss and death—the cessation of work and the death even of those proverbial for industry. More especially, in the maelstrom of social change, it is about the loss of an inherently poetic language of a people, their texts and their meanings; about their inability, finally, to leave any lasting imprint on the text of nature, at most leaving behind a parable in a "straggling heap of unhewn stones" and a sign, a corner stone/head stone without an epitaph, an object in which the eternal is called into the temporal realm as part of an enigmatic palimpsest, which one "might see and notice not."

The poem's parabolic method, with its naming and plotting, and its web of intertextual allusions, concludes not with human action as in Luke 15, especially not with "making merry," but with landscape, an elsewhere of "utter solitude" whose landmarks consist of a tree of fallen language and a fragmentary text in stone scrawled across a barren hillside. Neither of these objects speaks for itself; their significance requires a parable-maker who will name them and give them a story. The story tells of what remains at the end of the human story, when the heavenly light fails or has failed: "The Cottage which was named The Evening Star / Is gone, the ploughshare has been through the ground / On which it stood" (485–7). The human actors, Matthew, Isabel, and Luke, are dead or lost. The pastures have been transformed into fields and the sheep scattered:

"great changes have been wrought" (487). All that remains are the heap of stones and the old oak tree—obscure text and fallible language.

As already suggested, Wordsworth's metaparabolic enterprise in *Michael* anticipates the metapoetic concerns in Book 5 of the *Prelude*. The stone heap and the naming tree are early versions of the dream's stone and shell (which both are and are not books). Both *Michael* and Book 5 have an apocalyptic bent, and, to use Wallace Stevens' phrase, a tone of "literate despair" about the failure of the human—individuals, their significance, and their texts—in the face of enduring nature. The parabolic form permits its narrator to assume a timeless posture, to stand above his own narrative before a largely uncomprehending audience and speak of human beings and texts, of obscure things, of objects with hidden significance, of what passes and what remains. It permits the poet, through his text, to inscribe the "head stone of the corner," which may survive itself as the stone survives its ruin, "rescued," rather than refused, by its own inscription, living on as its own epitaph.[11] In this enterprise the poet-narrator addresses "a few natural hearts" (36), his own alter-egos in the "youthful Poets . . . / Who will be [his] second self when [he is] gone" (38–9), those not fed on the dead letter. For this audience of disciples he uses the mysterious language of parable within whose naming and plotting letter and spirit merge. In offering the parable of *Michael* to his readers, Wordsworth has given his own covenant, his own mysterious text, his own "Sheep-fold," wherein the dead letter may survive, both to veil and reveal the spirit of things.

Chapter 6

Wordsworth's Song of Songs
"Nutting" as Mystical Allegory

A garden inclosed is my sister, my spouse,
a spring shut up, a fountain sealed.
Thy plants are an orchard of pomegranates
with pleasant fruits. . . .

—Song of Solomon 4:12–13[1]

This thy stature is like to a palm tree, and thy breasts to [its] clusters.
I said, I will go up to the palm tree, I will take
hold of the boughs thereof.

—Song of Solomon 7:7–8

The allegorical nature of "Nutting" is well recognized. Readers frequently focus on the poem's sexual allegory, finding in the boy's expedition to gather nuts a sort of Freudian manifest content to mask a latent content of sexual aggression, Oedipal passions, psychic maturation, rape, and/or murder. Daniel P. Watkins takes the allegory to a further level at which "the story of the rape includes within it a commentary on the relations between masculine sexuality and imperialist conquest" (56). M. W. Rowe, borrowing a term from Gerard Manley Hopkins, calls the allegorical level the "underthought"—"conveyed chiefly in the choice of metaphors etc. used and often only half realised by the poet himself" (23 n1), a claim that implies a rather artless poetry and a poet not only influenced by, but in thrall to, unconscious forces that produce the poem for him. Post-Lacanian linguistic readings, as Rachel Crawford points out, have seen the poem again as unconscious art, "the effort to recuperate the discourse of the original, phallic mother" (198). Most recently, Kenneth R. Johnston has found in "Nutting" a record (among several) of Wordsworth's attempts to "gain control of his passion for Dorothy" and of hers for him (*The Hidden Wordsworth* 648–52). Understandably, the focus of discussions of the poem's sexual implications is often the poet, rather than the poem.

Although details of its significance are subject to debate, that a sexual allegory operates in "Nutting" may be acknowledged. However, I want to consider this level as only one of a number of increasingly complex and resonating stages that, acting together, constitute the intricate art of the poem and its presentation of a physical, epistemological, creative, and spiritual process. To understand the process to which the poem alludes, "Nutting" may be seen as a system of strata, with the more superficial layers partially concealing, even as they partially reveal, those lying beneath. At least four levels can be exposed: the literal level (the narrative of a boy's gathering hazel nuts), the sexual allegory (often explored by critics), the more intriguing metapoetical allegory, and, finally, borrowing a phrase from Robert Lowth, the "mystical allegory." Recognizing several levels of meaning acknowledges the complexity, the careful art, and the sheer Wordsworthian genius of the poem. One might say of "Nutting" what Francis Landy said of the Song of Songs: "If the Song were a continuous allegory of sex, no matter how ingenious the techniques or subtle the allusions, it would be nothing more than a riddle or a tease." I want to claim that the sexual allegory of "Nutting" is like that which Landy claims for the Song, which speaks of something that happens, a process, that is "beyond speech," and that "enters language only through displacement" (305). The process beyond speech exists in its various forms in the allegorical layers, each layer revealing an aspect of the process. As the strata lie adjacent to one another, they exchange particles, each stratum by this means enriched with and complicated by the "materials" of the others. At one plane of meaning, a word, detail, or image may suggest one sense or attitude, ironic or otherwise, and at another, some entirely different sense or attitude, so that a reader is likely to undergo repeated cycles of mystification, disequilibrium, and recovery as the text unfolds.

I shall argue that "Nutting" is extraordinarily evocative and complex because it is Wordsworth's subtle and ironically admonitory revision of the biblical Song of Songs. In revising the Song, Wordsworth joins a number of other poets, including Edward Taylor ("The Reflexion"), Michael Drayton ("The Third Chapter from The Most Excellent Song which is Solomon's"), and, most interestingly, Henry Vaughan, whose "Regeneration" eerily forecasts figures, themes, and images of "Nutting." So numerous are the echoes between the two works that it is very likely that Wordsworth had the example of Vaughan's poem in mind when he composed his own poem.[2] I shall explore the intertextual implications of the Vaughan poem in the sections on metapoetic and mystical allegory. Another important figure in this tradition is Thomas Percy, whose translation of the Song of Solomon, with commentary and notes, was published in 1769. While I do not find external evidence that Wordsworth read Percy's translation, textual evidence suggests that he was familiar with it, another matter to which I shall return below. In his own revision, Wordsworth displaces the Song's literal (sensual/sexual) level to the first allegorical level of "Nutting" and continues through subsequent levels to construct what Robert Lowth calls mystical allegory, because its ultimate system of reference is inarticulable. As I shall show, the language and images of "Nutting" call the Song of Songs and the figure of Solomon, as well as biblical and Miltonic Edens, into Wordsworth's poem.[3] The effect is to create a complex intertextuality among the various allegorical levels that results in an extraordinary orchestration of signs and meanings. The literal story of a boy's gathering nuts represents on successive levels: (1) a complex, partially physical, partially mental event or epistemological process, originary and universal; (2) a metacritical mythopoetic enterprise, the poetic process itself; and (3) the metaphysical intimations. As the metaphors operate among and between the various allegorical levels, each is a shape-shifter. For example, the youth on his nutting expedition is, as Wordsworth tells us, a "Figure": he is a boy who seeks nuts, but he is also pilgrim, king, prophet, and poet. He is one who finds in the nutting expedition the power of language, the nuts he gathers having grown on the bard's tree; he is the king who discovers the source of creativity and his own allegorical relationship to it. The nuts he gathers are food, but also wealth, and at the same time they are knowledge—physical, mental, and spiritual.

ROBERT LOWTH AND THE SONG OF SOLOMON

I am persuaded by Stephen Prickett's exposition of Robert Lowth's influence on Wordsworth,[4] and I will use as my point of departure Lowth's comments on the Song of Solomon (2:298–344). Lowth explains that some readers have chosen to see the Song as literal and some as allegorical (2:310). Of those who see it as allegorical, some find it to be simple allegory; others, the more complex and mysterious "mystical allegory."[5] Lowth announces that he "feel[s] irresistibly inclined to that side of the question which considers this poem as an entire allegory." Of the three classes of allegory that Lowth identifies—continued metaphor, parable, and mystical allegory—he finds that the Song is properly seen as mystical allegory, "which, under the veil of some historical fact, conceals a meaning more sacred and sublime" (2:326–7). He explains:

> Those . . . who are conversant with the writings of the Hebrew poets will easily perceive how agreeable the conduct of this poem is to the practice of those writers, who are fond of annexing a secret and solemn sense to the obvious meaning of their compositions, and of looking through the medium of human affairs to those which are celestial and divine. (2:328)

Of the sorts of mystical allegory, Lowth identifies the Song as a type he calls anthropopathy, which he describes as an allegory resulting from a divine attempt to accommodate itself to human understanding:

> The narrowness and imbecillity of the human mind being such, as scarcely to comprehend or attain a clear idea of any part of the Divine nature by its utmost exertions; God has condescended, in a manner, to contract the infinity of his glory, and to exhibit it to our understandings under such imagery as our feeble optics are capable of contemplating. *Thus the Almighty may be said to descend, as it were, in the Holy Scriptures, from the height of his majesty, to appear on earth in a human shape, with human senses and affections, in all respects resembling a mortal*—"with human voice and human form." This kind of allegory is called anthropopathy and occupies a considerable portion of theology . . . as delivered in the Holy Scriptures. (2:312; emphasis supplied)

Years after writing "Nutting," Wordsworth voices a similar idea, a version of the theory of accommodation,[6] where he asserts that "The commerce between Man and his Maker cannot be carried on but by a process where much is represented in little, and the Infinite Being accommodates himself to a finite capacity" (*Pr. W.,* "Essay, Supplementary to the Preface" 3:65). It is important to notice that the imagery of anthropopathy is "derived from the passions." Moreover, "there is no affection or emotion of the human soul which is not, with all its circumstances, ascribed in direct terms, without any qualification whatever, to the supreme God" (2:312–13). Through his discussions of the marriage metaphor as employed in the Song and by various of the prophets (2:314–20), Lowth makes it clear that he includes in human affection or emotion the sexual passions. In the marriage metaphor, Lowth argues, an analogical relationship is established between God and husband and between Church and wife, who experience passions, the spiritual passions expressible only as sexual passions. In partial support of this claim, Lowth cites Chardin on the Persian poets: "Debauchery and licentiousness . . . are the common topics of these compositions; but I must not omit remarking, that the most serious of their poets treat of the sublimest mysteries of theology, under the most licentious language . . ." (2:321n). Lowth's interpretation of the Song as anthropopathy argues that the sensual and passionate discourse of the lover and the beloved operate at the literal level of meaning, representing the "contracted" and encoded form of a metaphysical, and ultimately unspeakable, mystery to which they refer. Therefore, each "licentious" word, act, or image of the literal Song, each metaphor drawn from nature or elsewhere, carries a message of the sublimest mysteries.[7] This point will prove relevant to the sexual imagery of "Nutting." Just how readers may apprehend and comprehend sublime mysteries in the form of contracted infinity and glory Lowth leaves unspecified. Undeniably, modern metaphor theory would insist that sublime mysteries suffer the normal transfer of particles between the tenor and vehicle of the metaphor, leaving the imagination simultaneously to embrace and reject the notion of God as a passionate, sexual mystery.

Given the allegorical understanding of the Song of Songs, it would follow that at the literal level Solomon is himself, wise and wealthy king of Israel, but also bridegroom, prophet, and poet; at the allegorical level, he is the figure through whom the anthropopathy functions. His is the "human voice," his the "human form," in which the Almighty, contracted, appears to human senses in the world. Thus, in Lowth's analysis, the overt sexuality and sensuality of this mystical allegory, understandable to "the narrowness and imbecillity of the human mind," are merely hints of sublime and largely incomprehensible mysteries. This allegory offers its message partially hidden—"under the veil of some historical fact"—not so much to make a difficult meaning accessible, but actually to conceal "a meaning more sacred and sublime." This hiddenness raises the question of whether the meaning must be concealed, or must be "shown" as not directly presentable. The tradition that makes Solomon the poet-author of the Song functions as a part of the allegory, making him, a human author, representative at the metapoetic level of God, supreme Author, ultimate source of the Song and indeed of all Holy Scriptures.

"UNDER THE VEIL OF SOME HISTORICAL FACT"

As Bruce Bigley notices, a question "that invariably arises in discussions of 'Nutting' is why the poem is not part of The Prelude" (448). After analyzing and rejecting other explanations, Bigley offers his own theory: the reasons lie in "the constantly shifting tonality of the poem . . . , constantly shifting from playful to ecstatic to moral, as well as from the voice of the boy . . . to the voices of the adult" (449). Bigley's discussion of the poem's tones and voices is perceptive and instructive. However, the reasons he offers do not, to my mind, account for the exclusion of "Nutting" from the *Prelude*. For me, the question is not, Is the tone wrong for the *Prelude?* but, Is the tone indicative of another sort of verse and function? My claim is that "Nutting" is excluded because it evolved into another sort of verse, a richly intertextual, mystical allegory. However it began, it is not autobiography (even excluding the question of whether it is possible to write autobiography in verse and ignoring the curious mode of the *Prelude* as autobiography[8]). The false start to the poem[9] is evidence, certainly, that at the outset Wordsworth wrote of an incident thematically linked to other incidents in the 1799 *Prelude*. Indeed he claims as much when he says that the poem was originally "intended as part of a poem on my own life, but struck out as not being wanted there" (cited in *P. W.* 2:504). Furthermore, if we consider the radical changes from the cancelled verses of the poem's false start as we have it—for example, from Lucy as ravager of the nut grove to speaker as ravager—it is clear that something other than personal history is being recorded. A further indication that the poem is not autobiographical lies in the poet's claim that "the verses arose out of the *remembrance of feelings* [rather than incidents] I had often had when a boy" (cited in *P. W.* 2:504; emphasis supplied). "Feelings" is a richly suggestive term, for it may encompass all the passions of the poem, from sexual excitement and aggression to mystical awe. Wordsworth's claim of their frequent recurrence suggests a sort of haunting over time, which feelings, couched in figurative language, are reified in the narrative of "Nutting." Further, the poem's intricate web of intertextuality, particularly the numerous parallels with Vaughan's "Regeneration," argues against autobiography. But, finally, the best argument for Wordsworth's "not want[ing]" the poem in the *Prelude* is the central claim of this discussion—that in its final form the poem is a complex, multilayered allegory, the poet's appropriation and "translation" of the Song of Songs.

Yet the poem comes to us *as though,* to use Lowth's phrase describing the disguise of mystical allegory, "under the veil of some historical [autobiographical] fact." As the allegory of the Song of Songs presents itself under the veil of the historical marriage of Solomon, but in essence speaks of the mystical relationship between God and Israel, so "Nutting" presents itself under the veil of the boy William's nutting expedition, but in essence speaks of far other matters.

THE "LITERAL" LEVEL: NUTTING EXPEDITION

At the first level of significance, the poem relates how the speaker as a boy had gone seeking hazel nuts, found them, and gathered an abundance, resulting in feelings of pride in his accomplishment and perhaps regret that in the process he had broken many branches of the trees. Yet even at this level, the language pulls readers away from the literal, being richly suggestive of the depths of significance the poem will encompass. It tells of a protagonist in old clothes, which constitute a "disguise," or rather multiple disguises: knight, pilgrim, beggar, and clown. A disguise is a false appearance. One must be wary of one in disguise, for he is not what he seems. More interestingly, however, the boy is a "Figure quaint." A protagonist who is a "Figure" may be an "illusion or a fantasm," but he is not a literal human being. He is a walking trope. The adjective *quaint* complicates the matter, for it is a word of paradoxical meaning. Like "uncanny," it designates both the unfamiliar and the familiar simultaneously. *Quaint* can suggest something "curious, unfamiliar, or strange," but its origins go back to the Latin *cognoscere*, referring to something known or with which one is acquainted. While the evocative language of the opening lines invites this sort of speculation, the apparently ironic playfulness and self-mockery of the description allow readers to pay attention or not, as they wish. But having paid attention, one finds oneself confronted with a strange, unknown, illusory, but oddly familiar "Figure" in disguise setting out to gather nuts. Although he seems strange, we have met this "Figure" many times before.

Moreover, the fact that the boy is seeking *hazel* nuts is telling. In the northern tradition, the hazel tree has mythic properties. It is most frequently seen as a tree of wisdom, inspiration, and knowledge; it is the poet's tree, "an emblem of concentrated wisdom" (Graves 181), but it may also serve as a tree of life (J. C. Cooper 80). In Celtic lore, "those destined to partake of the [hazel] nuts or of the salmon [which has eaten the nuts] obtained the gifts of the seer and the poet" (Rees and Rees 161); the salmon of knowledge is one that has "fed on nuts fallen from the nine hazels of poetic art" (Graves 75). A growth of hazel trees is a sacred grove or sacred orchard wherein one obtains wealth and wisdom in meeting with the divine. Rods of the hazel are thought to have magical properties, being used as divining rods. In a similar function, hazels were said to bend and stretch on the earth toward gold mines. The arrival of summer, the advent of love, and the springing of hazel nuts are contemporaneous events (*OED* under *hazel*). In its richness of associations, the nut may be used as a metaphor for allegory itself; the shell representing the literal level, concealing the kernel of the matter.

Thus even at this literal level, in his portrait of the artist as a young man and description of his quest, Wordsworth has disguised his protagonist, who is both strange and familiar, rendered him figurative, and sent him into a sacred grove or orchard to gather the fruit not only of wisdom, but of life, of poetic art, and of prophetic inspiration. The grove with its hazel trees of life and wisdom expands to implicate other groves, orchards, and gardens wherein such trees flourish, and where consuming the trees' fruit changes everything: As in the Garden of Eden, here one can move in a moment from innocence to experience, from ignorance to wisdom (becoming "like God, knowing good and evil"), from childish to adult consciousness, suddenly realizing as the scales fall from one's eyes that one is a sexual being and that one is naked. One might say of the hazels what Milton's Eve ironically says of the biblical fruit of wisdom: the fruit "feed[s] at once both Body and Mind" (*Paradise Lost* 9:779). In "Nutting," the boy appears to undergo a transformation merely by eyeing the fruit, in anticipating but not actually consuming it. Yet as in *Paradise Lost,* the protagonist's first response after the radical physical and epistemological transformation is one of aggressive passion (*Paradise Lost* 9:1011–14).[10] The boy's change is internal, evidenced outwardly in his astonishingly rapid move from benign observer to violent actor. The transformation occurs mid-line in the brief break between sentences: "Then up I rose, / And dragged to earth both branch and bough, with crash / And merciless ravage." Such violence directed against an implicitly feminine hazel grove or orchard (this "virgin scene") may begin as greedy destruction but is quickly transformed by the language used to describe it into brutal sexual assault, whose object is not so much the trees themselves, as a feminine identity encompassing the grove to which the boy claims possession. All these considerations "at the literal level" mean that the poem is too evocative to permit any but the most determined readers to remain satisfied with the manifest story.

THE PERSONA OF SOLOMON

Solomon's name is proverbial first for wisdom, and then for wealth. As a wisdom figure, he is poet-prophet, one who was said to have written both philosophy (or wisdom literature—Proverbs and Ecclesiastes, as well as the apocryphal Wisdom of Solomon), and poetry (psalms and the Song of Songs). As a seer and poet, he is the one biblical figure whose life and works represented for Wordsworth the bardic calling. For example, it is Solomon who composes the biblical "spousal verse" (the Song of Songs), a prototype of the poem Wordsworth projects in *Home at Grasmere* as his own life's work. In the section of *Home at Grasmere* that later became the

"Prospectus" to the *Excursion,* Wordsworth echoes Solomon's words in his dedication of the temple ("But will God indeed dwell on the earth? behold, the heaven and the heaven of heavens cannot contain thee; how much less this house that I have builded?" [1 Kgs 8:27]). Wordsworth suggests a similar divinity, vastness, and elusiveness of the human mind to which the "Heaven of heavens is but a veil" (979). A bit later Wordsworth claims that "Paradise, and groves / Elysian, fortunate islands" need not be a dream, for "minds" wedded to nature "in love" can find these as "the growth of common day"; in celebration of such nuptials, the poet will sing the epithalamion:

> I, long before the blessed hour arrives,
> *Would sing in solitude the spousal verse*
> *Of this great consummation,* would proclaim—
> Speaking of nothing more than what we are—
> How exquisitely the individual Mind . . .
>   to the external world
> Is fitted; and how exquisitely too . . .
> The external world is fitted to the mind.
>   (*Home at Grasmere* 996–1011, emphasis supplied)

This theme of the marital relationship of mind to nature is Wordsworth's "great argument" (1014), his poetic enterprise expressed in a marriage metaphor, just as, traditionally read, Solomon's great argument of the relation of divine to world is expressed in the extraordinary and difficult marriage song of Solomon. In the Song, Solomon as husband or bridegroom is understood in his earthly roles of king, wise man, and poet, but allegorically he is also a figure for the divine. In Lowth's analysis, Solomon is the human form through whom the divine attempts to accommodate itself to human understanding. The bride is likewise a human woman, a Shulamite, but within the mystical allegory of the Song, she is Israel, a chosen and beloved people and, more interestingly, from a Wordsworthian perspective, through repeated and insistent identification in the images of the Song, she is also nature or world. God and the bride/Israel/nature in the Song are analogous to the vast individual mind and nature, marriage partners in Wordsworth's projected work, *The Recluse.* Albeit transformed and deformed, they are also analogous to the boy and the hazel grove in "Nutting," which can be seen as a first, brief, ironic or bemused annunciation of this nuptial theme. The fitting of mind to nature, as Wordsworth suggests in "Tintern Abbey," results from the fact that both are "deeply interfused" with that scarcely nameable "something," a "presence," a "motion and a spirit" (94–103). In "Nutting," that this entity may be called to haunt about the sacred grove is intimated in the undersong of metaphor and image and announced in that apparent non sequitur of the last line, which insists that "there is a Spirit in the woods."

Solomon's associations with wisdom and wealth arise from his dream conversation with God soon after he has assumed the throne of David. When God asks Solomon what he wants, Solomon, characterizing himself as "but a little child," asks for an understanding heart to discern between good and evil (which raises an echo of the admonition to Adam against eating of the fruit of the tree of knowledge). In response God grants Solomon a "wise and understanding heart" unparalleled in human experience—a wisdom associated with both philosophical and poetic skills; wealth and honor to exceed that of all other kings; and long life (1 Kgs 3:7–14). These gifts from God to Solomon are just those that pass from nature to the boy William in "Nutting." The boy, like Solomon as "a little child," comes away from his experience "Exulting, rich beyond the wealth of kings." (Solomon was given riches "so that there shall not be any among the kings like unto thee all thy days.") The wealth is in the form of hazel nuts, the fruit of wisdom or knowledge, the fruit of prophecy and poetic inspiration, so that Solomon's separate gifts of wisdom and wealth are conflated in "Nutting." For the boy William, wisdom is wealth; wealth is wisdom. Both abstractions are given concrete form in the hazel nuts, the fruit of the mythical poet's tree of inspiration and wisdom, identifiable with both of the Edenic trees of life and of the knowledge of good and evil, an abundance granted to and gathered by one in disguise, a figure quaint.

THE SEXUAL ALLEGORY:
"A GARDEN INCLOSED IS MY SISTER, MY SPOUSE" [11]

The scene of "Nutting," like that of Wordsworth's poetic enterprise, discussed earlier, is familiar from the literary tradition of the earthly paradise. This is a tradition in which classic (Wordsworth's "groves Elysian" and "fortunate fields") and biblical (Wordsworth's "paradise") sources converge in depictions by medieval, Renaissance, and later poets of a place of harmony and repose, earthly or celestial, real or apparent, holy or enchanted. A. Bartlett Giamatti says of this tradition, "The desire for a state of perfect repose and life eternal has always haunted mankind, and poets have forever been the spokesmen for the dream" (3). The Judeo-Christian tradition (with which I am chiefly concerned here) offers as archetypes the gardens in Genesis and in the Song of Songs. Both of these are pristine, "virginal," and associated with a woman as "unravish'd bride." In his commentary on his translation of the Song of Solomon, Thomas Percy explains that in referring to the bride as "a garden shut up" or "a fountain sealed," the bridegroom has used "great delicacy" in making the requisite public declaration "that he has received her pure and inviolate" (xxviii–xxix). The parallel declaration in "Nutting" that the "dear nook" is a "virgin scene" (and a virgin seen) is apparent and constitutes the bridegroom's acceptance of the inviolate bride. Both Eve and the beloved of the Song are associated with trees—Eve with the trees of life and of knowledge of good and evil, and the bride of the Song with the palm tree (of life). Both are gardens of love; and in both the progress is from an apparently platonic or linguistic love, to the physical. In each case this progress is associated with the tree (the sexual knowledge gained from eating the forbidden fruit of Eden, and, in the Song, the lover's intention to "go up to the palm tree [woman]" and to "lay hold of the branches thereof"). In both instances this is the moment when the "virgin scene" (the inviolate bride) is to be irremediably changed and, especially in the case of Eden, with it/her, everything else, for here the sexual event is associated with an epistemological event, and both with the fall and the loss forever of the perfect place.[12] Since that initial fall and exile, humanity has been seeking to reenter the garden of beginnings and all that it represents of love, life, knowledge, peace, and communion with the divine. But now it seems remote, inaccessible, "inclosed," "locked up," to all but the one singled out for "blessing" or a particular allegorical role. In part, the power of "Nutting" results from its plotting the reentry into the garden, its subsequent loss and inaccessibility, and the radical epistemological transformation triggered by the consumption of the fruit.

In "Nutting," the tree (of life, wisdom) and the sacred garden or grove (the "virgin scene") are made woman, the beloved, or the desired, whether the desire be physical lust or transcendent longing, motives that lie at different levels of the allegory and converge in the language of the nutting expedition. This feminizing of the natural scene in "Nutting" has a counter-allegorical movement in Song of Solomon, whereby the human woman is "naturalized," becoming garden, tree, nature.[13] The feminine presence in both Song of Songs and "Nutting" is nature (the garden or grove) and the beloved, although her aspect is rather more natural than feminine in "Nutting" and rather more feminine than natural in Song of Solomon. In both works, however, the impulse or desire to move and the actual action of moving beyond the self to that which is not self—whether to the "inclosed garden" of nature, to the beloved, or to divinity—is couched in the language of human sexual passion (literal in Song of Solomon and figurative in "Nutting"). This is a linguistic maneuver that results in the creation of simultaneously articulated physical and metaphysical libidos that compete with each other and assert their disparate claims and meanings in a complex double entendre through the shared language. The physical desire (lust, greed, aggression) and the transcendental desire (to alleviate personal isolation, ignorance, and spiritual longing, complicated by the insoluble mystery of an inherent incommensurability of self and other, indeed the desire to become like God, "knowing good and evil") converge in the language of allegory in an expression of a complex, overriding, and irresistible bodily lust.

"Nutting" makes use of the language of sexuality and sexual assault in describing the boy's gathering of nuts. The speaker says, "Among the woods / And o'er the pathless rocks, I forced my way" into the enclosed garden. This entry, as Roberts W. French points out, is like Satan entering Eden disguised (as the boy William is disguised) as a "stripling Cherub" (43). Thus he forcefully enters the grove, "a virgin scene," a "dear nook / Unvisited," to encounter a (tree-)tall and erect virgin hung with "milk-white clusters." Much has been made of Wordsworth's use of the word "erect" in this description, with the suggestion that the word implies something phallic, and therefore some curious gender ambiguity. While one cannot deny that such connotations may be present, even so, looking at similar imagery and language in Song of Solomon and in "Three years she grew in sun and shower" makes it clear that this language suggests both the beloved of the Song and Lucy of Wordsworth's poem. In all three cases similar features are singled out for attention: the height and the breasts of the maiden. Here is the pertinent passage from the Song:

> This thy stature is like to a palm tree, and thy breasts to [its] clusters.
> I said, I will go up to the palm tree, I will take hold of the boughs thereof. (Song of Solomon 7:7–8)

There is a similar description in "Three years she grew," wherein Nature, in the process of appropriating Lucy, making her "a Lady of [his/her] own," declares that, "vital feelings of delight / Shall rear her form to stately height, / Her virgin bosom swell. . . ." In "Nutting," therefore, the description of the hazel trees feels familiar: "the hazels [the trees] rose / Tall and erect, with milk-white clusters hung, / A virgin scene!" The passage of the Song begins with an analogy: as woman is to palm tree, so are her breasts to its clusters. The passage from "Three years she grew" similarly associates Lucy's being reared to "stately height" with breasts, the swelling of the "virgin bosom." And in "Nutting" (although there is no literal woman, only trees), they, like the beloved and Lucy, are "tall and erect"; like them they have breasts—"milk-white clusters," the word *milk* certainly evocative of breasts and lactation; finally, they constitute an innocent femininity—a "virgin scene." What is encountered in each case is a virginal, treelike, tree-tall woman or womanlike tree with breasts. In "Nutting," it is this "quiet being" whom the boy "with merciless ravage" deforms and sullies. As with Adam's taking the fruit of the tree of knowledge (fruit that is said to make him "like God," knowing good and evil, figured apparently in his becoming sexually conscious, aware of his own nakedness), the boy in seizing the hazels gains an uncanny, godlike knowledge figured largely in sexual terms (it is the adult speaker who employs the language of rape to describe the harvesting of hazel nuts); at the same time (again as with Adam), an irreparable change has occurred and something is lost, although the realization of loss may not occur at once:

> [U]nless I now
> Confound my present feelings with the past,
> Even then, when from the bower I turned away,
> Exulting, rich beyond the wealth of kings
> I felt a sense of pain when I beheld
> The silent trees and the intruding sky.

Wordsworth has given us a "Figure quaint," a strange but familiar persona whom he has ambiguously linked not only with Solomon (and, through the anthropopathy, with God), but with Satan and Adam, and through Adam with the Fall, as well as with sexual knowledge and rape, a persona who forcefully enters the Edenic shady nook and with emotions expressed as scarcely contained sexual excitement voluptuously contemplates the garden/grove/woman before his sudden act of "merciless ravage."

THE METAPOETIC ALLEGORY

The action of the poem is, at another allegorical level, a tale of the making of a poet and of a poem, telling of how with the shaping, linguistic, text-making powers of the poetic mind, a neophyte poet confronts nature's scene of poetry, a text in its own right, the second of the two books of God, but one already revised by the namings and texts of countless past and present poets.[14] From the outset the youth acknowledges this intertextual dimension of nature, invoking sacred poetry and assuming, through disguise, multiple personae in order to explore the nature of poetry, of poetic inspiration, and of composition. Henry Vaughan's interpretation of the Song, "Regeneration," and the quest of his pilgrim offer intriguing parallels. The "virgin soile" encountered by his youthful quester is called "Jacobs Bed," an allusion to Jacob's unlikely act of placing his head upon a stone to sleep, whereupon he experiences the vision of a ladder reaching into heaven, with angels on the ladder and God standing above (Gen. 28:10–12). Wordsworth's persona repeats Jacob's curious act by placing his head "on one of those green stones / [that] Lay round [him] scattered like a flock of sheep." Vaughan says that Jacobs Bed is a place where "only go / Prophets, and friends of God." Wordsworth has apparently brought his protagonist to Jacobs Bed, as a potential prophet and friend of God. It is a place of vision and conversation with the divine, the bed situated in a place Jacob calls "awesome," "house of God," and "gate of heaven" (Gen. 28:17).

The poet-prophet role is repeated in the figure of Solomon. As mentioned, in the Song we encounter the bardic, wise figure as bridegroom ("Solomon") whose song speaks of unarticulated and perhaps inarticulable mysteries in the sensual language of love, sexuality, and marriage. The bride is woman, nature, chosen people. His Song is the great prototype for Wordsworth, the "spousal verse" that Wordsworth will later determine to revise as his own poetic enterprise. "Nutting," however, is a first, ironic articulation of that spousal verse. In "Nutting," as in the Song, language is the only meeting place between mind and nature, between self and not-self. The mind, or husband of the spousal verse, is represented in "Nutting" by the poet-speaker-persona as a youth. He is a disguised Figure who goes out into a world-as-text and thus into an abyss of language, external and internal, where he finds a bride, the not-self. The bride is muse, embodied in the hazel grove, the trees of wisdom and poetic inspiration, and soon revealed as a nature knowable only through and as language, and consequently comprised of language. The meeting is an epistemological event in which the would-be poet recognizes for the first time his power to *make,* sheer word power, and he comes to know that understanding and knowledge are the result of expression. One knows what others have said (the textualized world) or what one has said or can say. This language, as the medium between mind and nature, is not an abstract, philosophical language, but a poetic, sensual language that speaks from and through the feelings, the language of blood and nerves and bones.

Hence the boy's delight at the discovery of the poet's trees and his potential poetic power is expressed in the language of sexual excitement, temporarily suppressed and restrained:

> A little while I stood,
> Breathing with such suppression of the heart
> As joy delights in; and with wise restraint

Voluptuous, fearless of a rival, eyed
The banquet.

The banquet, this fruit of wisdom and poetry, is, he announces, his alone. This is his muse, his bride, his garden enclosed, his fountain sealed. He calls this banquet a blessing, a word-gift bestowed on a favored being, and he experiences that "temper known to those, who, after long / And weary expectation, have been blessed / With sudden happiness beyond all hope." The language here is not sexual, but suggestively religious, speaking of blessings and happiness and hope. These implications, together with the preceding language of greedy voluptuousness, constitute some of the rich, complex reality of the poetic wealth discovered in his own self-generated sacred grove.

The neophyte or would-be poet encounters a radically metaphorical nature in the hazel grove, whose parts he names and whose reality he himself determines through his own language. In this world, reality *is* linguistic and hence polysemous, endlessly equivocal. Each named part or aspect is this, but also something else, and something else, none and yet all at once. Everything is "known" through language. The stones are green stones, yet they are at the same time Jacobs Bed, and also sheep, "fleeced with moss," lying "scattered round," and, as in the Song of Songs, the stones-sheep become aspects too of the beloved, as are the flowers: "beneath the trees I sate / Among the flowers, and with the flowers I played." It is rewarding to compare this complex of images with a passage from the Song. Here the lover speaks first, and then the beloved:

> As the lily among thorns, so is my love among the daughters.
> As the apple tree among the trees of the wood, so is my beloved
>   among the sons. I sat down under his shadow with great delight,
>   and his fruit was sweet to my taste.
> He brought me to the banqueting house, and his banner over me
>   was love. (2:2–4)

The speaker of "Nutting" might almost be paraphrasing these ideas, conflating the language of lover and beloved, since in "Nutting" the beloved is given voice only as the eternal murmur of the water: "I sat down under her shadow with great delight, and knew that her fruit, this banquet, would be sweet to my taste."

Here waters flow not in streams, but in something the speaker names "fairy water-breaks," *breaks* suggestive of discontinuities, silences, that nevertheless both precede and fill this "text" with their own language as they "murmur on / for ever." The enclosure is a hazel grove, yet the youth has called it woman, a "virgin scene," a muse. The trees are nut trees, but they have been named trees of inspired language, of prophecy and poetry. The stones have been called sheep and treated like Jacobs Bed. That is, the would-be poet through his language and the borrowed language of others has created the scene, its meaning, and its life. Nevertheless, there comes a moment when the youth steps back from the implications of his language, his naming, resisting the "reality" of his poetic creation by asserting, oddly, that this is merely a place where one can waste his "kindliness on stocks and stones / And on the vacant air." "Stocks and stones" is a derisive phrase suggesting that the trees and green stones are lifeless and senseless, only "gods of wood and stone" [OED under *stock*]), that is, "mere" trees and stones; moreover, he claims, the air is empty, "vacant," without spirit. It is precisely this unexpected repudiation of the figurative nature and life of the place that prompts the sudden and remarkable change in the youth's behavior toward the grove: "Then up I rose, / And dragged to earth both branch and bough." If the scene is untextualized, neither kindliness nor brutal attack are, in a strict sense, possible. Yet when the scene is textualized, rendered "real" through the language of figure and metaphor, the crimes are apparent; the boy's act (as the mature persona asserts) is one of "merciless ravage" as "the shady nook / Of hazels, and the green and mossy bower, / Deformed and sullied, patiently gave up / Their quiet being."

Both the action of the poem and its composition are ultimately a single process in which a poet is born. He is one whom we see actually in the process of *becoming,* still discovering or receiving his power, then denying that power, and finally once again acknowledging it—the power to shape reality through words—and then both reaping the benefits and suffering the consequences of the new word-reality he has made for his habitation. The poet-prophet's power is awesome yet dangerous, as Wordsworth's narrator, and possibly the neophyte poet himself, realizes, as exultation and (perhaps) pain characterize the triumph of the boy. Yeats appears to have a similar idea of the birth or initiation of the northern poet in mind when in "The Song of Wandering Aengus" he sends Aengus into a hazel wood "because a fire was in [his] head," from which wood he emerges with the salmon of poetry, which has consumed the hazels of wisdom, soon to be transformed into a "glimmering girl" whom Aengus will pursue forever "through hollow lands and hilly lands." Yeats' "fire in [the] head," like the Wordsworthian boy's greed and lust, is at this metapoetic level of allegory the creative impulse expressible in the language of sexual desire, an impulse that drives the would-be poet into the hazel wood, there to discover the poet's trees and calling, and the beloved, the maiden muse, transformation or effluence of the trees.

What "Nutting" reveals about the poet's art is that it is one in which the feelings speak their language, and language itself determines the narrative, rather than the reverse. Once the stocks (the grove) are feminized through the language used to name them, "she" will behave like a woman; once the lifeless idols of the stones are animated as sheep, they will sprout green fleece and "lie" about. When this figurative "reality" is denied—when the trees are stocks and the stones mere stones, not "real" gods, not living, not mystical—they may with impunity become subject to brutal attack and deformation.

"Nutting" demonstrates that the word-power of the poet can be devastating as well as creative. The poem is composed in 1798, the year that produced the "Prospectus" to the *Excursion,* discussed earlier, and "Tintern Abbey." Speaking of the "Prospectus," Harold Bloom claims that in it Wordsworth reveals extraordinary power, taking on "Jehovah and Milton together," only a few months before writing "Tintern Abbey," a poem in which, on the contrary,

> Power is being repressed . . . , a power so antithetical that it could tear the poet loose from nature, and take him into a world of his own, restituting him for the defense of self-isolation by isolating him yet more sublimely. Wordsworth defends himself from his own strength through repression. . . . (*Poetry and Repression* 76)

"Nutting," with its two personae—the neophyte and the mature poets—may be seen as exemplifying what Bloom calls power, but it is also cautionary in Bloom's sense as well. The boy's seizing of power, his gathering of the fruit of the poet's trees, his brutal domination of nature—all leave him "Exulting, rich beyond the wealth of kings," but also threaten to separate him from nature, whose texts and powers as he discovers are subservient to his own. He can create and decreate their reality with his words. Therefore, the youth's triumph is mitigated by the man's sense of pain and his not-altogether-persuasive suggestion that maybe the boy felt a similar pain even in his extreme blessedness. The youthful poet seizes a poetic power over nature, a power greater than he knows, one that he repudiates for a time, but over which he has incomplete control. The effects are creative (the poem is written) yet destructive (a fall is reenacted in verbal deformation and sullying as the broken branches of the poet's trees respond in "silent" witness, their devastation laid open to the vaguely ominous "intruding sky").

The poem permits the mature poet-persona to express an ironic admonition not to himself, or to the youthful poet, to whom it should properly be addressed, but to a sexually and poetically innocent bystander, the "dearest Maiden," another "figure," who suddenly "appears" in the poetic environs. This maiden might almost be a restoration in some figurative sense of the muse or "virgin scene": "Then, dearest Maiden! move along these shades / In gentleness of heart; with gentle hand / Touch,—for there is a Spirit in the woods." As the mature poet now knows, the air is not "vacant," for he himself has invested it with Spirit. In the "Prospectus," Wordsworth expresses his desire to write the "spousal verse" that will announce that the power to restore paradise to earth lies in the "blended might" of "minds . . . wedded to this outward frame of things / In love"; what that wedding accomplishes is "creation (by no lower name / Can it be called)" (*Home at Grasmere* 999, 1014). In the metapoetic allegory of "Nutting," a figuratively sexual meeting has occurred between neophyte poet and grove—a productive but painful parody of the wedding, characterized not by gentleness and love, but by "merciless ravage." The would-be poet and the virgin scene are analogous to the pair "mind" and "this outward frame of things," but here there is no marriage, for language slips, the stocks and stones and air are denied their life and spirit, lust overcomes love, and power is too blatantly, too forcefully, wielded. If the Wordsworthian marriage is the means for regaining paradise, this rape is a sort of fortunate fall; paradise not lost exactly, but exchanged for poetic power, knowledge, and, most importantly, for the poem that strives so intriguingly to express that multilayered process that occurs at the boundary between the language of the poet and the silence of the trees.

In many ways the poetic scene of "Nutting" is like that of Vaughan's poem. It is complexly intertextual and textualized. It is as though the youthful poet—that "Figure quaint"—had indeed assumed the identity of countless precursors to wander through ancient, language-made sacred sites—Jacobs Bed, Solomon's garden, Eden. In disguise, he acts many parts—spiritual quester, wandering minstrel, dreaming and visionary Jacob, Miltonic Satanic denier, prophet and friend of God, wise Solomon, through whose persona God accommodates himself to human understanding. At the metapoetic level of allegory, the quester seizes an abundance from the poets' trees and discovers at last that the woods are full of words, and the Spirit in the woods is breath, voice—a spirit of poetry, summoned from the ages by the inept (yet strangely competent), violent, unschooled coupling of the shaping, creative, linguistic mind of the neophyte poet and nature.

THE MYSTICAL ALLEGORY: "A SPIRIT IN THE WOODS"

> *I heard*
> *A rushing wind*

Which still increased, but whence it stirred
  No where I could not find. . . .

—Henry Vaughan "Regeneration"

Discussion of the mystical allegory returns me once more to the intertextual implications of the Song of Songs and of Henry Vaughan's revision—"Regeneration." A closer analysis of parallels between Vaughan's and Wordsworth's poems is instructive. Both poems are structured as quests—Vaughan's as an overtly and Wordsworth's as a covertly spiritual quest. Like Wordsworth's, Vaughan's youthful persona "steals abroad" on a sort of pilgrimage in an ambiguous condition of sin appearing as innocence (youth) to enter a spiritual garden. Like Wordsworth's traveler who encounters a "virgin scene," Vaughan's youth after a difficult journey arrives in a "fair, fresh field," a "virgin-soile, which no / Rude feet e'er trod." (The processes in Wordsworth's virgin scene proceed "unseen by any human eye.") Vaughan's youth, like Wordsworth's, reposes here, and then enters a grove of "stately height"[15] in which he, like the youth of "Nutting," is the recipient of treasure—vital gold from the sun (emblem of God). Vaughan's youthful quester then comes, like Wordsworth's, to a sacred grove. As in "Nutting," the language used to describe the grove presents figurative sheep (in the clouds as "snowy fleeces") and a fountain that speaks ("on the dumb shades language spent"); Vaughan's quester "fe[eds] his eye" on the "air all spice" and the blossoming bushes; Wordsworth's feeds through the eye as he "eye[s] the banquet" of the hazel nuts. Vaughan's quester "mus[es] long" on a "bank of flowers"; Wordsworth's lies in a bower with violets and mossy stones. At this point in "Regeneration," Vaughan's poem comes quickly to a climax, as his youth hears "a rushing wind" whose origin he cannot discover. The poem concludes with the search for this mysterious wind that can move through the grove without disturbing a leaf, and invokes the winds of the Song of Songs:

> But while I listening sought
>   My mind to ease
> By knowing, where 'twas, or where not,
>   It whispered; Where I please.
> Lord, then said I, *On me one breath*
> *And let me die before my death!*

Vaughan's poem thus ends with the recognition of *a Spirit in the woods*, borrowed from the Song of Solomon, which his persona interprets as the mysterious breath of God, moving through the garden, and which raises intertextual echoes of God's breathing the breath of life (or soul) into Adam, as well as the explicitly cited passage from the Song. By contrast, Wordsworth's poem at the same point moves to a denial of the word-made reality and the astonishing act of "merciless ravage," as the youth seizes (rather than receives) the treasure of the grove-beloved and in the process deforms and sullies it. In "Nutting," it is only after the violence that the spirit/breath/wind is named and recognized.

Vaughan, in imploring the wind to blow on him, implicitly takes on the feminine persona of the bride-as-garden of the Song: "Awake, O north wind; and come, thou south; blow upon my garden, that the spices thereof may flow out. Let my beloved come into his garden, and eat his pleasant fruits" (S. of S. 4:16).[16] The implicit sexuality of the beloved's invitation appears ambiguously in Vaughan's poem in his desire to "die [the little death] before [his] death," but also links sexual desire with spiritual longing to die to mortal existence in the union with the divine breath of eternal life. Thomas Percy comments concerning the bride's being compared to and speaking as a garden: "She, catching up the metaphor [herself as garden], wishes that this garden, for which [the lover] has expressed so much fondness, might be so breathed on by the kindly gales, as to produce whatever might contribute to his delight" (xxix). Wordsworth's grove is given no voice; she cannot invoke the wind; she instead "patiently" gives up her "quiet being," the trees remaining "silent." Wordsworth's evocative "Spirit in the woods" thus enters a web of intertextual meanings in which understanding is further complicated by the fact that Wordsworth interposes the "merciless ravage" between the idyllic musing among the flowers and the realization of the presence of the Spirit in the sacred grove.

At the level of mystical allegory, the Spirit in the woods takes on a metaphysical character that must be contrasted with false gods, "stocks and stones." The events of "Nutting" occur, as in Vaughan's poem, in a language-made sacred time and space in a grove serving as a kind of fane or temple. These dimensions recall the garden of beginnings, a paradisal setting that like other such places is out of time; the events occur in a period that "seems a day," but that is nevertheless eternal, "one of those heavenly days which cannot die." The timelessness suggested here is reinforced later when the boy enters a "dear nook / Unvisited," where "fairy water-breaks do murmur on / For ever." To step into this timeless, perfect place is to fulfill the dream of much of Western humanity—to recover the serenity, repose, and innocence of the lost garden of beginnings; it understandably brings "sudden happiness beyond all hope."[17]

The Song of Solomon, Lowth found, is a mystical allegory, veiling sublime truths about the relationship of divine and human with the sensual language of sexual desire and marriage. Vaughan's "Regeneration" invokes the Song to speak of spiritual regeneration in a desired union of the pilgrim with the divine. These two texts form a great part of the background for and the intertextual complexities of Wordsworth's "Nutting." In invoking these intertexts (along with others), Wordsworth "plays host" to them in Miller's sense. But the host may encounter risks. The intertext is always subject to interpretation and revision, to be sure, but the text itself is likewise subject to interpretation and revision by the older texts. For one thing, they tend to bring with them their intertextual lint, old meaning realms and metaphysical hauntings, which may settle right in and eat the host text out of house and home. Some recognition of the power of old namings may account for the youth's denial of the rhetorical reality of the grove and his dismissal of the trees and stones as "stocks and stones." The mature poet comes to realize that a wind that rises in ancient Hebrew texts and circles through a seventeenth-century English ode, bears traces, spices of the gardens and groves through which it has moved, when it appears at last in an English grove of hazels. The "Spirit" (breath, wind, words) in the woods is an enigmatic, but a voluble and voracious guest. As part of the mystical allegory it illustrates that feature of Wordsworth's theory of accommodation discussed earlier: "The commerce between Man and his Maker cannot be carried on but by a process where much is represented in little, and the Infinite Being accommodates himself to a finite capacity." The entire poem certainly represents much in little. And the Spirit in the woods speaks volumes.

I have argued that "Nutting" is a multilayered allegory that implicates many sources (among them Milton), but that takes its primary inspiration and form from two sources: the Song of Songs, archetypal "spousal verse" of Solomon (poet, prophet, and wisdom figure), and from Henry Vaughan's "revision" of the Song, "Regeneration." The various levels of meaning in "Nutting" tell several tales: one of ordinary physical activity (the nutting expedition); one of dawning, violent sexuality (the rape of the bower/woman); one of the gaining of wisdom (and the recognition that knowledge lies in words); one of creativity (the gaining of the nuts of poetry and wisdom and the making of the poem); and one of metaphysics (the spiritual quest for some connection with a voice, a wind, a breath, a Spirit in the woods). The result is a many-voiced marvel of a poem, and one, I would argue, that is central to Wordsworth's poetics and poetry.

CHAPTER 7

Wordsworthian Apocalyptics

DEFINITIONS AND
BIBLICAL INTERTEXTS

Nothing! thou elder brother even to Shade:
Thou hadst a being ere the world was made,
And well fixed, art alone of ending not afraid.

—Rochester, "Upon Nothing"

If nothing is interpreted as no thing, it turns out to be nothing other than the fullness of
being. . . .

—Mark C. Taylor 205

Wordsworthian apocalyptics welcome a veritable swarm of biblical ghosts, along with phantoms of religious discourse, which appear often unobtrusively and depart with scarcely a trace, yet which nevertheless "adjust" the texts to accommodate their force and presence. One may wonder, for example, how to make room for the holy ghost–spirit-breeze that comes as a messenger in the opening lines of the *Prelude* and speaks a blessing on the rededicated poet, or the semidivine cloud that will guide the poet on his way, or the insistent voice of waters heard throughout the works, suggesting the poet's encounter with the Merkabah, as in "It was an April morning." Once recognized, such biblical intrusions are impossible to dismiss.

Apocalypse and apocalyptics demand attention in a work such as this, so I began reading in order to obtain some sort of critical consensus from which I might work. What I found was that different writers address different parts of the whole, different "meanings" of *apocalypse,* and find, predictably, different truths. Therefore, in what follows in this chapter and the next, I shall try to sort out these different perspectives so as to present an image of the whole. In doing so, I shall argue that Wordsworthian apocalyptics are deeply marked by biblical intertextuality and what may be called a form of biblical iconography (with the result that Wordsworth's apocalyptic depictions often have a sort of painterly quality); that they employ the long-established rhetorical techniques of negative theology, which "circumscribe the unsayable by means of exclusions, metaphors, and negations" (Eco, *Kant and the Platypus* 24–5); and, going further, that they depend upon what Mark C. Taylor describes as "parapraxical writing," writing that engages in "indirect communication" (225), of which more presently.

In chapter 1, I introduced briefly the Wordsworthian encounter with Nothing, and I reiterate part of that discussion here in the context of Wordsworthian apocalyptics. Harold Bloom's claim is that Wordsworth inaugurated modern poetry through his insight that "poems are 'about' nothing," by which Bloom means that "Their subject is the subject herself or himself, whether manifested as a presence or as an absence" (*The Western Canon* 239). Bloom has in mind a form of ontological "nothing." Mark C. Taylor's chapter, "How to do Nothing with Words," is pertinent both to the metaphysical issues raised in chapter 1 and to Bloom's claim of poetic originality for Wordsworth. As Taylor explains, a metaphysical nothing—that which is no thing and not thing—is what is left at the end of ontology and theology: "Nothing lies 'beyond' ontotheology. This nothing is the unthought that we are now called to think. The nothing that remains to be thought is not simply the opposite of being but 'is' *neither* being *nor* nonbeing" (205). To encounter the unimaginable and unrepresentable and depict that experience calls for extraordinary linguistic maneuvering. As Taylor says, "That which is unrepresentable cannot be approached directly but must be approached indirectly through linguistic twistings and turnings that can never be straightened out." To describe such linguistic twistings and turnings, Taylor uses "parapraxis" and "parapraxical writing," in which there is always a sense of failure, slip, or error,[1] and contrasts it with performative discourse that "always does *something* with words," whereas "parapraxis struggles to do *nothing* with words," thus staging "the withdrawal of that which no text can contain, express, or represent." Taylor distinguishes between the *nothing* of parapraxical writing (neither being nor nonbeing) and the *nothing* of negative theology (the opposite of being) (225). That Wordsworth interweaves both sorts of language into his texts contributes to one's perception of tension or two-sidedness, as discussed in the Introduction. Both negative theology and parapraxis take the powers of language seriously, as does Wordsworth: "Words are too awful an instrument for good and evil to be trifled with" (*Essays Upon Epitaphs, Pr. W.* 2:84). The linguistic maneuvers of parapraxical writing include a pervasive tropology characterized by excess, catachresis (that most aggressive and impertinent of figures), paradox, and distressed or contorted syntax—all of which seek to bring into language "the trace of what was once named God" (Taylor 228). For Wordsworth the transformed, deformed, or absent God has often seemed to have abandoned the sacred, the uncanny, and the mystical as language-crafted intertextual orphans on the doorsteps of nature and mind, amorphous progeny of the Unfather, the Nothing. Hence the object(s) that the poet struggles again and again to represent appear in psychological, "natural," and poetic (dis)guise, rather than spiritual and theological, even though Wordsworth's echoing lexicon, quasi-sacred images and events, and clearly religious intertexts lend their mysteries to the endeavor, creating a dense texture woven of the (a)theological holy and the mundane. To reveal what has never been said or even thought takes Wordsworth to the very limits of language—to apocalypse—where he interweaves the discursive maneuverings of negative theology and parapraxis to suggest the boundary beyond which one may be called as an act of faith to see, to think, to speak nothing, or Nothing or (the) No Thing.

Wordsworth's language, characterized by negation, ambiguity, intimation, tension, and contradiction, is made to speak, as in St. Paul's definition of faith, "the substance of things hoped for, the evidence of things not seen," a definition based on the understanding that "worlds were framed by the word of God, so that things which are seen were not made of things which do appear" (Heb. 11:1–3). The poetic reverse of this precept is that invisible things must be made in the language of things that are seen. The substance and evidence of the invisible world and the self, in which Wordsworth invests a kind of faith, can only be made to appear in words: "Visionary power /Attends upon the motions of the winds /Embodied in the mystery of words." Within the mystery of words and the "turnings intricate [the twistings and the turnings, both the distressed syntax and tropes] of verse," the sacred orphans, the visionary, the dark unknown, and myriad ghostly shadows find something like a "proper home" in which to perform their tasks—to "work their changes" (*Prelude* 5:619–27).

As a result of this curious Wordsworthian faith—in words, if not in the Word—the verse offers apocalyptic, yet blinding, flashes of recognition that display the invisible world through the language not of nothing, not of infinity, eternity, and invisibility, but of the something, the finite, and the timed—nature and natural images. Wordsworth's language is thus distressed, as words for nature and natural objects are subtly warped out of their natural attitudes, highlighted by enigma, and contorted by allusion to or imitation of the invisible, unbounded, untimed, and ultimately unspeakable that (almost) emerges just as it is said. In their reworking of the biblical texts and their themes, Wordsworthian apocalyptics present a series of extraordinarily evocative visions and re-visions in which, both literally and figuratively, Nothing is revealed. Their effect is to bring readers, in their turn, also to a kind of faith, to implicate them in the difficult enterprise of thinking the unthought, of confronting that Nothing that is neither being or nonbeing embodied in the mystery of words.

Before I attempt to make this case, I want to sort out an array of senses in which the terms *apocalypse* and *apocalyptic* are used.

THE PROBLEM OF DEFINITION

Blake's [humanism] is apocalyptic, Freud's is naturalistic, and Wordsworth's is— sometimes sublimely, sometimes uneasily—blended of elements that dominate in the other two.
                                        —Harold Bloom, *The Ringers in the Tower* 13

Writers use "apocalypse" and "apocalyptic" to mean several things. As Douglas Robinson points out, *apocalypse* can grow to encompass all of literature, secular as well as sacred.[2] He observes that "apocalyptic" can describe, on the one hand, a collocation of images—often "visionary"—(of war, destruction, renewal, mysterious symbols, mythologically represented "good" and "evil," etc.) or, on the other, a structure, a plot requiring an ending. Moreover, "apocalyptic" is difficult to separate from literature itself: "It is . . . ultimately impossible . . . to draw clear-cut distinctions between 'literature' and 'apocalyptic' . . ." (364). Here *literature* means roughly "secular" and *apocalyptic* means roughly "religious." Robinson identifies five hermeneutics for approaching *apocalyptic*:

> (1) the *biblical* prediction of an imminent end to history, controlled by God so as to provide for a paradisal continuation; (2) the *annihilative* prediction of an imminent end to history controlled by no God at all and followed by oblivion; (3) the *continuative* prediction of no end at all, but of simple secular historical continuity . . . ; (4) the *ethical* internalization of apocalyptic conflict as a figure for personal growth in ongoing history; and (5) the *Romantic* or visionary internalization of the fallen world by an act of imaginative incorporation, so that the world is revealed as the paradise it already is. (373)

Robinson says of the Romantic hermeneutic that it "mediates between 'apocalyptic' visions of an imminent, final, and total end (biblical/anni-hilative) and 'anti-apocalyptic' visions of historical continuation (ethi-cal/continuative) by imagining a total transformation of reality, an end to the old and a new beginning, that takes place in the mind and therefore involves no radical historical upheaval" (375). In "The Idiom of Vision," Kenneth Johnston likewise links "visionary" and "apocalyptic": "The words 'visionary' and 'apocalyptic' are sometimes used as loosely in con-temporary interpretations of Romanticism as the words 'transcendental' and 'mystical' were a generation ago" (1).

The extraordinary versatility of the term leads Stephen Goldsmith to identify what he calls a "constellation" of definitions:

> Apocalypse can mean many things: a particular text (the Book of Revela-tion); a biblical and intertestamental genre that includes many texts; the eschatological events that occur at the end of history; an internal, psycho-logical event usually referred to as a *revelation* or an *epiphany*; and in the most general usage, any catastrophe that seems incommensurable. (xi)

Moving from all "apocalyptic" texts to Romantic texts, Goldsmith em-phasizes not images, but the "psychological event"—often an experience called "illumination"—that the images attempt to represent. This differ-ence in focus can be accounted for, in part, by what Goldsmith identifies as a tendency in Romantic texts for various meanings of *apocalypse* to in-tersect. Examining the history of representations and emphasizing the notion of the end of both history and book, Goldsmith finds in texts a tendency to represent that end in spatial terms, terms in which stasis and eternity supersede process, diversity, strife, and the polyglot babble of earthly tongues, and, rid of those whose names are not written in the book of life, permits a conservative and monoglot harmony of voices and a uniformity of attitude and behavior in eternal worship.[3]

In Wordsworth studies, however, the terms have understandably taken on a particular coloring to the extent that they have become iden-tified with key terms of Wordsworthian scholarship. Geoffrey H. Hart-man's explanation of the term is still one of the most useful:

> By "apocalyptic," as in "apocalyptic imagination," I intend the Apocalypse of St. John (the Book of Revelation), and, more generally, the kind of imagination that is concerned with the supernatural and especially the Last Things. The term may also describe a mind which actively desires the inauguration of a totally new epoch, whether preceding or following the end of days. And since what stands between us and the end of the (old) world is the world, I sometimes use "apocalyptic" to characterize any

strong desire to cast out nature and to achieve an unmediated contact with the principle of things. (*Wordsworth's Poetry* x)

As the Hartman definition suggests, the most frequently encountered meanings of Wordsworthian *apocalypse* and *apocalyptic* are two: (1) To suggest a biblical intertextuality, especially to the Book of Revelation, or to suggest a biblical model for the shape of a plot, and (2) to serve as synonyms for *vision* and *visionary*, for *revelation* and *revealing*, for *imagination* and *imaginative*; and, at the same time, to serve as antonyms for *Nature* and *natural*. While the intersections of these several senses make the attempt to separate them decidedly problematic, for purely expository purposes—and recognizing the need at times to retrace my steps—I will review these matters later. In the remainder of this chapter I shall consider "Biblical Intertextuality." Then, in chapter 8, I shall turn my attention to "Apocalypse and Nature." My purpose in each of these discussions will be to demonstrate how various occurrences as they accumulate disclose a pervasive apocalyptic mode to Wordsworth's exploration of the relationships between mind (with its interior geography) and nature, and among language, world, and thought. I shall also be interested to examine some of the ways in which the apocalyptic mode is integral to the development of key Wordsworthian themes and contributes in indispensable ways to much that is most original and most difficult in Wordsworthian poetics. In the concluding section of chapter 8, "Apocalypse in Which Nothing is Revealed," I shall gather up salient points from previous sections of chapters 7 and 8 in order to elaborate the argument that Wordsworthian apocalyptics perform the impossible task of revealing Nothing.

BIBLICAL INTERTEXTUALITY

The golden bird will not always sing the same song, though a primeval pattern underlies its notes.
—Frank Kermode, *The Sense of an Ending* 31

Of importance here are biblical eschatological texts, chief among which are opening and closing chapters of Ezekiel, late chapters of Isaiah and Daniel, Mark 13, 1 Corinthians 15:51–55, and, most influentially, the last book of the Christian Bible, the Book of Revelation, whose name is a translation of the Greek *apokalypsis* and therefore provides a narrow sense of the term—simply "unveiling" or "revelation." Through the particular dream vision of John of Patmos and his subsequent "writing" of his revelation, the term *apocalypse* comes to mean a prophetic text whose subject is End-times. Revelation speaks of the utter destruction of both heaven and earth (rendered through mysterious symbolic images of beings and battles), the eternal punishment of those whose names are not written in the book of life, and the creation of a new heaven and earth, free of death and sorrow, free of the separation between humankind and God, and free too of time and of the natural emblems of time—sun, moon, and sea. The new creation is figured in the marriage of Jesus (the Logos, the Lamb), and his bride (the New Jerusalem), a woman, but also a timeless, coherent, monoglot community outside time, in whose city is found once more the tree of life that grew in the garden of beginnings.

THE BIBLICAL PLOT

M. H. Abrams points out that by the closing years of the eighteenth century, after these biblical texts had undergone a long tradition of literary treatments, *apocalypse* had come to mean "a prophetic vision, set forth in arcane and elaborate symbols, of the imminent events which will bring an abrupt end to the present world order and replace it by a new and perfected condition of man and his milieu" (*Natural Supernaturalism* 38). Considering *apocalypse* narrowly in its aspect of biblical intertextuality, Abrams' extended argument emphasizes biblical plot and shows that over centuries the reading of biblical texts was influenced by Neoplatonism and that the Neoplatonic circle of emanation from God and return when "assimilated to Christian history, is temporalized and given a specific historical beginning and end"; the Christianized circle begins in Eden in unity and perfection, moves into division and evil, and returns to unity and perfection in the New Jerusalem:

> This design of a temporal and finite great circle is applied not only to the world and all mankind (whose history is conceived as a long circuitous detour to reach its origin) *but also to the life of each redeemed individual* (whose "conversion" is conceived to occur at the moment at which his direction changes from a movement out to a movement back to his lost integrity). (*Natural Supernaturalism* 132; emphasis supplied)

This Christian great circle, rooted in apocalypse and Neoplatonism, with its plot of a journey in which unity is lost and regained is, Abrams argues, adapted by Wordsworth to secular and individual purposes in a mode of autobiography that owes something to Augustine: "Wordsworth's [the *Prelude*] . . . converts the wayfaring Christian of the Augustinian spiritual journey into the self-formative traveler of the Romantic educational journey" (284). In the Christian great circle, the regaining of unity corresponds with the biblical apocalypse's representation of the marriage of Jesus and the New Jerusalem. In Wordsworth's representation in "The Prospectus," the marriage that signals restored integrity is that between the mind and nature, to sing whose "spousal verse" is Wordsworth's announced poetic enterprise, a claim that not only makes language the point of join between mind and nature, but also casts a decidedly and characteristically Wordsworthian apocalyptic light on the whole of his work.

The biblical eschatological texts conclude the biblical "plot," which Abrams describes as "right-angled": "The key events are abrupt, cataclysmic, and make a drastic, even an absolute difference"—the sudden creation of perfection, followed rapidly by the Fall of humanity and nature into time, labor, and mortality; the advent of the Redeemer (the turning point in the plot), to be followed after his second coming by "the abrupt termination of this world and of time and their replacement, for all who shall be deemed worthy in the Last Judgment, by a heavenly kingdom in eternity" (*Natural Supernaturalism* 36–7). In the last stanza of his curiously reiterative, quasi-orthodox,[4] yet revisionary "On the Power of Sound" (1828–29), Wordsworth recapitulates in 16 lines the biblical plot from creation to apocalypse. The poem is addressed to the ear "as occupied by a spiritual functionary, in communion with sounds, individual or combined in studied harmony" ("Argument"). All earthly and human sounds and voices, Wordsworth speculates, are echoes of an "Art / Lodged above the starry pole; / Pure modulations flowing from the heart / Of divine Love, where Wisdom, Beauty, Truth / With Order dwell" (108–12). A spirit of sound— music, voice—controls "all things," and "Innumerable voices fill / With everlasting harmony" the "Heavens" (177–84). The final stanza reiterates the world plot from creation through human history to the last judgment and destruction, as the product of sound, in particular of poetic divine speaking: It is "A Voice" that "to Light gave being" and to "Time, and Man his earth born Chronicler." Wordsworth sees human texts—chronicles, as their name implies—as products of time and in time. It is, therefore, the eternal Voice that will end time and with it human texts; a Voice that "shall finish doubt and dim forseeing, / And sweep away life's visionary stir," where "visionary" suggests not clear seeing, but obscurity. Another sort of music, that of the archangel's trumpet (a sort of military speaking), will raise the dead and "quench the stars." At this point, the "Silence" of the "Intimations Ode" is addressed and denied eternal status. Eternity is marked not by silence, but by noise, by Harmony, by the divine whose nature "is in the WORD," origin and end of all speaking, all music:

O Silence! are Man's noisy years
No more than moments of thy life?
Is Harmony, blest Queen of smiles and tears,
With her smooth tones and discords just,
Tempered into rapturous strife,
Thy destined Bond-slave? No! though Earth be dust
And vanish, though the Heavens dissolve, her stay
Is in the WORD, that shall not pass away. (209–24)

Voice, Word, and Harmony mark the extratemporal margins of this late Wordsworthian reiteration of the biblical plot, ending in the destruction of earth and heaven. A similar treatment is found in the *Excursion* as the Wanderer recounts that before the Fall "Man" was not alone, for the eternal voice was still audible: he "heard, borne on the wind, the articulate voice of God" (4:432–5). The Book of Revelation would add at the end of the plot the conditions of immortality, felicity, ease, and a peculiar stasis or static recursion, a condition (music, poem) prohibitive of all plots. Eternity (and the Voice) *is* before the beginning of all stories of time and *is* after the end of human narratives of time and in time—the condition of both the beginning and the ending of the human story, a plot whose course is a circle, and whose end is a cataclysmic return to its beginning.

This structure identifies time with both book and history: The Bible tells the story of time. History from creation to destruction is that story. Of time and in time, the Book ends where time ends, with the account of the end of both history and time. Structural apocalyptic representation therefore rests on the issues of history and writing, of time and narrative. As a result, as Frank Kermode, Paul Ricoeur, Northrop Frye, M. H. Abrams, Stephen Goldsmith, and others have shown, the Bible furnishes a model—a "paradigmatic fiction" (Kermode, *The Sense of an Ending* 24)— not only for individual human lives and human history, but for texts and narrative structure.[5] The Fall is a lapse into time, process, history, and mortality; the End is a redemption from time, process, history, and mortality. Life and history occur, in Kermode's phrase, "in the middest," between birth and death, between first divine fiat and last syllable of recorded time, between Alpha and Omega, Genesis and Revelation, always in the shadow of an approaching End. Kermode illustrates this "middest," the space of history and life, by the example of a clock that speaks to us, saying "*tick-tock*":

> *Tick* is our word for a physical beginning, *tock* our word for an end. We say they differ. What enables them to be different is a special kind of middle. We can perceive a duration only when it is organized. . . . The interval between the two sounds, between *tick* and *tock* is . . . charged with significant

duration. The clock's *tick-tock* I take to be a model of what we call a plot, an organization that humanizes time by giving it form; and the interval between *tock* and *tick* represents purely successive, disorganized time of the sort that we need to humanize. . . .

Tick is a humble genesis, tock a feeble apocalypse. . . . (*The Sense of an Ending* 44–5)

According to Kermode, the human task is to find significance in or give significance to that disorganized time between beginning and ending. What Kermode does not say is already implicit in what he does say: Apocalypse stops all time and all narrative. For, as Ricoeur states, his working hypothesis "amounts to taking narrative as the guardian of time, insofar as there can be no thought about time without narrated time" (*Time and Narrative* 3:241).

What may be said of time, of life, of history, and of nature may therefore be said as well of literature. Ricoeur, following Kermode, observes that "Apocalypse can . . . signify both the end of the world and the end of the book at the same time":

This congruence between the world and the book extends even further. The beginning of the book is about the beginning and the end of the book is about the end. In this sense, the Bible is the grandiose plot of the history of the world, and each literary plot is a sort of miniature version of the great plot that joins Apocalypse and Genesis. In this way, the eschatological myth and the Aristotelian muthos are joined together in their way of tying a beginning to an ending and proposing to the imagination the triumph of concordance over discordance. (*Time and Narrative* 2:23)

Discordance—the Aristotelian peripeteia—whether in a life, in history, or in plot, is a crisis signaling an imminent end, resulting in resolution and concordance. Kermode finds that over the last two millennia, and even into the present, although "changed by our special pressures [and] subdued by our skepticism, the paradigms of apocalypse continue to lie under our ways of making sense of the world" (*The Sense of an Ending* 28). Our concern with time and with End-time grows from the human desire to find some sort of significance in the interim that is ours.[6]

As Ricoeur argues, "there can be no thought about time without narrated time," emphasizing the essentially linguistic nature of time.[7] Time and language stand, as it were, face to face. Genesis 11 tells the story of what is often referred to as the second Fall, one occurring shortly after time begins in a country later known as Babylon. The temple builders of Babel retain their prelapsarian language, "one language and one speech"— perhaps that spoken by God as he decrees, "Let there be light." Their project is to build a tower, "whose top may reach unto heaven." Of this activity the Lord observes, "Behold, *the people is one, and they have all one language, and this they begin to do: and now nothing will be restrained from them, which they have imagined to do*" (Gen. 11:1–6; emphasis supplied). Seemingly fearful of this monoglot assembly of people for whom imagination, speech, and achievement are congruent, the Lord confuses their tongues and scatters them and their now mutually incomprehensible languages abroad over all the earth. In the polyglot chaos that follows, the people, unable to complete the tower, name the place Babel, "to confuse," emblematic of the inauguration, in Wordsworth's terms, of the terrible power and fearful inadequacy of human language, of "doubt and dim forseeing, / And . . . life's visionary stir," which will be swept away at the end of time. Thus the perpetual plight of language users in time is sanctioned. Wordsworth's comment on human language is poignantly appropriate. Even in the most solemn circumstances—"rendering to our friends . . . testimony of our love"—our "thoughts cannot, even upon this impulse, assume an outward life [i.e., be expressed in language] without a transmutation and a fall" (*Essays Upon Epitaphs, Prose Works* 2:85). It is only at the end of time that the one perfect language will be restored and, as Goldsmith argues, the Logos will prevail over the Whore of Babylon (Babel), and the blessed who surround the throne of God will sing in perfect unison one song. Within the reaches of historical time, between Babel and apocalypse, human beings must suffer the confusions of multiple tongues and inadequate speech, of words never quite up to their task of translating imagination into speech and speech into work. It is only after Babylon, labeled "Mystery" (Rev. 17:5), is defeated by the sword-tongue of the Word or Logos that time may end and the kingdom come in the marriage of Jesus and the New Jerusalem, wherein language, like humanity, is redeemed. One place, Babylon, is earthly, timed, and marked by the confusion of fallen language; the other, New Jerusalem, is heavenly, eternal, and characterized by ritualized speech, the chanted words of an immutable song (a kiddusha), which represents what Goldsmith calls "a postapocalyptic social and linguistic identity" (*Unbuilding Jerusalem* 58).[8]

The kiddusha (from *kiddush,* "holy"), this one song, this "postapocalyptic social and linguistic identity," is characteristic of traditional apocalyptic literature—both canonical and apocryphal. It is closely associated with the Merkabah tradition in which a prophet "sees" the chariot-throne of God (as do Isaiah, Ezekiel, and John of Patmos), flanked by seraphim or surrounded by four cherubim, and sometimes by 24 elders, hosts of angels, and/or companies of the redeemed. The song is a prayer of praise sung by those surrounding the throne, the sound of the song frequently compared to the "noise of great waters" (Ez. 1:24) or the "voice of many waters" (Rev. 14:2). Isaiah's seraphim sing, "Holy, holy, holy, is the Lord of hosts: the whole earth is full of his glory" (6:3) or, in Revelation, the cherubim "rest not night and day, saying Holy, holy, holy, Lord God Almighty, which was, and is, and is to come" (4:8). The kiddusha is a song out of time, one associated with triumph, joy, and piety. After Babylon (the whore/city, the place of human speech) has fallen and earthly music silenced within her, John of Patmos hears again "a great voice of much people in heaven" praising God, "the voice of a great multitude, and as the voice of many waters" (Rev. 19:1, 6). Goldberg argues cogently that the Book of Revelation "describes the sublime rupture" that occurs when process gives way to stasis, "when time becomes space, when history meets its final antithesis in both a heavenly city and a book." He continues:

> At the same time, the Book of Revelation describes a fundamental change in the nature of language. The interdependence of these two narratives is the necessary foundation of Revelation's authority, since the representation of the end of history must in a convincing way seem already to participate in a language beyond history. In order to have a decisive impact, the words of the book must seem to have their origin not in any ongoing, circumstantial debate about how to act and what to do, but in that space already outside of mere contingency, that end-space where historical conflict will have been definitively resolved. Revelation can command such authority because it claims to speak from the end with perfect hindsight; it therefore requires a language commensurate with its vision. (56)

The "fundamental change in the nature of language" of which Goldsmith speaks, consists of reducing polyphony to one voice; holiness and membership in the heavenly chorus of praise "consist[] in one's ability to speak precisely the same words as others [and] such scenes creat[e] the impression that the fulfillment of providential history . . . lies in . . . the distilling of social polyphony to the purity of one ritual voice" (58). The implication is that the confusion of the fallen world, its nations and tongues, initiated at Babel, will at last be replaced by ritual speech, whose words, spoken in unison, are eternal and unalterable. An inevitable side effect, not lost on Wordsworth, is that this situation of "perfected" speech makes the earthly poet-prophet of necessity a citizen of Babylon, the place of confusion, whose music—including his own—will at last be silenced, when in Babel the "voice of harpers, and musicians, and of pipers, and trumpeters, shall be heard no more at all . . ." (Rev. 18:22). This silencing of the poet is one of the pervasive themes of the dream and Boy-of-Winander episodes in Book 5 of the *Prelude,* a matter to which I shall return.

The kiddusha or one song so closely associated with the apocalypse is, I suggest, an important theme of Wordsworth's poetics and the primary theme of Wordsworthian apocalyptics. The song, often depicted by Wordsworth as a song of Nature or participated in by Nature, is the ground bass, the motif endlessly repeated under the changing harmonies and melodies of human "songs." In the "Argument" of "On the Power of Sound" (1828–9), Wordsworth goes so far as to invoke as a version of the one song the "Pythagorean theory of numbers and music, with their supposed power over the motions of the universe," imagining that "By one pervading Spirit / Of tones and numbers all things are controlled," that "Innumerable voices" fill the Heavens "With everlasting harmony" (177–84). The unchanging permanence of the one song is to be contrasted with mutable and ephemeral human expressions. The one song is, therefore, a Janus-faced theme exhibiting two quite different appearances. Over time Wordsworthian representations of the theme evolve, generally moving closer in spirit and import to the biblical and Miltonic expressions. Among the early examples, quite different poetic attitudes and stances are exhibited.

THE WORDSWORTHIAN KIDDUSHA

One manifestation of Wordsworthian apocalyptics is his own preoccupation with the kiddusha, a figure for poetry—natural, human, or divine; it may be heard early and late as a recurrent theme in the poetry about poetry. The early examples represent what may be called a natural kiddusha, presenting the world as, on the one hand, invested with an implicate harmony and joy concealed beneath the appearance of things, the song of an inspirited, self-referential, metapoetic Nature whose music may at times be heard; and, on the other, the at times stern, admonishing voice of a powerful, mysterious Nature, capable of evoking sublime terror. This indwelling, early, natural kiddusha in its two aspects anticipates the doubleness of the eternal harmony of which the poet speaks in "On the Power of Sound," that harmony that administers both joys and sorrows ("blest Queen of smiles and tears"), concord and strife ("With her smooth tones and discords just"). The early kiddusha, however, has no origin or goal antecedent or external to nature, and it is devoid of image:

> I would walk alone
> In storm and tempest, or in starlight nights
> Beneath the quiet heavens, and at that time
> Have felt whate'er there is of power in sound
> To breathe an elevated mood, by form

Or image unprofaned; and I would stand
Beneath some rock, listening to sounds that are
The ghostly language of the ancient earth,
Or make their dim abode in distant winds. (*Prelude* 2:321–9)

What the young Wordsworth hears is not the divine originary Word, to
which the heavenly kiddusha conforms, but an indwelling natural power
of sound, a language, the "ghostly language of the ancient earth." By contrast, the later manifestations of the theme present the song of a created
and separate nature, directed toward the Uncreated; not, it seems, producing the song, but echoing one whose ultimate source is God and
whose duration is eternal.

"It was an April morning: fresh and clear" (1800) typifies the first
sort. As discussed in chapter 4, the poem describes an apocalyptic experience of the divine, with intertextual echoes to the visions of the Merkabah seen by Ezekiel and John of Patmos. Wordsworth's experience, like
theirs, involves hearing the "voice of waters," associated by Ezekiel with
both the voice of God and the song of the "living creatures" who surround the throne, moving it or moving with it, and by John of Patmos at
times with the voice of God, but more usually with the universal kiddusha: "And I heard a voice from heaven as the voice of many waters, and
as the voice of a great thunder: And I heard the voice of harpers harping
with their harps: And they sung as it were a new song before the throne,
and before the four beasts and the elders" (Rev. 14:2–3).

In a condition of thoughtless but heightened perception, "Alive to all
things and forgetting all," Wordsworth's narrator hears the voice of waters, its "sallies of glad sound," which reduce all previously experienced
sounds to "the voice / Of common pleasure." The implication is that the
alive and attentive ear may be privy to an otherwise imperceptible natural music. Nature's music, its one song, is an undersound, often drowned
out by what Wordsworth calls in the *Prelude* the "passionate sounds" of
the times, which "might often make / The milder minstrelsies of rural
scenes / Inaudible" (11:247–50). All creatures answer this voice, and
"ma[ke] a song" that *seems* "like the wild growth / or like some natural
produce of the air / That could not cease to be." This natural song, the
"wild growth" of the air, responds to the song of the waters—itself also
apparently a wild, i.e., "natural," growth. Perceived as immanent and self-
generated, this natural produce is a song of joy, a Wordsworthian revision
of the biblical kiddusha in the form of an eternal antiphonal chant between voice of waters and natural creatures. At the same time, however,
the biblical intertextuality with its apocalyptic, End-times theme, although here nearly stripped of otherworldly trappings, cannot help but

invest the Wordsworthian natural song, that seemingly collaborative effort of the perceiving mind and nature, with a mysteriously religious and *unnatural* grandeur. A similar significance invests the scene in which the Boy of Winander participates in the "wild" song of the owls and its "doubled and redoubled" echoing through the valley, then to be invaded in the succeeding silence by the voice of waters—"the voice of mountain torrents" (*Prelude* 5:399–409). The natural song, like the boy who participated in it, seems subject to death, to end with the natural and human.

The contrast of early and late versions of the Wordsworthian kiddusha may be seen by comparing a description from "It was an April Morning" (1800) to one from "On the Power of Sound" (1828–9). The opening lines of "It was an April Morning" will serve to demonstrate the character of the early, or natural, kiddusha:

> It was an April Morning: fresh and clear
> The Rivulet, delighting in its strength,
> Ran with a young man's speed, and yet the voice
> Of waters which the winter had supplied
> Was softened down into a vernal tone,
> The spirit of enjoyment and desire,
> And hopes and wishes, from all living things
> Went circling, like a multitude of sounds.

Everything here appears to be of nature and in nature, the song of "all living things" (oddly echoing the description of the cherubim as "living creatures") taking a "vernal tone" from the spring morning itself. The song expresses life's "spirit of enjoyment," self-circling, self-delighted and -delighting. The oddness of the simile is easily overlooked: The imperceptible "spirit of enjoyment and desire" circles (a visual image) "like a multitude of sounds" (an auditory image), yet Wordsworth's parapraxical writing renders the source of the spirit ambiguous (does it arise from man or nature?) and conceals within natural images the fact that spirit (of enjoyment and desire) is neither visible nor audible. The form of the poem is narrative-descriptive, the poet himself participating in the scene he observes. The song of nature is a heterodox revision of the kiddusha, an effusion of joy rather than an other-directed song of praise.

By contrast, the later version of the kiddusha may be seen in stanza XIII of "On the Power of Sound":

> Break forth into thanksgiving,
> Ye banded Instruments of wind and chords;
> Unite, to magnify the Ever-living,
> Your inarticulate notes with the voice of words!

> Nor hushed be service from the lowing mead,
> Nor mute the forest hum of noon;
> Thou too be heard, lone Eagle! freed
> From snowy peak and cloud, attune
> Thy hungry barkings to *the hymn*
> *Of joy, that from her utmost walls*
> *The six-days' Work, by flaming Seraphim,*
> *Transmits to Heaven!* As Deep to Deep
> Shouting through one valley calls,
> All worlds, all natures, mood and measure keep
> For praise and ceaseless gratulation, poured
> Into the ear of God, their Lord! (emphasis supplied)

Both mood and message here are quite different from those of "It was an April morning." In the later poem, exhortation and exposition replace narrative. The "inarticulate notes" of natural song are now to be "united" with the human ("the voice of words"). No longer a spontaneous, self-circling effusion of natural growth, the song is directed away from creation, a work of time and in time (a "'six-days' Work") into the ear of the timeless, the "Ever-living," who abides in so distant a heaven that the song must be conveyed by angels, those beings who traditionally sing the kiddusha at the throne of God.

Similar contrasts may be illustrated by passages from the 1805 and 1850 versions of the *Prelude*. In Book 2, for example, the passage in question reiterates themes from "It was an April morning" and comes in a context in which Wordsworth is describing his youthful interaction with nature. He has spoken of a habit of mind, which he calls "poetic, . . . resembling . . . / Creative agency," whereby he rears "that interminable building . . . / By observation of affinities / In objects where no brotherhood exists / To common minds" (1805, 400–05). He uses rather Aristotelian terms to speak of that greatest of poetic gifts, an eye for resemblances, and of the creative power of metaphor.[9] It is perhaps due to this disposition of "Creative agency" or it might be "from excess / Of the great social principle of life / Coercing all things into sympathy," that Wordsworth may have "transferred / [His] own enjoyments [to nature]." But, alternatively, it may be that what he saw and heard was actually "revealed": "the power of truth / Coming in revelation," which permits him to "converse[] with things that really are" (1805, 2:407–13). Implied in both the metaphors of an "interminable building" and of the coercion of "all things into sympathy" is the concept of a universal composition—whether created by the poet or existing externally and "revealed" to him. Neither possibility is rejected; neither is preferred.

He says that at that time he was "contented" only when that composition beyond thought, knowledge, and perception was somehow "felt," when

> with bliss ineffable
> I felt the sentiment of being spread
> O'er all that moves, and all that seemeth still,
> O'er all that, lost beyond the reach of thought
> And human knowledge, to the human eye
> Invisible, yet liveth to the heart,
> O'er all that leaps, and runs, and shouts, and sings,
> Or beats the gladsome air, o'er all that glides
> Beneath the wave, yea, in the wave itself
> And mighty depth of waters. Wonder not
> If such my transports were, for in all things
> I saw one life, and felt that it was joy;
> *One song they sang, and it was audible—*
> *Most audible then when the fleshly ear,*
> *O'ercome by grosser prelude of that strain,*
> *Forgot its functions and slept undisturbed.* (1805, 2:419–34; emphasis
> supplied)

The sentiment of being is like that "quickening soul" in which the "great mass" of nature "lies bedded" (*Prelude* 3:127–8). It infuses everything with life and joy; it is song—one universal song, a natural kiddusha, an undirected outpouring, audible, not to the "fleshly" ear, but to some ear of the mind or spirit.[10] In this case, as elsewhere, the physical senses are not implicated in the perceptions; the poet experiences a sense of election and revelation, a *natural* analogue of John of Patmos' heavenly seeing and hearing of the one song sung at the throne of God. Most interesting in this and others of Wordsworth's early representations of the kiddusha is the fact that he makes no mention of the possibility that the song, which celebrates coherence, the natural composition, "the great social principle of life / Coercing all things into sympathy," is directed toward a supreme auditor.

A somber and more problematic version of Wordsworth's one song is heard in the Simplon Pass passages of Book 6 of the *Prelude*. After learning that he and his companion have unwittingly crossed the Alps, the travelers proceed slowly through the "gloomy pass." It is a paradoxical scene where time and eternity struggle together, exhibiting at once both change and permanence, process and stasis: "Woods decaying, never to be decayed, / The stationary blasts of waterfalls," of "Winds thwarting winds." At the same time, it is full of voices, not singing a song of joy, but offering a darker sort of music that like the song of joy seems to coerce "all things into sympathy":

The torrents shooting from the clear blue sky,
The rocks that muttered close upon our ears—
Black drizzling crags that spake by the wayside
As if a voice were in them—the sick sight
And giddy prospect of the raving stream,
The unfettered clouds and region of the heavens,
Tumult and peace, the darkness and the light,
Were all like workings of one mind, the features
Of the same face, Blossoms upon one tree,
Characters of the great apocalypse,
The types and symbols of eternity,
Of first, and last, and midst, and without end. (554–72)

Wordsworth's allusion to *Paradise Lost* in the last line of the quoted passage is instructive. In the passage alluded to, Milton presents Adam and Eve at their morning prayers in an Edenic dawn that illuminates "in wide Landscape all the East / Of Paradise and Eden's happy Plains":

> These are thy glorious works, Parent of good,
> Almighty, thine this universal Frame,
> Thus wondrous fair; thyself how wondrous then!
> To us invisible or dimly seen
> In these thy lowest works, yet these declare
> Thy goodness beyond thought, and Power Divine. . . .

God's prelapsarian works in Milton's version, as in Wordsworth's revision, speak; they "declare" God's goodness "beyond thought." Adam and Eve then invite the angels of heaven, who in sight of God sing the kiddusha (who "with songs / And choral symphonies, Day without Night, / Circle his Throne rejoicing") to join with all earth's creatures "to extol / *Him first, him last, him midst, and without end*" (*Paradise Lost* 5:142–65; emphasis supplied). Milton's allusion is to the song of the four cherubim surrounding the throne of God, who say, night and day, "Holy, holy, holy, Lord God Almighty, *which was, and is, and is to come*" (emphasis supplied). These are joined by the 24 elders who "worship him that liveth for ever and ever . . . saying Thou art worthy, O Lord, to receive glory and honor and power: for thou hast created all things, and for thy pleasure they are and were created" (Rev. 4:8–11). Adam and Eve further invoke the stars, sun, planets, elements, winds, plants, and fountains to join their voices with those of all living souls in the song of praise (*Paradise Lost* 5:166–204), as Wordsworth does in "On the Power of Sound."

While Wordsworth hears a sort of song—the muttering rocks, the speaking of the black drizzling crags, and the raving of the stream—it is a song of the earth, neither of praise nor of joy, but a natural song repre-sentative of the gloomy pass with its diluvial apocalyptic scars. This song and near quotation present a far different message from those of Milton and John of Patmos. A simple inventory of vocabulary in the passage sug-gests dreariness, illness, and incomprehension: *gloomy, slow, immeasurable, hollow rent, bewildered, forlorn, sick sight,* and *giddy prospect.* The near quotation from Milton is therefore remarkable not only for the language it includes, but for what it leaves out: the object of praise—not "Him first, him last, him midst, and without end," but "Of first, and last, and midst, and with-out end." *Him* (God), reiterated so dramatically in Milton's line, is absent from Wordsworth's or present as the merest trace—excluded, effaced if not quite wholly obliterated. Without recipient, the song of Simplon Pass remains natural, ambient, and ominous. Its apocalyptic intima-tions—"like workings of one mind, the features / Of the same face, blos-soms upon one tree, /Characters of the great apocalypse, / The types and symbols of eternity"—suggest a sublime and terrifying mind-invested and unified immanence like a face, a single tree, or a text in which are in-scribed "characters" from "eternity" of the "great apocalypse"—at once a record of former devastation (the universal flood) and signs predicting an approaching End-time obliteration, but also the characters, the per-sonae, of the apocalyptic drama, including the Whore of Babylon and her destroyer, the Logos.

Wordsworth is content to leave the 1805 Simplon Pass passage and its song (with its divine absence) virtually unchanged, but between 1805 and 1850 he adds significantly to the "one song" passage from Book 2 dis-cussed above. The 1805 version merely presents the song: "Wonder not / If such my transports were, for in all things / I saw one life, and felt that it was joy; / One song they sang . . ." (2:428–30); whereas the 1850 ver-sion (revised in or after 1839) insists on a divine auditor:

> Wonder not
> If high the transport, great the joy I felt,
> Communing in this sort through earth and heaven
> *With every form of creature, as it looked*
> *Towards the Uncreated with a countenance*
> *Of Adoration, with an eye of love.*
> One song they sang. . . . (*Prelude,* 1850 2:409–15; emphasis
>   supplied)

Here the 1805 "one life," which is "joy" (which produces the "one song"), is replaced by the one song as a traditional kiddusha, expressing "adora-tion" for the "Uncreated," making it a far more orthodox song of praise, one very similar to that in which Milton's Adam and Eve, the heavenly beings, and all "Creatures" participate. Gone is the life- and spirit-infused, self-contained and -referential natural world that celebrates its own joyous or darkly sublime wholeness and unity, its common "sentiment of Being." In its place is the song of the creature and the created, a song of praise now directed toward the divine, named in the mode of negative theology, the eternal song originating from and returning to a kind of linguistic black hole—the "Uncreated."

In early enunciations of the theme of the one song, Wordsworth implies a natural, self-generated harmony inherent in the universe and perceptible in time to attentive ears; in later versions, origin and goal of the song are removed to a distant poetic source, the divine Word. Nevertheless, implicit in the concept of Wordsworth's "one song" in both its early and late versions is the notion of a universe whose primordial matter and temporal dimensions (its first and last and midst) are linguistic or, more precisely, poetic—song. In early versions, it is a song of time, a "wild growth," or natural effusion inherent in nature and animating it, directing its processes, and failing when nature—individual or universal—fails, making the "noisy years seem moments in the being / Of the eternal Silence" ("Intimations Ode" 157–8). In later examples, the song is an external ground of being, a speaking that creates the world, "A Voice" that has given "Being" to "Light" and "Time" and "Man"; a voice that will also end the language-created universe. And in this later view, when earth and heavens have vanished or dissolved, what remains is not the "eternal Silence" of the Ode, but divine poetry, harmony, whose "stay / Is in the WORD, that shall not pass away" ("On the Power of Sound" 217–24).

The one song appears in an intriguingly involuted form in Book 5 of the *Prelude,* the song uttered by the shell-book that the dreamer is instructed to hold to his ear. He says that, as he put the shell to his ear, he

> heard that instant in an unknown tongue,
> Which yet I understood, articulate sounds,
> A loud prophetic blast of harmony,
> An ode in passion uttered, which foretold
> Destruction to the children of the earth
> By deluge now at hand. (1805 5:94–9)

Here is a music of "articulate sounds" in an "unknown tongue"—unknown, but paradoxically "understood"—suggestive of the prelapsarian language confused at Babel. At the same time, it is a "prophetic" trumpet blast of "harmony," but also a song—an "ode in passion uttered." Its message is that delivered to John of Patmos: "Destruction to the children of the earth." Its message is spoken by "a god, yea many gods"; it has "voices more than all the winds," yet, despite its message of destruction, it is "A joy, a consolation, and a hope," a consolation that the text explicitly announces, yet implicitly denies. A late, simpler version of this configuration of images appears in "On the Power of Sound." Absent in the later poem are the conflicting intertextual implications and the rich chains of figure that form the fabric of the *Prelude* passage.[11] Yet the later passage, solely biblical in its allusions, suggests its relation to the earlier lines in merging "Voice" and "Trumpet" in a "prophetic blast"[12] announcing destruction (represented in the quenching of the stars), reinforced by the oblique reference to the battle of Armageddon (the war more deadly than human wars), and again linking consolation with apocalyptic destruction through the opening of the grave and resurrection:

> A Voice shall finish doubt and dim foreseeing,
> And sweep away life's visionary stir;
> The Trumpet (we, intoxicate with pride,
> Arm at its blast for deadly wars)
> To angelic lips applied,
> The grave shall open, quench the stars. (211–6)[13]

Despite the persistence in Wordsworth's work of the one-song theme, seen in the apparent similarities and imagistic connections between these early and late representations, radical changes in thought and poetics are apparent. Prominent themes of the *Prelude*'s book on Books are: (1) the characterization of Nature's poetry as eternal and self-renewing; (2) the antithetically fragile and transitory nature of human books; (3) regret that human books will perish; and, more interestingly, (4) sorrow that in any imaginable eternity the human as "immortal" being "No more shall need such garments"—the works "worthy of unconquerable life" (5:19–23).[14] Not to need such garments implies a radical and not altogether satisfactory transformation of both language and human being from time into eternity, from Babylon to New Jerusalem. The Wanderer seems to echo such misgivings when he speaks of St. Paul's "mystery" concerning flesh becoming spirit and corruptible becoming incorruptible, calling it "that most awful scripture which declares, 'We shall not sleep, but we shall be changed!'" (*Excursion* 2:577–8; 1 Cor. 15:51). Implicit in the misgivings is the question of whether in fact the "human" can survive immortality, whether humanity and human poetry require a mutable and timed existence. As an eternal being, whose language conforms to a single, changeless song, would a man be a man? Probably not, for both dreamer and narrator desire to share the Arab-Quixote's desperate enterprise to save human works from apocalyptic destruction, an apparently mad endeavor in which "reason did lie couched" (5:116–66). The language-trumpet blast-song issuing from the shell has an ambiguous nature. Its instrument is natural (the shell), but its message is that of "a god, yea many gods," and it has "voices more than all the winds." It seems an odd precursor of the "Voice" in "On the Power of Sound" that creates and destroys the world. In the *Prelude* it would regrettably interrupt and silence human songs, recorded in volumes revealed as "Poor earthly casket[s] of immortal verse" (165). In "On the Power of Sound," the song is the eternal Harmony/Word from which all things flow and to which they return. The *Prelude* values human songs, the works "worthy of unconquerable life," and would resist their inevitable loss in apocalyptic destruction; divine and human songs are somehow incompatible, at odds. "On the Power of Sound" makes all sound—natural and human (including, implicitly, the "consecrated works of bard and sage" [*Prelude* 5:41], and the "still, sad music of humanity" ["Tintern Abbey" 92])— mere reverberations of the originary "Voice" that precedes, creates, destroys, and endures. The later poem does not grieve for, but anticipates—even celebrates—the apocalyptic silencing of mortal songs in favor of the universal Harmony whose "stay / Is in the WORD, that shall not pass away." It is important to observe that Wordsworth's early stance is repudiated in "On the Power of Sound," which is in its entirety itself a kiddusha whose essential theme echoes that of Milton's Adam and Eve, who with all creation "extol / *Him* first, *him* last, *him* midst, and without end."

Wordsworth's poetry reveals that the theme of the one song persists, undergoing through the years both transformation and deformation. The early song celebrates nature and poetry (and the power of imagination); the later song—unrelievedly and joyfully a kiddusha—enthusiastically celebrates the destruction of nature (heaven and earth, "though Earth be dust / And vanish, though the Heavens dissolve her stay") and the silencing of human poetry in favor of a primordial and eternal Harmony. The contrast in attitude between a rather orthodox anticipation of the End in "On the Power of Sound" and the clearly heterodox grief over lost human texts in Book 5 of the *Prelude* illustrates the radical transformation that the theme of the one song undergoes in Wordsworth's poetry. Gone without a trace from the late poem are the "tremblings of the heart" at the thought that immortal human beings might suffer an apocalyptic destruction of their works, "things worthy of unconquerable life," only to "survive / Abject, depressed, forlorn, disconsolate" (5:19–27). Of what value, the lines from the *Prelude* implicitly ask, is immortality without human texts, without the consecrated works of bard or sage, without the music of Babylon? The earlier vision is original, mystical, tragic, heroic, and grander, I think, than the traditional and almost complacent surrender of the later.

DREAM VISIONS OF END-TIMES AND THE THRONE

The Revelation tells the story of the throne.

—D. L. Moody[15]

Two notable Wordsworthian dreams depict visions of the apocalypse. The one, discussed above, is from Book 5 of the *Prelude,* and the other occurs in the sonnet, "Methought I Saw the Footsteps of a Throne" (1802). As mentioned, the kiddusha, or one song, is closely linked to the Merkabah, the divine throne-chariot, toward which the kiddusha is directed and that provides the imagistic center of several prophetic theophanies, including the entire Book of Revelation. Wordsworth's dream sonnet takes up this crucial image, an image that sustains both presence and absence in a poem that deals ironically with the traditional kiddusha, the prophetic vision of God on his throne, and, indeed, the throne itself. In these respects, Wordsworth's sonnet illustrates Alan Bewell's point that Wordsworth believed that the inherited "tradition and poetry had become ossified and needed to be remade" (230). The sonnet invokes and then transforms, as both human and aesthetic issues, traditional cultural constructs of life, death, and afterlife.

The poem is written against a long tradition of dream visions that reaches back, most importantly, into the highly symbolic dream vision of Revelation, flourishes in medieval literature, and finds a briefer but more specific expression in dream vision sonnets (the dream signaled typically by identical opening words, "Methought I saw") in which the speaker observes a dead beauty or beloved. For example, Sir Walter Ralegh offers, "Methought I Saw the Grave Where Laura Lay," a witty sonnet whose subjects are the life and death of poets and their poetic creations. Here the world of death seems not metaphysical but, as in the mode of Chaucer's *House of Fame,* literary; its concerns are those of the dream of the Arab-Quixote. Its scene is the place of dead poems and the figures who "lived" in them. The poet-dreamer observes the tomb of Petrarch's Laura within the temple of virginity and celebrates succession to the vestal throne by Spenser's Faerie Queen. Meanwhile, Oblivion lies on Laura's grave, with grim finality consigning her beauty and virtue to that obscurity which is poetic death. As a result, the society of dead poets grieves:

stones bleed, ghosts groan, and Homer's spirit trembles. By contrast, Milton's sonnet, "Methought I Saw My Late Espousèd Saint," although marked by classical and biblical allusions, presents a rather more traditional and religiously orthodox vision of death and afterlife and is concerned with personal rather than literary bereavement. The dreamer sees his dead wife as though "rescued from death by force" to be "Brought . . . like Alcestis from the grave" and restored to her husband. She has been purified in death, "washed from spot of childbed taint," and appears virginal, veiled, and "vested all in white." Her person "shined / So clear, as in no face with more delight." As the vision "incline[s]" to embrace the poet, he wakens: "she fled, and day brought back my night."

In these precursor poems, the poet makes traditional use of the medium of dream to see into the realms of death. Ralegh's poet encounters the place of dead poems and poets, finding the virginal, literary beauty not only entombed, but forgotten and displaced, and with the art also the artist. Milton's blind poet "glimpses" in dream his dead wife in all her restored beauty. She does not molder in obscurity as does Laura, but "lives" in heaven, having been enhanced by death: she is not only alive, but purified. Through her example the poet trusts that his eyesight will likewise in death be restored, so that he will have "Full sight of her in heaven without restraint." The dream visions of Ralegh and Milton represent part of the tradition that Wordsworth confronted; both conform to certain conventional myths. Their images reflect poetic or Christian commonplaces. Poetic fame and oblivion occupy Ralegh's effort, while Milton's dead wife enacts the Christian myth and in her purified spiritual body appears resurrected and "washed in the blood of the Lamb" (Rev. 7:14). Milton's sonnet is a touching enunciation of loss and longing, but it, like Ralegh's, remains within fairly conventional parameters. One of those conventions is a certain death orientation, marked by contempt for the world (a world of death) and its (bodily) pleasures and pains and a longing for "life," stripped of mortality and sorrow and perfected in the eternal realms of the spirit. Wordsworth's sonnet treats both themes of death in a richly equivocal and ironic work that owes something to both the literary and Christian traditions of his precursors.

As a dream poem, Wordsworth's sonnet presents yet further matter for thought. Such a poem, as often the dream itself, may be dismissed as "only a dream," and therefore as inconsequential, incapable either of being taken seriously or being held against the dreamer. In another view, however, the dream may seem to provide access to otherwise unavailable wisdom or truth—a glimpse, for example, of the afterworld, as in Revelation. Furthermore, a poem purporting to be a report of a dream may be just that—an attempt to describe in verse an actual dream, and that in itself raises two issues of interpretation. First, there is the problem of the effect of transcription into poetic language of highly visual and figural dream matter, and the related question, once the translation is complete, of which figures belong to the dream and which to the verbal transcription.[16] Second, and following from the first, is the question of the extent to which the order of versification (especially that of the highly formal sonnet) can in any way render intact the shapeless matter of dreams. On the other hand, the poem may not present a "real" dream at all, for the dreamer and/or the dream may well be fictional (as is the dream of Book 5 of the *Prelude*), in which case it is pertinent to ask why the mode of dream is appropriate to this subject and this poem. Ralegh's sonnet is intended to be read as a fiction: the reported dream is not at all dreamlike, but, rather, logical, literary, and purposeful—to extol Spenser's ascendancy over Petrarch, which is made possible by the view of Laura's grave. It might be claimed that Milton's more personal sonnet speaks of a "real" dream, but nevertheless it too strikes one as undreamlike, a work whose progress is narratively sound and whose purport and images are conventional, suggesting that if it is the report of a dream, either the poet's sleeping imagination or his waking editorial inclinations have been mythologically and culturally shaped and determined.[17] In a sense, the dream provides its own interpretation.

Thus Wordsworth's sonnet must be considered against the intertextual tradition while keeping in mind the special problems posed by the genre. Like the intertexts, Wordsworth's sonnet, through the medium of dream, reveals a vision of the afterworld. It thus represents a unique moment in Wordsworth's poetry when the linguistic space between life and death in which poet and poem so often abide is apparently transgressed. Those older visions of similar transgressions not only echo in Wordsworth's poem, but they furnish the ground against which it can be seen in stark contrast, for "Methought I saw the footsteps of a throne" is radically revisionary (and re-visionary), presenting a scene to which neither reason nor convention has easy access. Miller, discussing the dream in Book 5 of the *Prelude,* points to the essentially figural nature of dreams and makes observations that apply here: that through the dream, the mind "celebrate[s] its dominion over things as they are" and that, in dreams, that dominion "is affirmed not as figures of speech but as the paradoxical reality beheld by the dreamer. . . . since dreams enact as vivid images what poetic language performs in overt tropes." Miller comments, "in dream as in the language of poetry, nothing is its solid self. It is neither what it is nor the thing whose name or whose image displaces it, but is both at once. It is nothing but the interchange between the two" (*Linguistic Moment* 91). The process Miller describes is parallel to that which

Wordsworth explains in the "Preface to Poems" discussed in chapter 2, whereby through the language of contrasting images an intermediate thing comes into being. If dream images are to reality what figures of speech are to literal language, the poetic transcription of the dream renders it doubly challenging—figure expressed in figure, the poetic wrapped in poetry, the paradoxical, tropological visibility of dream figures interpreted and further figured in words. This imbrication of dream figure with verbal figure produces a density of meaning through which a semantic static emerges—the sort of "anasemia" involved in parapraxical writing (Taylor 226). That is, to present the matter as a dream provides the poet not only with a hedge (it is only a dream), but with the special dimensions of signification provided by the genre (the mutually implicating visual and verbal figures).

The initial scene of Wordsworth's sonnet occurs in a space hollowed out by words between life and death, made "visible" in the poem as a stairway obscured by "mists and vapours." The opening two lines ("Methought I saw the footsteps of a throne / Which mists and vapours from mine eyes did shroud") place Wordsworth's dreamer in a situation similar to that of John of Patmos, whose first glimpse into heaven reveals the divine throne. But Wordsworth's lines are disorienting, for almost immediately the "seeing" implied in the formulaic "methought I saw" is contradicted by the dream images themselves and the assertion that neither throne nor footsteps are visible; they are "shroud[ed]" in mists and vapours. The winding sheet or *shroud* of mists (which belongs to the verbal figures) hides from sight the dream figures of footsteps and throne and "interprets" the dream images, by associating both mists and the hidden throne with death. Neither dreamer nor reader can "see" the footsteps that nevertheless through their mere naming prepare the mind for the view of someone—a god or king—seated on a throne to which the footsteps lead. But he too is hidden: "Nor view of him who sate thereon allowed." The poem speaks of perceptions (of signs presented not by nature but by the mind in dream, not "I saw," but "methought [i.e., 'it seemed to me'] I saw"). It contains both report and interpretation as it weaves a combination of three orders of representation: (1) *the seemingly literal report* of dream image (the view of "mists and vapours"—which image, as the dream's figurative form of "reality," will not stay "its solid self" but, transcribed into poetic language, augments its already tropological import [e.g., m(i)stifying] with the connotations of the verbal metaphor, "shroud"); (2) *the verbal images* (the god represented as absence in the hidden "footsteps," "throne," and "him who sate thereon"), which hover between dream and poem, even as the syntax both affirms and denies their status first as visual images and then as word-things; and, finally, (3) *tropes or figures* ("shroud," "nor view . . . allowed") which seem to belong to the interpretation, investing the dream-figures, the "reality," with additional tropological significance.

After these opening lines, the sonnet moves into an allegorical and critical mode, as further details of the visionary landscape are revealed. Wordsworth's dreamer and stairway are ironically evocative of Jacob and his dream vision of a stairway or ladder with angels ascending and descending on it, touching the ground at what Jacob calls the "gate of heaven" (Gen. 28:11–17); John of Patmos also has seen a kind of gate, an open door in heaven (Rev. 4:1). Wordsworth's dreamer, however, does not see immortal or angelic beings, as do Jacob and John, but mortal human subjects, a "miserable crowd," who assemble at what is shown to be not the gate of heaven but the door of Death:

> But all the steps and ground about were strown
> With sights the ruefullest that flesh and bone
> Ever put on; a miserable crowd,
> Sick, hale, old, young, who cried before that cloud,
> "Thou art our king, O Death! to thee we groan."

The entirety of the human population ("Sick, hale, old, young") blindly inhabits the scene and the transcendent steps, presenting the "ruefullest" sight ever assumed by body—"flesh and bone"—and, in a curious parody of Christian privileging of death over life, paying obeisance to their king, Death, a curious *deus absconditus.*

While Death's subjects are "visible" in the dream imagery and interpreted in the verbal imagery, Death is not. They cry *before the cloud,* that mystifying impenetrable shroud of mists that conceals whatever exists above the steps, even as their discourse designates their king as Death. The primary images of the dreamscape are thus humanity, the stairway or ladder, and the obscuring, dominating, intimidating cloud/shroud. The theme of blindness (suggestive of Milton's disability—literal and figurative) is subtle, but pervasive. Neither dreamer nor dream figures are able to see.

It is at this point (as the sonnet moves into its sestet) that the dreamer receives his "revelation":

> I seemed to mount those steps; the vapours gave
> Smooth way; and I beheld the face of one
> Sleeping alone within a mossy cave,
> With her face up to heaven; that seemed to have
> Pleasing remembrance of a thought foregone;
> A lovely Beauty in a summer grave!

Dream "logic" prevails here (as it does not in the Ralegh and Milton sonnets). Nothing will stay "its solid self." The earth-bound blindness represented by the cloud easily dissolves (gives "smooth way"), and—in a
remarkable reversal of expectations and ironic anticlimax—the dreamer
ascends to find neither the expected masculine presence (the king Death
to whom all cry) nor the "divine" throne, but instead a feminine *figure* ("a
lovely Beauty") and a "mossy cave." In dream fashion, displacement occurs, as king becomes sleeper/corpse, as throne becomes a cave, and the
cave at the same time a "summer grave." The figures suggest the indeterminate conditions of both dream logic and metaphor. And in this place
of slippage there is neither life nor death and yet both life and death. In
her grave Beauty lies, not precisely dead but "sleeping," perhaps dreaming within the dream, her expression one of "pleasing remembrance of a
thought foregone," where present memory of past feeling remains
stamped on the features, though the thought is "foregone." Both life and
death are suggested in the mossy "summer" grave (green like the graves
of "The Three Graves" or like those of the dead-but-living children of
"We Are Seven"). The enigmatic, Mona Lisa–like expression both hides
and reveals; it hides the content of the thought while revealing its associated pleasure. The figure is in that Wordsworthian state of remembering
how it felt, but not *what* it felt (*Prelude* 2:334–7). The identity of the
sleeper is mysterious. She seems an image of the soul, yet in her mossy,
summer grave, she suggests also something of Mother Earth or Nature in
whom life and death are inextricable. She is not in heaven, but she faces
toward heaven. She seems to have a name—"Beauty"—and may be identified with the figure of *Home at Grasmere*—that "Beauty, whose living
home is the green earth, / Surpassing the most fair ideal Forms / Th[at]
craft of delicate Spirits hath composed / From earth's materials"
(991–4). The "delicate Spirits" who compose ideal Forms from earth's
materials may well be human philosophers and poets.

   This Beauty surpasses ideal forms, an idea, of course, associated with
Plato's Allegory of the Cave, forms that transcend their earthly appearances and are not to be found in the cave of material existence, but in a
transcendent realm "above" it. Wordsworth seems to answer Plato and
his distrust of "imitators," human poets. Wordsworth's Beauty sleeps
content *in* the cave of materiality, facing a perhaps transcendent
"heaven" but independent of it, the mysterious smile providing stark
contrast to the terrified groans of those who clamor toward an unseen
throne, a grim deity, apocalypse, End-times, and the eternity of ideal
forms. One implication is that if the footsteps (representing human life
and aspiration) lead to something permanent, it is not a masculine presence on a heavenly throne, but this Beauty of and in the earth, a figure

for art or poetry who makes her home in the "middest" between the tick and tock of human time.

The most interesting precursor text of Wordsworth's sonnet is Revelation. As mentioned, John's dream vision opens with a view of an open door in heaven; he hears an invitation to "come up hither." Immediately he is "in the spirit" and sees a throne and one "who sat on the throne." Surrounding the throne are four "beasts" or cherubim and 24 elders who sing a kiddusha to God. John can be said to represent a Christian tradition (to which Milton belongs) that privileges death over life and prefers End-times to present or past times. Revelation closes with a sense of urgent expectation of the impending fullness of times and the imminent End. Jesus says, "Behold I come quickly. . . . I am Alpha and Omega, the beginning and the end, the first and the last." A series of invitations is issued to "come" into the End-time community, and John reiterates Jesus' assertion, "Surely I come quickly," and adds, "Even so, come, Lord Jesus" (Rev. 22:7–17). The rhythms of the closing verses suggest the swift approach of the prophesied end of heaven and earth, the death of earth's creatures, and the resurrection to eternal life of the worthy. A death longing is prevalent.

Reading Wordsworth's dream vision against this text reveals further ironies. Obviously, Wordsworth's stairway and open door seem to lead to Death, whom the people, like John, worship. Ironically, however, this Death, as I said, is not the King in glory seated on his throne, worshipped in eternal song; he is not one who offers eternal, perfected "life," as in Revelation. Rather these "footsteps of a throne" lead to something that can only be understood aesthetically or poetically—an indeterminate "sleep" in which the past "lives" in nature's green, in the cave of consciousness, and in traces of memory observed in the face of Beauty. The bleak kiddusha sung by the people is not a song of rejoicing and praise, not "Alleluja; Salvation, and glory, and honour, and power unto the Lord our God" (Rev. 19:1), but a chanted, agonized Thanatos, "Thou art our king, O Death! to thee we groan." Wordsworth's dream vision discloses no city of God, no divine throne, no marriage of Jesus and the New Jerusalem, no promise of felicity and eternal life. There is only that enigmatic soul figure, a sleeping Beauty in and of the earth and earthly works; an image of enduring human artifacts, called by Wordsworth "Godlike, a humble branch of the divine," and "Art divine, / That both creates and fixes, in despite / Of Death and Time" ("Lines Suggested by a Portrait from the Pencil of F. Stone" 89, 76–8). She is a figure suggestive of the poetic tradition, of Petrarch's art, embodied in the "dead" Laura, or of Wordsworth's own Lucy—of the earthly muse in all her forms, represented most dramatically in Revelation by the woman associated with Babel and fallen human language, the woman called "Mystery, Babylon the Great, the Mother of Harlots and Abominations of the Earth" (Rev. 17:5), whose music must at last be silenced before the power of the Word. Finally, read against the several pretexts that converge in Wordsworth's sonnet, "Methought I saw the footsteps of a throne" answers the traditions of dream vision—contempt for things earthly and apocalyptic longing—with an ironic validation of the human, the aesthetic, the natural, and the timed.

Wordsworth would not sustain his ironic stance beyond the Great Decade. He presents a far more traditional representation of the afterlife in the vision of the Solitary, an embittered, isolated man, who has an "infidel contempt of holy writ" (*Excursion* 2:249) and reads Voltaire's *Candide* (2:443–4). As he travels his own road to Damascus, following along behind shepherds who carry home a dying man through "a dull mist" (2:829), the Solitary is not struck blind, as was Saul of Tarsus, but he is, like Saul, given (in)sight. He emerges in a single step from the "blind vapour"—a significantly altered representation of the obscuring mist in "Methought I saw the footsteps of a throne," to see, like the "Hebrew Prophets" (2:867), a vision of heaven and the New Jerusalem ("a mighty city" [2:835]), and in the center of the city, the divine Merkabah-throne and surrounding cherubim ("forms uncouth of mightiest power" [2:869]). He is struck with "admiration and Mysterious awe," claiming that what he "saw was the revealed abode / Of Spritis in beatitude." He cries, "I have been dead . . . / And now I live!" His immediate reaction to his vision and recognition is a rejection of earthly life (as a form of death) and an apocalyptic death-longing for "life" like that of John of Patmos, of Milton, and of the people of "Methought I saw the footsteps of a throne." He prays "to be no more" (2:869–77).[18]

The early and late Wordsworths are quite clearly of two minds and radically different visions. Nevertheless, as is clear from the late examples of "On the Power of Sound" and the *Excursion,* apocalyptic themes and modes endure in his poetry, while their meanings and expressions change utterly. A short lyric of 1802, "It is no Spirit who from Heaven hath flown," expresses a desire that can represent the Wordsworthian apocalyptic attitude, one that persists over time through periods of revolutionary and visionary optimism, heterodox uncertainty, and into a late, not altogether settled, orthodoxy. "There came to me a thought," he says,

> That I might step beyond my natural race . . .
>   might one day trace
> Some ground not mine; and, strong her strength above,
> My Soul, an Apparition in the place,
> Tread there, with steps that no one shall reprove!

The lines manifest an apocalyptic wanderlust, a longing for a "place" somewhere beyond nature and the poet's "natural race" where his soul can "tread," tracing the alien topography as he has traced the contours of his native England. The place beyond nature is imaginable and speakable only in the language of nature. The poet requires soulish *feet* to tread the metaphysical hills and bottoms of the *beyond*.

It is to this linguistic relationship of nature and apocalypse that I turn my attention in the next chapter.

CHAPTER 8

Wordsworthian Apocalyptics in Which Nothing Is Revealed

[Nature] is the path or temple through which one approaches the veiled shrine of the "mystery of man."

—Johnston, "The Idiom of Vision" 10

---

*A*pocalypse as used by scholars more often than not serves as a synonym or near synonym for a number of key concepts of Wordsworthian criticism—*imagination, vision, prophecy*—and, at the same time, as an antonym for *nature*. In the passage cited at the end of chapter 7, Wordsworth himself seems to distinguish between nature and some other sort of place—"Some ground not mine"—that might be the realm of, or accessible to, vision and hence in this context "apocalyptic," some place his "Soul" might explore. The natural realm is in this case to be contrasted with the visionary or apocalyptic realm. In a discussion of the Simplon Pass episode of Book 6 of the *Prelude* (composed in 1804), Geoffrey Hartman underscores what he sees as a new opposition in Wordsworth's thought between nature and apocalypse, describing "a conversion," an abrupt turn of mind, as the poet rejects nature and accepts imagination as his "hidden guide." Hartman believes that Wordsworth's about-face is accompanied by "apocalyptic feelings." He continues, "By 'apocalyptic' I mean that there is an *inner necessity to cast out nature,* to extirpate everything apparently external to salvation, everything that might stand between the naked self and God, whatever risk in this to the self" (49; emphasis supplied). In this same context, Hartman opposes perception and vision, associating perception with nature and vision with apocalyptic imagination. The opposition Hartman identifies as a new discovery in 1804 "prophesies against the world of sense-experience [perception] . . ." (48).

Wordsworth's method, however, was (and here the biblical model is apparent) to use not nature, but the *language of nature* (rather than, for example, theo-philosophical language) to represent or, if that is too strong a term, to intimate the proximity, the presence, and the sheer ineffability of something/nothing nearby, capable of emerging only as the mind interacts with the natural world, and that perceives and translates into human, natural language the product of that interaction.[1] That which seems to lie hidden within or lurking beyond nature, the not-natural, is unknown and unknowable in an empirical sense, but expressible, if at all, *through empirical terms;* penetrating beyond nature, still one obeys figurative natural laws and uses natural language—treads "some ground" "with steps that no one shall reprove." The point is important: the problem implicit in Hartman's observations is that of understanding how not nature but *the language of nature* can be made to serve Wordsworth's apocalyptic and visionary verse, how the language of perception can be parapraxically contorted or twisted so as to serve vision, how nature can be made to take on the mental patina of spirit, thought, and feeling.

APOCALYPSE AND NATURE

To reiterate, in thinking about the relationship of nature to apocalypse, one may lose sight of the fact that it is never nature (or Nature) in the poems, but rather the poet's verbal transformation and thereof, a (re)presentation of selected aspects, which constitutes a reading and interpretation of that which, itself meaningless, achieves significance through carefully shaped, even contorted, highly figurative, necessarily ambiguous and indeterminate poetic language. And it is this language that requires attention. For example, in a passage from "A Night-Piece," a poem whose "fitness as a visionary paradigm is established by scholarly precedent" (Johnston, "The Idiom of Vision" II), Wordsworth's "pensive" traveler, with his "unobserving eye / Bent earthwards" is startled by a sudden change of light, which triggers what is generally agreed to be a "visionary" or "apocalyptic" experience:

> he looks up—the clouds are split
> Asunder,—and above his head he sees
> The clear Moon, and the glory of the heavens.

There, in a black-blue vault she sails along,
Followed by multitudes of stars, that, small
And sharp, and bright, along the dark abyss
Drive as she drives: how fast they wheel away,
Yet vanish not!

In attempting to analyze just what aspects of language contribute to the judgment of the poem as a visionary paradigm, it is instructive to compare Wordsworth's language with that of Dorothy Wordsworth. As becomes clear, Wordsworth has at least one eye on Dorothy's prose, for the *natural* scene appears to be the same for each writer:

> January 25th [1798]. . . . At once the clouds seemed to cleave asunder, and left her [the moon] in the centre of a black-blue vault. She sailed along, followed by multitudes of stars, small, and bright, and sharp. Their brightness seemed concentrated (half-moon). (*Journals* 2)

Dorothy's version is not a strictly objective rendering of the natural scene, and yet it cannot be described as visionary. The percipient's role is foregrounded twice in the verb *seemed:* The clouds "seemed to cleave asunder," a construction that insists upon the observer and makes the clouds the underlying subject of the infinitive *to cleave;* and again, the brightness of the stars "*seemed* concentrated." While a clearly poetic rendering of the sailing moon as feminine implicates the following "multitudes" of stars as well in the personification, one understands that an implicit *seeming* governs as well the personification and action of moon and stars.

Given the similarities between Dorothy's prose and William's poetic rendering, one must ask how to account for their very different effects, the one natural, the other apocalyptic. My answer is, in short, that in articulating the visionary or apocalyptic experience, the poet depends upon what I have identified as the interwoven linguistics of negative theology and parapraxical writing, in this case with a particular dependence on the manipulation of the negative combined with a certain syntactic legerdemain. One of the first differences one notices is that in Wordsworth's lines subtle grammatical shifts introduce a mysterious absence. Dorothy says that "the clouds seemed to cleave asunder." The subject clouds (seem to) perform the action of cleaving. By contrast, in "A Night-Piece" there is no "seeming"; instead the clouds "are split asunder," the shift to a passive construction making the clouds the object of "to split" and eliding the agent of the splitting. Almost without the reader's noticing, and certainly without the aid of philosophical or theological language, a sort of

No-thing is introduced by a trick of syntax as the absent actor in a passive construction who/which splits the clouds asunder to reveal the personified moon and stars in a "dark abyss" through which they "sail" and "drive" and "wheel away, / Yet vanish not." Although William borrows images and even exact language from Dorothy's journal entry, and his moon sails, as does hers, with its following stars in a "black-blue vault," William's vault quickly takes on the character of a "dark abyss" (*abyss* meaning "bottomless"—the *a-* meaning "without"—and used to refer variously to a watery primeval chaos, the pit, hell, or an immeasurably profound void or depth). Coupled with the sailing metaphor with its suggestion of travel over water, the effect of the dark abyss is to disorient one in space—to upend the universe as the traveler looks *up* to see into that which is bottomless; time is similarly disrupted as the hurrying drive of moon and stars whirls them away, and yet not away: they "vanish *not.*" To see the movement of moon and stars as "fast" implies an intrusion of mental or apocalyptic time upon natural time, for *as perceived,* the moon and stars move slowly; to see them as whirling away and yet not away implies a visionary psycho- or polychronological perspective.

Wordsworth's technique displays what Kenneth Burke refers to as the "feeling for the *principle of the negative*" (18), the principle by which language as symbol system "transcends" nature, enabling the description of the unnatural and the supernatural that are, as Burke says, "*not* describable by the positives of nature" (22).[2] Wordsworth's poetic task and his negative apocalyptic linguistics are apparent in the absent agent of the passive construction, the "not" of *abyss,* the "vanishing *not*" of moon and stars, as well as the implied negative in the figure of sailing (the moon is *not* a boat, and its movement is *not* sailing). He continues with such devices in the following lines:

> —the wind is in the tree,
> But they are silent;—still they roll along
> Immeasurably distant; and the vault,
> Built round by those white clouds, enormous clouds,
> Still deepens its unfathomable depth.
> At length the Vision closes; and the mind,
> Not undisturbed by the delight it feels,
> Which slowly settles into peaceful calm,
> Is left to muse upon the solemn scene.

The moon and stars are "silent," a word that can only be defined in negative terms—making no sound—and understood in contrast to the natural—the sound of the wind in the tree. They are "immeasurably distant"—another negative, evoking a distance incapable of being measured, a concept picked up again in the word *unfathomable*. The white clouds of nature are pushed to the very limits of the natural in the term "enormous," meaning "exceeding" or "out of" the normal. The apocalyptic vault is itself defined by the unnaturally distended clouds and revealed by them, but it cannot be confined either by nature or the language of nature, as it becomes an agent—almost animate—paradoxically extending still deeper its own limitlessness; in the process, it seems to give access to that unthought, unknown Nothing beyond the limits not only of language and of measure but of understanding (*unfathomable* meaning, of course, "immeasurable" but also incapable of being penetrated intellectually or understood). "At length" (another term suggesting distance), in a counteraction of the unfathomable expansion, the "Vision closes," a phrase that grants to vision an odd agency, and the mind that has expanded to glimpse the boundless with the help of and at the very cliff-edge of negative linguistics (yet unable to measure, to describe, or to understand what is glimpsed) is left "Not undisturbed by the delight it feels." What emotion can lie between the *not* and the *un-* of this phrase? Certainly the phrase does not mean simply "disturbed," even if "disturbed by the delight it feels" could be readily understood. Rather it seems to express the barely namable metaphysical response by creating a linguistic space between the two negatives (*not* and *un-*) for a congruence of the incommensurates *delight* ("great pleasure or joy") and *"disturbed"* ("troubled emotionally or mentally"). The *not-un* construction is an extension of the artistry of the entire passage whose achievement, through negative linguistics and syntactic twistings, is to force language to speak the "unspeakable." Through such devices, not nature, but the *language of nature* can be made to accommodate the apocalyptic Nothing that is neither presence nor absence, neither being nor nonbeing.

It is a subtle distinction, but an important one. I want to agree with Kenneth R. Johnston, for example, when he claims that "[Nature] is the path or temple through which one approaches the veiled shrine of the 'mystery of man'" ("The Idiom of Vision" 10), but with the proviso that is it not Nature per se, but the *language of nature* yielding to Wordsworth's poetic maneuvers that provides the path that leads beyond the thing. This assumption, then, forces me to abandon Hartman's idea that there came a moment when Wordsworth moved from nature to imagination as poetic guide—simply because a poetic guide or muse is a creature of language (a figure), one who cannot be consistently located either internally (with the imagination) or externally (with nature), either before or after 1804, the year when Hartman notices Wordsworth's "conversion." What is clear is that Wordsworth's muse, having assumed body in language, in turn resists abstract, philosophical, or theological lexicons and insists for the most part on using the language of nature and of the mind's interaction with nature. Hartman is correct in his claim that Wordsworth often signals the change from natural to visionary through the figure of perception: "Wordsworth's journey as a poet can only continue with eyes, but the imagination experienced as a power distinct from nature opens his eyes by putting them out" (*Wordsworth's Poetry* 48). But the visionary eye is itself a figure based on the physical eye, and what it sees is typically expressed in the idiom of physical nature, the natural language given an apocalyptic accent. In my view it is more useful to recognize an extended period of Wordsworthian labor to discover ways of representing ineffable thought, of forging the elusive shapes of eternity, of mere being and nonbeing, from the material of nature, and of sorting out the linguistic relationships between something and Nothing.

Imagination and nature, mind and world: "How exquisitely," Wordsworth announces, "the individual Mind . . . to the external world is fitted; and how exquisitely too . . . / The external world is fitted to the mind" (*Home at Grasmere* 1006–11). *Exquisitely,* uncommon in Wordsworth's lexicon, repeated as it is, along with the passive *is fitted,* invites attention. *Exquisite* suggests the carefully sought or chosen, ingeniously devised, uncommon, and *exquisitely* is associated with the manner of crafting, "with delicate accuracy," "in a highly finished manner; with perfection of detail; elaborately, beautifully, excellently" (OED at "exquisite" and "exquisitely"). The etymology winds back to the Latin *quaerere,* "to seek." Who is the absent agent of the passive construction who seems so casually excluded? Who (or what) seeks carefully and crafts with perfection of detail the "fit" of the mind to external world? Does the same agent create the "fit" of the external world to the mind? What possible instrument or medium can accomplish a fit between a mysterious, abstract interiority of mind and the concrete exteriority of the world?

The first part of Wordsworth's claim, that the individual mind is fitted to the external world, is a form of Lockean-Hartleian orthodoxy. In his *Observations of Man,* David Hartley explains the working of the mind by means of the "Doctrines of *Vibrations* and *Association*":

> The First of these Doctrines is taken from the Hints concerning the Performance of Sensation and Motion, which Sir *Isaac Newton* has given at the End of his *Principia,* and in the Questions annexed to his *Optics;* the Last from what Mr. *Locke,* and other ingenious Persons . . . have delivered concerning the Influence of *Association* over our Opinions and Affections and its Use in explaining those Things in an accurate and precise Way. . . . (1:5; Hartley's emphasis)

For Hartley, the universe, man, and his mind were joined in a vibrating, unifying motion of imperceptible particles, all subject to natural law in the Newtonian sense. Through time the natural state of the mind at birth, with its so-called natural vibrations, is modified by perception or sensation, "the Ideas which are presented to the mind," i.e., "experienced" (1:79–80). The mind, by this view, is a product of the world, indeed of the entire universe, and is explainable in purely materialistic terms. Hartley explicitly discounted theories that allowed an immaterial soul influence over the material body, including the brain (1:110–11). The effect of the doctrine is to produce a passive mind subject to constant, involuntary molding or shaping from birth to death by the world's action upon it through the organs of perception. Although it is apparent throughout his work that Wordsworth, like Coleridge, recognized a determinism implicit in associationist views of the mind,[3] he does not wholly reject Hartley's epistemology, but seeks to correct it by augmenting it. The Hartleian doctrines are explicitly incorporated in the first half of his "great argument": "How exquisitely the individual Mind / (And the progressive powers perhaps no less / Of the whole species) to the external world / Is fitted." The passive mind fitted to the world is shaped by the world, gradually advancing, as Hartley said, "in Spirituality and Perfection"—Wordsworth's "progressive powers"—so as to find happiness in "the Improvement of . . . Understanding and Affections" (Hartley 1:208). The second part of Wordsworth's argument supplements the Hartleian theory by audaciously reversing the relationship between world and mind, active and passive, shaper and shaped, investing the mind with a reciprocal power over nature: "and how exquisitely too—/ Theme this but little heard of among men—/ The external world is fitted to the mind."

In an early essay, Harold Bloom ruled out any external source of the "apocalyptic," finding that what Wordsworth learns in "Tintern Abbey" is that apocalypse emerges as a result of "a principle of reciprocity between the external world and his own mind," a reciprocity indicated in the phrase, "all the mighty world / Of eye, and ear,—both what they half create, / and what perceive" (105–7) (a restatement of Wordsworth's augmented Hartleian psychology); and further that "the story of that reciprocity becomes the central story of Wordsworth's best poetry" (*Visionary Company* 132).[4] While the source of the apocalyptic remains problematic, shifting, and ultimately indeterminate, certainly *reciprocity* is a useful concept for understanding Wordsworth's poetic argument. It is through this reciprocity that mind and world are "married" as partners in a process by which world shapes mind and mind shapes world to make some new thing or *new world,* a "creation . . . which they with blended might / Accomplish: this is my great argument" (*Home at Grasmere* 1006–14). According to Hartley, mind is fitted to world through perception, and Wordsworth agrees; according to Wordsworth, however, world is fitted to mind through vision, imagination, apocalypse; moreover in this marriage of mind and world, the mind is or may be or should be "lord and master" of the "outward sense" (*Prelude* 11:270–1).

Yet the lexicon of perception—especially of sight and vision—proves problematic, for, on the one hand, it is only through experience of the sounds and sights of nature that "vision" may occur, or that something deeper, something "unnatural" may be "perceived"—the "sentiment of being," or the "presence" (that rolls through all things, mind and world), or the "life of things." On the other hand, Wordsworth often suggests that the physical senses are despotic and the action of the world on mind overwhelming, so that only by obliterating sense experience, shutting down the physical eye and ear, can "the power of truth" be "seen."

Whence the fit between mind and world? How are the senses implicated in that fit? More to the point, how are the senses implicated in "vision," if at all? A matter that complicates any easy solution to the problem is, as stated, that Wordsworthian representations of "vision" evade, for the most part, a metaphysical rhetoric, employing instead language descriptive of physical perceptions of nature, particularly those moments of odd coincidence when sights and sounds arrange themselves so as to permit momentary, stunning glimpses of depth, power, or beauty, whose origin lies in the fit of the world and the mind to each other. One language is made to serve two poetic ends, a language in which ordinary perceptions of nature's sights and sounds manage to make the Hartleian world play host to profound mystery, thus creating access to or implicating the apocalyptic in nature.

Andrzej Warminski traces the origin of the critical opposition of nature and apocalypse to a 1909 comment by A. C. Bradley. Bradley, he remarks, "inaugurates a tradition of Wordsworth interpretation by setting up the opposition (and the synthesis) in terms of 'natural' and 'apocalyptic,'" going on to suggest the virtual synonymy of "apocalypse" and "imagination" (986). Bradley's comments are brief, but intriguing. After citing a passage from the *Prelude* (1850 12:317–23) (a passage unchanged from 1805 [11:375–81]), he comments, "Everything here is natural, but everything is apocalyptic." That he uses "apocalyptic" as a synonym for "visionary" is clear, for he continues, "The visionary feeling has here a peculiar tone; but always, openly or covertly, *it is the intimation of something illimitable, over-arching or breaking into the customary 'reality'*" (134; emphasis supplied). The character of this "something" and the means of its intimation Bradley leaves unspecified. His comments suggest, however, that this something is utterly opposite and external to nature—breaking into it, "something illimitable" and "overarching" the "customary 'reality,'" the nature with which it is to be contrasted. Yet it is important to keep in mind that both the character and the position of this apocalyptic something change in Wordsworth's poetry from passage to passage and from early to late expressions. "Breaking into" is quite different from dwelling within, and while both the extrinsic and intrinsic "something" may elicit vision, those visions are of necessity quite different. In addition, the "something," when implicate in nature, produces a far different *nature* from that into which the apocalyptic something must break, and both of these versions are different from the nature through which apocalyptic imagination must find expression, intimating its presence, becoming visible, like the Word made flesh, as it assumes a body in natural forms. Even more complexity is introduced when the apocalyptic something invests both nature and mind, as in this famous passage from "Tintern Abbey":

> I have felt
> A presence that disturbs me with the joy
> Of elevated thoughts; a sense sublime
> Of something far more deeply interfused,
> Whose dwelling is the light of setting suns,
> And the round ocean, and the living air,
> And the blue sky, and in the mind of man. . . . (94–100)

This something—here called "presence"—is, on the one hand, implicate, indwelling, in what may be called nature. On the other hand, this same something inhabits the human mind. There is something Hartleian and deterministic about this something that Wordsworth calls "power," a master universal mover; it "impels /All thinking things, all objects of all thought, / And rolls through all things" (101–3). From this passage it is impossible to choose between, or even to separate, nature and mind (or imagination), for they constitute parts of a unity that in its entirety is driven by one ineffable something (or Nothing) through which they are connected as gears of the same universal machine.

Nevertheless Bradley claims that the apocalyptic is external to both nature and mind. By contrast, Hartman finds that the Wordsworthian apocalyptic is not an external phenomenon, but "something" that existed for Wordsworth first in nature and later in mind, claiming, as discussed above, a Wordsworthian "conversion" in 1804 from nature to mind. Between the two scholars, we have three ways of understanding the source of the apocalyptic, if not its precise nature: (1) it is external to nature (including mind) and breaking into it; (2) it is implicate in nature; and/or

(3) it is implicate in mind. Each of these views may be supported by different texts.

The most common and often only shared characteristic of the different apocalyptic representations is that they are triggered by eerie coincidence and couched not in psychological or metaphysical terms, but in the language of nature. The interpreter's task is always to discover the means by which the language of nature is made to express the un-natural, the psychological, metaphysical, or, in common critical usage, the apocalyptic. Bradley, discussing the *Prelude* passage already mentioned, suggests that the intimation of the apocalyptic through the natural occurs because "Wordsworth is describing the scene in the light of memory," which, cognizant of the imminent death of his father, causes the scene in retrospect to be "charged with the sense of contrast between the narrow world of common pleasures and blind and easy hopes, and the vast *unseen world* which encloses it in beneficent yet dark and inexorable arms" (134; emphasis supplied). Taking this claim further, Warminski finds that the apocalyptic *feeling* "breaks down into three identifiable moments: it is 1) the remembrance in a present of 2) a past event with its own 'natural' aura, which (past event) retroactively gains an 'apocalyptic' aura because it anticipates 3) another intervenient past event between 'now' and 'then'" (987).

While Bradley's observation and Warminski's elaboration are pertinent, one is still left with only Wordsworth's language and the question of just how the apocalyptic can be implicated in the language of nature; how, that is, he is able to provide a door in the strict language of nature through which something "apocalyptic" or "visionary" may enter. To seek an answer to this question is a necessary task if one is to understand the artistry of Wordsworth's remarkable and admittedly shifting apocalyptics. Intriguingly, in an echo of Wordsworth's own view of the need to read both letter and spirit, Warminski suggests that a solution lies in a double reading of natural and apocalyptic: "To take the past event as 'natural' is to read it literally, whereas to take it as 'apocalyptic' is to read it figuratively. . . . In other words, a double reading—simultaneously literal and figurative—constitutes the visionary feeling and its peculiar tone" (987). The notion of double reading is, I believe, useful. It suggests that apocalyptic or visionary intimations lie in the figurative; natural, in the literal. The difficulty is that the double reader Warminski has in mind is the poet writing, not the poet's readers reading.[5] Yet it is the host of Wordsworth's readers who are led to acknowledge with Bradley that, "Everything here is natural, but everything is apocalyptic." This reaction induced in Wordsworth's readers has nothing to do with the poet's own memory or the poet's "reading" of events as natural or apocalyptic and everything to do with his "writing" of events, his configuring of details, the words on the page, their sounds, rhythms, and order, the intricacy and art of their relationships—in other words, everything to do with the poetry per se. What aspects of the poetry prevent a strictly literal reading and demand the figurative reading that Warminski proposes? The literal and figurative readings occurring simultaneously would produce something like a strobe light effect that flickers between natural and apocalyptic, between perception and vision.

To attempt to answer this question, I want to return to the passage Bradley examines. Those lines reiterate in part the details of an earlier passage of the same episode, describing a scene in which Wordsworth, then a schoolboy, watches from a crag for horses that will take him home for Christmas holiday. Despite Bradley's assertion, there is little sense here of "blind and easy hopes." Wordsworth describes his mood as "feverish, and tired, and restless . . . impatient." Climbing a crag, he observes the place where two roads meet, by either of which his horses might come. The stormy, inhospitable natural scene, the boy's anxiety, and his concern over the exact route of deliverance are almost prophetic of impending disaster:

> 'Twas a day
> Stormy, and rough, and wild, and on the grass
> I sate half sheltered by a naked wall.
> Upon my right hand was a single sheep,
> A whistling hawthorn on my left, and there,
> With those companions at my side, I watched,
> Straining my eyes intensely as the mist
> Gave intermitting prospect of the wood
> And plain beneath. (1805 11:344–63)

The boy watches from his summit in an oxymoronic "anxiety of hope" (371).

Although unaware at this point of the sad events to follow, attentive readers will recognize the boy's fatigue, impatience, and apprehension, states that exist uneasily with and undermine the advisability of hope, states moreover that appear mirrored in the natural world. Contributing to a reader's inclination toward double reading is what I would call an iconographic quality to the scene emerging from the naming of its stark details; the scene's absence of action further enhances the sense that here is a tableau whose details constitute in themselves a significant representation. Furthermore, the scene and the boy's mind are "fitted" to each other through a tonal language that creates resonances between them: the storm in nature mirrors and is mirrored by the boy's anxiety. In a Freudian reading of the scene, Harold Bloom comments that this

anxiety is an "expectation," which, "as if hastening the event, is of the father's death" (*Ruin the Sacred Truths* 135), hence the boy experiences an
unconscious and semi-Oedipal "anxiety of hope" prompted by the coincidence of storm, mists, and roads—the place where two (rather than
the Oedipal three) roads meet. The scene is set in a bare catalogue that
displays but does not analyze the odd configurations and curious coin-
cidences in world and mind: the storm and wind that accent the boy's
vulnerability and mirror his anxiety; the mist that partially obscures the
view and reflects the boy's only partial vision; the cold, inadequate shelter of the naked wall that suggests the boy's lack of defenses; and at the
center, the isolated, curiously assorted trio on the wind-buffeted crag—
the feverish, restless, anxious boy, the single sheep, the whistling
hawthorn—configured so as to suggest a crucifixion.

The only action to disrupt this dreary tableau is the boy's attempt to
see—*straining his eyes*—through the obscuring mist (a natural hindrance to
both sight *and* vision) as he watches the place where the roads meet.[6]
While each of the details of the scene, described in the language of nature, seems strictly "natural," a bleak foreboding is evoked by their accu-
mulation; by the odd specular character of nature and boy; by the way in
which the reader's eye is directed from image to unadorned image, which
together constitute an ominous iconographic arrangement through
which may be heard the chill white noise of the storm and the sinister
whistling of the hawthorn. It is this configuration and its dis-ease that
compel readers to perform the sort of double reading that Warminski
describes; willy-nilly, they must read figuratively as well as literally.
Bradley's illimitable something intrudes as a prevailing mood mirrored
between world and mind, both in the boy's anxiety and nature's tempest,
a mood whose import—whose prophecy—reveals itself as implicate in
coincidence of details if they are rightly "read."

Although the boy, caught up in the scene, may read literally at first,
looking back, he will read it—and misread it—figuratively. He will suffer
an Oedipal angst as he imagines that he is in fact responsible for his father's death, that the death is a "chastisement," an admonishment from
God for faulty desires (1805 11:374). If the boy's reading of the scene
were correct, it would indicate that what he experienced was a natural
text written by an idiosyncratic and arbitrary "God" to "reveal" through
obscure signs in the natural scene his intent to kill the boy's father to
chastise the son for his "desires"—conscious or unconscious. While this
reading is intriguing, it does not seem to hold up, for the man—the
poet—finds the boy's reading somehow inadequate or incomplete, and
although he does not specifically substitute another, he returns again and
again to the inscrutable details of the scene. The plain natural language

as it creates the dreary configuration is made to approach the limits of the natural in order to disclose "something" beyond nature, a mystery (like the mist-shrouded scene) partially revealed, partially concealed. The hawthorn, for example, stands at the natural boundaries of time and space; and just "beyond" is another, enigmatic "something," which for lack of an *un*natural vocabulary is called "tree," but it is a tree that conveys an apocalyptic message: it is one tree of many—a tree of the borderland of life and of death. Companion to sheep and boy, it is an almost animate solitary that/who, like Lucy Grey, whistles in the wind. "Afterwards," the poet, as he looks back on the scene and reiterates its details, presents it rather differently than initially, for he foregrounds the "business" and noisiness of the scene, suggesting that now he can and does "see" and "hear" and, further, that there is a deep significance in the natural text if he could just learn to read it. If, as I have suggested, the boy reads the scene at first naturally and then later misreads it figuratively (although the boy's dark understanding of the scene is never explicitly rejected), now the man returns for further readings, figurative and apocalyptic, never certain of the accuracy or fullness of his reading, as demonstrated in the important passage that, as Bloom points out, would have been "the conclusion of a five-book Prelude that Wordsworth contemplated in 1804" (*Ruin the Sacred Truths* 136):

> the wind and sleety rain,
> And all the business of the elements,
> The single sheep, and the one blasted tree,
> And the bleak music from that old stone wall,
> The noise of wood and water, and the mist
> That on the line of each of those two roads
> Advanced in such indisputable shapes—
> *All these were spectacles and sounds to which*
> *I often would repair, and thence would drink*
> *As at a fountain.* (11:375–84; emphasis supplied)

In this almost paradigmatic passage, as so often elsewhere, the poet tells us *that* he reads the scene, but not *what* he reads there; the ineffable whole and all its parts remain charged with meaning, intimations at the edge and just beyond the capacity of natural language to express. Moreover, the entire scene, figured now as a fountain, suggests an abysmal reservoir of significance from which one may drink, perhaps forever, without exhausting its possibilities, but also, as the omission to specify the scene's meanings suggests, without necessarily being able to articulate in human language its messages.[7]

THE ADVANCING MIST

An important Wordsworthian metaphor bearing on the question of apocalyptics is to be found in mists, vapours, and clouds, images that recur
often and are everywhere connected paradoxically with both vision and
"blindness." In the quoted passages, the mist obscures not only space, but
time—that is, the roads beneath the boy, but also the obscurely prophesied
future in which his father will die; however much he strains his eyes, mist
prevents not just perception but "revelation." Yet looking back years later,
the poet notices that it advanced in mysterious, vaguely threatening,
unidentified but "indisputable shapes." Does the mist simply conceal, or
does it in fact reveal something through its "shapes"? Should one, like the
boy, "strain one's eyes" to see through or beyond it, or should one make the
mist itself and its shapes the focus of attention? The poet sees in the mist
shapes, forms, "something"—of which the boy was apparently oblivious.

In "Methought I saw the footsteps of a throne," the mysteries of death
are concealed from humans by "mists and vapours" that nevertheless give
"smooth way" as the dreamer climbs above them to "behold" the ambiguous image of "a lovely Beauty in a summer grave." The process of
climbing (here the footsteps of a throne) is also the Wordsworthian maneuver for overcoming the obscuring mists in the climactic vision of the
Prelude on Mount Snowdon. Other times, as in "A Night-Piece" or the
Solitary's vision in the *Excursion,* the simple act of walking seems to dispel
the mists or clouds, leading to vision. The Solitary, traveling through "dull
mist," remarks that "a single step . . . freed me from the skirts / Of the
blind vapour, opened to my view / Glory beyond all glory ever seen / By
waking sense or by the dreaming soul!" (*Excursion* 2:829–33). The vapour
is "blind"; the step that takes the Solitary beyond it "open[s] to [his]
view" the glory of glories—not just light, but a light "beyond" any ever
seen. The Solitary, like the narrators of "A Night-Piece" and "Methought
I saw the footsteps of a throne," and like the Wordsworth of the *Prelude,*
emphasizes the suddenness and ease with which blindness gives way to
vision through natural processes. The light that falls "like a flash" (e.g.,
Prelude 13:40) in each case signals the dispelling of the mists, the transformation from blindness to (in)sight, from sense perception to vision,
through nature's language and images to apocalypse.

Yet the association of mists, vapours, and clouds with earthbound per-
ception and blindness is curiously called into question in the Simplon
Pass episode of Book 6, in the passage that in the 1850 version, Hartman
argues, signals a Wordsworthian shift to antinaturalism and marks
Wordsworth's conversion from nature to imagination as his poetic guide.
Here is the passage from the 1805 *Prelude:*

> Imagination!—lifting up itself
> Before the eye and progress of my song
> Like an unfathered vapour, here that power,
> In all the might of its endowments, came
> Athwart me. I was lost as in a cloud,
> Halted without a struggle to break through. . . . (6:525–30)

The passage is often viewed as representative of Wordsworth's visionary and antinatural, hence "apocalyptic," posture. There is something Pauline about the occasion, for its archetype is that of Saul of Tarsus, halted and stricken (physically) blind on the road to Damascus after which he becomes able to "see" the imaginative reality of Jesus. As conversion and illumination, the passage poses some extraordinarily knotty problems of interpretation, for the magnificence of the lines disguises, *and is at the same time a function of,* an oddness that has not been fully appreciated. The ensuing discussion will consider, for the most part, the 1805 version.

UNFATHERED VAPOUR

> *For now we see through a glass, darkly.* . . .
>
> —1 Cor. 13:12
>
> *We see but darkly*
> *Even when we look behind us.* . . .
>
> —*Prelude* 3:491–2

The oddness of the lines illustrates Wordsworth's handling of the language of negative theology and parapraxis and is apparent from the beginning as the poet acknowledges in Pauline fashion an astonishing encounter with a heretofore unrecognized Other: "Imagination!—lifting up itself / Before the eye and progress of my song" (6:525–6). Incongruously, imagination is distanced from the poet and given a separate, almost personal being and volition: it lifts up itself. Just as Saul (soon to become Paul) is halted by a brilliant light and a presence, so is the poet halted dead in his tracks by an imagination that stirs and rises like an awakened beast or an angry god, opposing the poet's intentions, his perceptions (the poet's eye [I]), and even his act of composing—the "progress of [his] song." Unlike the mists that come in "indisputable shapes," this "being" is amorphous: "Like an unfathered vapour." Paul's perceptions are occluded by the blinding light. The poet is blinded by the vapourous imagination. The mists, clouds, and vapours that in Wordsworth's poems typically represent the limitations of perception and oppose vision here present a triple paradox: (1) blindness, (2) the figure of vision, *and* (3) the vision itself, a vision in which nothing can be seen and yet, as it seems, in which Nothing can be seen.

The strangeness of the phrase, "unfathered vapour," may go unnoticed. Hartman finds that *unfathered* means simply "self-begotten," itself a most problematic term: "In its purity the imagination is 'unfathered'—a self-begotten, potentially apocalyptic force" (*Wordsworth's Poetry* 67). But *unfathered* invokes, rather than banishes, the idea of parenthood, through the negative morpheme, *un-*, forcing one to conjure the specter of the equally elusive *fathered* vapour. Initially, the suggestion of absent parenthood in *unfathered* lends to the vapourous imagination the status of child or offspring, a status immediately denied by the negative morpheme, although as it disappears it leaves its trace. The unfathered seems a Logos figure just before the Word becomes flesh, (a)kin to the Uncreated, child of the Unfather. But even here, and also at the same time, this imagination-vapour is implicitly contrasted with other supposedly "fathered" vapours, although these, with which the unfathered vapour is to be contrasted, are themselves not only unknown but scarcely conceivable (no pun intended). "Like an unfathered vapour, here that power, / In all the might of its endowments, came / Athwart me" (6:527–9).

The imagination as an unfathered vapour is called a "power," a name difficult to reconcile with the formless, shifting, insubstantial character of vapour. As the terms *power* and *vapour* converge in the abstract term *imagination* (and its near synonym *vision*), Wordsworth's language performs the delicate work of transferring particles from one term to the other and from both to *imagination*. The formless natural image of vapour that obscures perception and vision is here not blind vapour, but in fact both the powerful instrument of vision and its very image. The narrator's paradoxical vision "shows" that he is not only lost and powerless, but blind: "I was lost as in a cloud, / Halted without a struggle to break through." Imagination's power and "personality" are emphasized, as it comes "Athwart" the traveler "In *all the might* of its endowments."[8] This vision blinds the poet or, put another way, "reveals" his blindness, and renders him powerless to proceed as either literal or mental traveler:[9]

> And now, recovering, to my soul I say
> "I recognise thy glory." In such strength
> Of usurpation, in such visitings
> Of awful promise, when the light of sense
> Goes out in flashes that have shewn to us
> The invisible world, doth greatness make abode,
> There harbours whether we be young or old. (6:531–7)

To recover generally implies that one has been stricken, knocked off balance, made ill either physically or mentally—as was Paul on the road to Damascus—and, in this context, the term specifically suggests that the assault by the imagination is not only irresistibly powerful and terrifying, but in some ways pathological. This sense is reinforced by the fact that the imagination's strength is exercised in usurpation—illegal seizure or encroachment. Its visitings are of "awful promise"—that is, while they may command respect or reverential fear, at the same time their promise (or prophecy) is *awful,* that is, terrible, dreadful, or appalling. It is only in light of the negative senses of *usurpation* and *awful* that need for recovery becomes understandable.[10] The effect of usurpation and awful promise by the vapourous, inhibiting imagination is, again, odd in the extreme. Like the heavenly light that blinds Paul, it causes the "light of sense" to go out in "flashes" that reveal "the invisible world." The "invisible," that which cannot be seen, is impossibly revealed, made visible, but the flashes in which it is disclosed belong not to the imagination that rises like a blinding, unfathered vapour, but rather to physical perception and to nature, to the "light of sense." Like a swan song, the flashes signal a sort of death—the end of seeing when perception in its failure transforms to "vision" and flashes of the light of sense *show* the *blinded eye* that which is in any case impossible to see—the *"invisible* world."

Recovering, Wordsworth says to his "soul," "I recognise thy glory" (or "light"). If *soul* here is a synonym for *imagination,* it is shown to exist apart from and even in opposition to the self, coming in the form not of glory (distinction, light, halo) but of vapour. It has power, autonomy, and volition. Is this division of soul and self an instance in which the mind (soul) is revealed as "lord and master" and "outward sense / . . . but the obedient servant of her will" (*Prelude* 11:270–2)? And if the flashes of ordinary perception reveal to the poet the invisible world, what image of that world, if any, do they offer to Wordsworth's readers? Approaching this problem, Johnston perceptively remarks,

> When we come fresh upon Wordsworth's descriptions of vision, or of his lesser "spots of time," we can be . . . perplexed. How can these moments possibly be sublime? We are often at a loss to say what, if anything, has happened. . . . *Especially, it is hard to tell when ordinary sight transmutes into vision in Wordsworth's poetry*—but this difficulty is, as much as anything else, the very essence of his genius. ("The Idiom of Vision," 3; emphasis supplied)

Not only is it difficult to say what has happened or to mark the boundary between "ordinary sight" and "vision," but the poetry, in fact, offers no description of the impossibly revealed but "invisible world." Yet the content of vision seems to "appear" at the blurred edges of the language of nature—if, for example, one stresses *world,* rather than *invisible.* And the language of nature *is* blurred—oxymoronic, ambiguous, suggestively figurative even at moments when it seems most "natural." Therefore, I find Johnston's identification of the reader's perplexity with "the very essence" of Wordsworth's genius to be one of those critical insights that can lead well beyond its immediate context, for I would argue that the reader's perplexity is necessary, a design of Wordsworth's use of language to approach the articulation of the unspeakable. His words are made to perform feats for which they are ill-equipped in a syntax that leads and misleads—in the present instance, through the many oxymoronic couplings of blindness and insight, of light and darkness, of invisibility and revelation; the impertinent attribution of qualities (*unfathered* vapour, *awful* promise); of evocative yet mystifying negatives (*unfathered,* the visible *invisible*). The linguistic devices of negative theology and parapraxis exert a force on readers as the language first creates and then obliterates images and expectations. To reiterate my earlier claim, the magnificence of the passage under consideration (as well as those other passages of which Johnston speaks) resides in a virtuoso management of words, Wordsworth's signature linguistic oddness.

APOCALYPSE IN WHICH NOTHING IS REVEALED

> *[Being] is pure indeterminateness and vacuity.—Nothing can be intuited in it, if there is any question here of intuition, or again it is merely this pure and empty intuition itself; equally there is in it no object for thought, or again it is just this empty thought. In fact, Being, indeterminate immediacy, is Nothing, neither more nor less.*
>
> —Hegel, *Science of Logic* 1:94

> *I should need*
> *Colours and words that are unknown to man*
> *To paint the visionary dreariness. . . .*
>
> —*Prelude* 11:307–09

Wordsworth's dilemma is that of the poet for whom natural images and human language are inadequate to express the "visionary," the essence and mystery of being—in Hegel's phrase, "indeterminate immediacy"— that is neither more nor less than Nothing, those thoughts and feelings that find no natural or linguistic correlatives, but merely intimate their existence beyond the realm of things, in thought empty of image or word, in primordial essences of light and darkness, in gleams and flashes and dark patinas fleetingly apprehended on or through natural surfaces, in "indisputable shapes" of the shapeless mist, and in duplicitous devices and tricks of language. Put another way, visions of Nothing cannot be captured in *things*, natural or linguistic; they rather momently and without warning subtly adjust the representation of the world of things, altering appearances and distending natural boundaries, or they slip almost unnoticed through semantic or syntactic chinks in linguistic structures— often in odd configurations of images, turnings (tropes, negatives, paradoxes) and twistings that can never be straightened out.

There is something in Wordsworth like Hegel's "pure intuiting," thoughts that resist human expression, that "lie too deep for tears," and though they be initiated by *something*, "the meanest flower," they are themselves no*thing*; there *is* a light not of nature, a "light that never was, on sea or land," a castle seen in that light capable of becoming a "chronicle of heaven"; there is a "visionary dreariness" that requires for its expression "Colours and words . . . unknown to man." The No*thing* associated with Being, "pure indeterminateness and vacuity," the subject of "empty thinking," can be articulated only through the ingeniously arranged language of *something*. Wordsworth's apocalyptic moment is just that instant when Nothing is intuited, noetically "glimpsed" in the afterimage of *something*, especially when the language of nature under stress of various Wordsworthian maneuvers thins to translucence and the formless shadows of the unspoken and unspeakable, the Nothing or the nothings of pure Being, are made to intimate their shapes and characters in the images and linguistics of time and space. Wordsworth's description of the descent of the Alps is illustrative; it is a passage when natural, irreconcilable images of "Tumult and peace, the darkness and the light" are made to speak the unspeakable in images and words known to man—"workings of one mind, the features / Of the same face, blossoms upon one tree." As the series moves from the abstract invisibility of thought to the visible features of a face, to the image of one blossoming tree, the implication is that the perceptible surface of things both human and natural—faces, trees—are texts in which something (the workings of one mind) may be read. In the language that follows, Wordsworth suggests the textual nature of the scene in the words "Characters," "types," and "symbols"—all of which may indicate systems of representation. These characters, types, and symbols reveal precisely Nothing: "the great apocalypse, . . . eternity, . . . first, and last, and midst, and without end" (*Prelude* 6:567–72). What remains after the apocalyptic instant passes is the poem, the verbal representation of a natural scene, but a scene forever changed and endlessly changing, distorted, contorted, or enhanced by artful articulation of the momentary intuition of Nothing.

THE ENDLESS WAY HOME

For Wordsworth and his many surrogate travelers, all roads lead to the invisible, to Nothing, often called infinity or eternity.

> I love a public road: few sights there are
> That please me more—such object hath had power
> O'er my imagination since the dawn
> Of childhood, *when its disappearing line . . .*
> *Was like a guide into eternity,*
> *At least to things unknown and without bound.*
> (*Prelude* 12:145–52; emphasis supplied)

For Wordsworth the natural image of a mundane public road becomes an object of power, drawing the mind into the invisible, the eternal, the unknown, and the boundless through a series of negative morphemes (*dis-, un-, -out*) that serve to transform the natural road into a way into the empty intuition of Nothing. The impossible revelation of Nothing, the invisible world briefly "seen" through nature in the dying flashes of the "light of sense," suggests every traveler's destination; it is the eternal and the infinite:

> Our destiny, our nature, and our home,
> Is with infinitude—and only there;
> With hope it is, hope that can never die,
> Effort, and expectation, and desire,
> And something evermore about to be.
> (*Prelude* 6:534–42)

The passage reiterates a persistent figure in Wordsworth's poetry—life as a journey whose destination is home, or Home. It is a peculiarly Wordsworthian expression of faith, a transformation of the manner of Paul, who, as mentioned earlier, defines *faith* oxymoronically as "The substance of things hoped for, the evidence of things not seen" (Heb. 11:1). For Paul, faith leads to God and the promised home, which is "seen" "afar off"; the faithful are "persuaded of [it]," and embrace it and confess "that they were strangers and pilgrims on the earth" (Heb. 11:13). The destination of which Wordsworth speaks is mysterious; and while it sometimes invokes the presence of God, this is not the personal, anthropomorphic God of Paul, but a kind of divine encompassing, akin to the Newtonian notion of the God that, being infinite and eternal, existing "always and everywhere," "constitutes duration and space" (Newton 4). The astonishing forward impetus of Wordsworth's lines, accelerated syntactically by the five repetitions of the word *and,* while driven forward semantically

by *hope,* by *"Effort,* and *expectation,* and *desire,"* mentally replicates the traveler's physical journey; it is an impetus that, like the road with "its disappearing line," guides readers to the very margins of physical space and
time: "something evermore about to be"—a something that is not yet and
always never will be and is, therefore, Nothing, "indeterminate immediacy."[11] Paul's meditation on faith asserts that "through faith we understand that the worlds were framed by the word of God, so that things
which are seen were not made of things which do appear" (Heb. 11:3). For
both Paul and Wordsworth, strangers and pilgrims on the earth travel toward the invisible, the things that do not appear, the home unseen but
from time to time intuited, glimpsed afar off, made to appear by way of
words through the natural mists.

"Stepping Westward" (1805) depicts the pilgrim's progress, the
Wordsworthian way leading from darkness toward light as a stranger asks
a question, "What you are stepping westward?":

> —'Twould be a wildish destiny,
> If we, who thus together roam
> In a strange Land, and far from home,
> Were in this place the guests of Chance:
> Yet who would stop or fear to advance,
> Though home or shelter he had none,
> With such a Sky to lead him on?

Here the sky, rather than the public road, serves as guide. The westward
direction of the journey, the evening gloom, and afterglow of the sunset—all quite natural—are transformed by sharing room in the same sentence with the oxymoronic "wildish destiny" (suggesting both a kind of
capricious fate and destination) and its semi-antonym, "Chance." Likewise, so do the phrases "strange Land," "far from home," and "guests of
Chance" metamorphose quietly, as they assume an allegorical aura. The
images become vehicles in which homeless wanderers in a strange land
may follow "such a Sky" to something that can never be reached, the place
of "something evermore about to be." The reader's eye is led from one to
another of the three nouns marked by capitals, from "Land" (a "strange"
land, a place of alien sojourn), to "Chance" (of whom the travelers may
be uneasy guests), to "Sky" (longed-for destination—and destiny; the distant "home"). The succeeding stanza makes explicit the revelatory alteration and extension of the details of the natural scene:

> The dewy ground was dark and cold;
> Behind, all gloomy to behold;

> And stepping westward seemed to be
> A kind of *heavenly* destiny. . . .

The journey toward "A kind of *heavenly* destiny" has been made possible through the coincidence of an odd question posed by a stranger in an isolated scene: "I liked the greeting," the poet says, because it was "a *sound* / Of something without place or bound." This "something" that manifests itself in the stranger's question, is again captured negatively; the sound is of the boundless and placeless, everywhere and nowhere, infinite and elusive, of the character of a "beyond," neither simply immanent nor transcendent, yet made somehow perceptible in nature to human senses as sound carried in language. This Nothing, this *sound* of the beyond, is only *something* in so far as it assumes the body of "something," the (mystery of) words of the question, "What you are stepping westward?" Even the form of the question invites speculation, for in place of the expected, "What, are you . . ." is "What you are . . . ," a more ontologically intriguing syntax. As phrased, the question may imply that one's essence—"what you are"—is simply this journey to the west. The sun *is* its journey; the human traveler *is* his or her westward movement through time to a "*heavenly* destiny." As in the "Intimations Ode," the life's journey is like that of the sun from east to west, from "God, who is our home" back to that home again. God-as-home is just that infinitude-as-home, or the "immortal sea" to which the path of the sun leads ("Intimations Ode" 71, 65, 166). As a result of the linguistic maneuvering, a visionary patina invests both scene and human figures of "Stepping Westward." The travelers move away from the gathering darkness led by that "glowing sky," the infinitude in which we find "Our destiny, our nature, and our home." Nothing is embodied in human language through which the infinite may be glimpsed: "The echo of the voice enwrought / A human sweetness with the thought / Of travelling through the world that lay / Before me in my *endless* way" (emphasis supplied).

READING THE FORMS OF THINGS

In *The Ruined Cottage,* Armytage (Wordsworth's prototypical pilgrim) speaks in naturalistic terms of Margaret's death and its devastating *natural* consequences:

> She is dead,
> The worm is on her cheek, and this poor hut,
> Stripped of its outward garb of household flowers,

Of rose and sweet-briar, offers to the wind
A cold bare wall whose earthly top is tricked
With weeds and the rank spear-grass. She is dead,
And nettles rot and adders sun themselves
Where we have sat together. . . . (103–10)

The scene, described with regret and grief, is one not of visionary but of
natural dreariness, the language reiterating Margaret's death and confin-
ing objects to time and its ruinous progress—the stark fact of death made
graphic by encroachment of an unfeeling, unappealing nature in the form
of the grave-worm on Margaret's cheek and the sprawling growth that
invades what was once the human abode, where it displaces the domesti-
cated flowers "with weeds and the rank spear-grass," "tricking" a crum-
bling wall abandoned to nature's processes, while "nettles rot" and adders
usurp the place of the former human inhabitants. All is natural here;
there is no sense of apocalyptic seeing.

What is particularly interesting is that the poem contains another
representation of this same scene and circumstances in which the
"natural" yields to the "visionary." Toward the end of the poem, after
he has narrated Margaret's story, Armytage admonishes his listener to
"Be wise and chearful, and no longer read / The forms of things with
an unworthy eye" as he describes once more Margaret and her ruined
cottage:

She sleeps in the calm earth, and peace is here.
I well remember that those very plumes,
Those weeds, and the high spear-grass on that wall,
By mist and silent rain-drops silvered o'er,
As once I passed, did to my heart convey
So still an image of tranquillity,
So calm and still, and looked so beautiful
Amid the uneasy thoughts which filled my mind,
That what we feel of sorrow and despair
From ruin and from change, and all the grief
The passing shews of being leave behind,
Appeared an idle dream. . . . (510–23)

This representation is one informed not by the "unworthy eye" of time,
not by perception, but by the "visionary" or apocalyptic eye to which the
Nothing of infinite intimates itself through the objects of time.
When properly "read," Margaret (or the form of Margaret) is not a
worm-eaten corpse decaying in the ground, but rather a sleeper: she
"sleeps in the calm earth, and peace is here." The worthy eye sees

through the "passing shews" and all the ruins of time to the eternal "forms of things," where everything is silent, tranquil, still, and beautiful. Even the spear-grass has taken on the patina of eternity, "By mist and silent rain-drops silvered o'er." The eternal image denies the validity of "sorrow and despair," experienced through perceptions in the realms of process, "From ruin and from change." To the worthy or apocalyptic eye, what the eye of time has perceived appears "an idle dream"—meaningless ephemera in an eternal tranquillity and beauty; the visionary eye reads not the "passing shews" but the forms of things and finds the formerly "rank" spear-grass revealed in its ideal form—"calm and still . . . and . . . beautiful."

This last description of Margaret and her ruined cottage constitutes for Armytage a Wordsworthian apocalyptic "spot of time"; revelatory, to be sure, but revelatory of that which remains after or beyond time and its processes—ideal objects, perhaps, Platonic forms, mere Nothings. At the time of his vision, Armytage, as he says, was suffering "uneasy thoughts which filled [his] mind," feelings of "sorrow and despair / From ruin and from change, and all the grief / The passing shews of being leave behind." As he "reads with a worthy eye," he penetrates beyond these to the "forms of things." Such a privileged "reading" constitutes, as Wordsworth says in the "spots of time" passage, "a renovating virtue," for the uneasy mind, "depressed / By false opinion and contentious thought, / Or aught of heavier or more deadly weight" (*Prelude* 11:259–61).

There is, without doubt, a Platonic aura to the Wordsworthian Nothing, implicit in his frequent use of "forms" to suggest those ideal objects or Nothings that seem to lie beyond nature and its processes. Nevertheless, there are important and telling contrasts. In an extended simile in a passage of the *Prelude* composed in 1804, Wordsworth offers an intriguing description of the visionary experience of the relationship of things to "forms," all within the context of an allegorical cave:

> As when a traveller hath from open day
> With torches passed into some vault of earth . . . ,
> He looks and sees the cavern spread and grow,
> Widening itself on all sides, sees, or thinks
> He sees, erelong, the roof above his head,
> Which instantly unsettles and recedes—
> Substance and shadow, light and darkness, all
> Commingled, making up a canopy
> Of shapes, and forms, and tendencies to shape,
> That shift and vanish, change and interchange
> Like spectres—ferment quiet and sublime. . . . (8:711–23)

Thematic similarities link this passage to the apocalyptic passage of Book 6 described above. Yet here Wordsworth's traveler may be compared to Plato's soul, which "has come out of the brighter life, and is unable to see because unaccustomed to the dark" (*Republic* 6:362–3). However, Wordsworth's traveler differs from Plato's soul in that he brings with him torches, representative of the sense of sight, by which he "looks and sees."[12] The cave is the cave of nature—for both Plato and Wordsworth—yet within the cave Wordsworth's traveler "sees, or thinks / He sees" not mere illusions, appearances, or "shadows of images" (*Republic* 6:358) observed by the Platonic soul who lives in "the prison-house of sight" (*Republic* 6:361), but a commingled vision of "Substance and shadow, light and darkness." Wordsworth's cave is a canopy not just of material objects, but of eternal forms as well. To enter the cave with torches, constituting a sort of double vision, is to observe not only the passing show of being, but some underlying and permanent essence, the "shapes and forms, and tendencies to shape," that within time and nature "shift and vanish, change and interchange / Like spectres." The visionary mix of things and No-things constitutes a Wordsworthian splendid agitation—"ferment quiet and sublime." The traveler's glimpse of pure being, of Nothing, is fleeting, occurring in a moment reduced to space, and soon obscured as the sublime ferment, "after a short space, works less and less":

> Till, every effort, every motion gone,
> The scene before him lies in perfect view
> Exposed, and lifeless as a written book. (8:711–27)

When vision fails, the cave, like Margaret, is simply dead. As the apocalyptic moment passes, the scene escapes its brush with eternity and "dies" into the wholly natural, the world of appearances, of process, of nettles, rank spear-grass, decaying corpses, and grave-worms—the view "perfect," over and done with, its life and action completed, "every motion gone." Nevertheless, the apocalyptic scene, as a story once told, has been, however inadequately, embodied in words and natural images. Though it lies exposed and lifeless—"a written book"—the figure insists that, like a book, the scene may be "read" again and again, revisited imaginatively countless times; that each rereading can trigger the chemical reaction, the "ferment quiet and sublime" through which the spot of time retains a "renovating virtue" by which minds are "nourished and invisibly repaired" (*Prelude* 11:259–64).

The metaphor "spot of time" reveals the apocalyptic tendency to nudge the timed and ephemeral toward permanency and stasis, to stop the "passing shews of being" in textual existence. In lines that immediately precede the "spots-of-time" passage of the two-part *Prelude* of 1799,

Wordsworth speaks of "numerous accidents," "tragic facts / Of rural history," which "impressed" his mind (like an inscription pressed in wax) with "images" and "forms" that "yet exist with independent life, / And, like their archetypes, know no decay" (First Part 280–7). These images and forms are exempt from change; silent icons, they wait like a painting or a written book to be read and reread. They are the "ordinary" moments that are seen "double," but must nevertheless be represented in natural images and human language. In the "murderer's grave" passage of the *Prelude,* the episode linked most closely to the "spots of time" passage, the boy William, not yet six, lost from his guide, has stumbled on the scene of an old execution and burial. Leaving the place disturbed and frightened, he encounters a scene that impresses his mind with visionary image and form:

> . . . reascending the bare common, [I] saw
> A naked pool that lay beneath the hills,
> The beacon on the summit, and more near,
> A girl who bore a pitcher on her head
> And seemed with difficult steps to force her way
> Against the blowing wind. (II: 302–7)

The lines offer a catalogue of images, the relationships among them iconographic or (for lack of a better word) tonal, their separateness resisting and yet requiring figural interpretation and composition. That Wordsworth understands such "spots" as iconographic and painterly is clear as the passage continues:

> It was, in truth,
> *An ordinary sight, but I should need*
> *Colours and words that are unknown to man*
> *To paint the visionary dreariness*
> Which, while I looked all round for my lost guide,
> Did at that time invest the naked pool,
> The beacon on the lonely eminence,
> The woman, and her garments vexed and tossed
> By the strong wind. (307–15; emphasis supplied)

The double seeing here is mirrored in the repetition of the catalogue—pool, beacon, hill, woman, wind; the visionary dreariness that would "compose" the scene is impossible to "paint" in natural images (colors) and human words. And yet Wordsworth approaches the impossible. Somehow that visionary dreariness is rendered in words that offer the merest outline of Nothing, neither more nor less.

THE ASCENT TO THE SUN

> *And suppose . . . that [the prisoner of the cave] is reluctantly dragged up a steep and
> rugged ascent, and held fast until he is forced into the presence of the sun himself, is he not
> likely to be pained and irritated? When he approaches the light his eyes will be dazzled,
> and he will not be able to see anything at all of what are now called realities.*
>
> —Plato, *Republic* 7: 359

In his painting *The Wanderer above the Mists* (1817), Caspar David Friedrich
presents a scene dominated by a figure who stands over and faces a mist-
shrouded abyss; from his vantage point the painted figure can see what is
tantalizingly just out of sight for the viewer. The painting presents a pic-
torial analogy for what Wordsworth does so often, not with paint but
with words. Although it could not have done so, his description of the as-
cent of Mount Snowdon might have served as inspiration for Friedrich's
Wanderer. As in the painting the viewer is kept from ever quite seeing what
the Wanderer sees, so is Wordsworth's reader denied a glimpse into the
real abyss of forms, of "ideal objects," of Nothing, which the poet experiences and strives to convey in colors and words that are known to men.

The episode takes the form of a journey and begins with stepping
westward once more (*Prelude* 13:4), as Wordsworth, with suggestively allegorical intent, sets out in darkness and mist to climb Mount Snowdon,
intending to see the sun rise. His movement is to be from darkness to
light, the anticipated sunrise suggestive of revelatory vision and enlightenment. The sun in Plato's Allegory of the Cave is emblematic of reason,
truth, and ideal reality ("the universal author of all things beautiful and
right, parent of light . . . and the immediate source of reason and truth"
[*Republic* 7:362]) toward which the soul, once free of the dark cave of nature, might ascend. One must, however, accustom one's vision gradually
to that ultimate light, moving from shadow, first to reflections in water,
then to the objects themselves, and, as the last step, to the moon and
stars, seeing "the sky and the stars by night better than the sun or the
light of the sun by day" (6:359–60).

Climbing Snowdon through the mist-entangled darkness,
Wordsworth experiences that apocalyptic and Pauline instant when "a
light upon the turf / Fell like a flash" (*Prelude* 13:39–40). Although his
purpose in climbing is to see the sun, he finds instead the moon, a body
that reflects not only physical but figurative sunlight—its dazzling ide-
ality, reason, and truth—in whose purity, according to Plato, prisoners
of the cave of nature are likely to be blinded to the material world, unable to see "anything at all of what are now called realities." The cave
dweller, the natural man, is better able to "see" by the lighted bodies of

the night sky, as does Wordsworth here, as the moon "st[ands] naked in the heavens at height / Immense above [his] head." Two archetypal emblems of time—the moon and the sea—dominate the scene. Wordsworth emphasizes both the temporal and the middle position of the traveler's physical body: above his head is the moon, at his feet, "a huge sea of mist, . . . meek and silent" (*Prelude* 13: 41–4), and the man stands poised between the moon (temporal reflector of realm of light) and material darkness, between vision and perception, apocalypse and nature. Seeing and not-seeing are thematic in the episode. Beneath him the obscuring sea of mist stretches "*as far as sight could reach*" and above him the moon "*looked down* upon this shew / In single glory" (*Prelude* 13: 51–3). Immersed in time and surrounded by the natural emblems of time, the poet's position between two worlds is precarious. From that vantage one can discern chasms and fractures in the encroaching sea of blinding vapour and hear the eternal voice of waters, a terrible apocalyptic kiddusha:

> we stood, the mist
> Touching our very feet; and from the shore
> At distance not the third part of a mile
> Was a blue chasm, a fracture in the vapour,
> A deep and gloomy breathing-place, through which
> Mounted the roar of waters, torrents, streams
> Innumerable, roaring with one voice. (*Prelude* 13:53–9)

What does this "homeless voice of waters" (*Prelude* 13:63) say? What words emerge from the deep and gloomy breathing-place? Are they all the human words of bard and sage? The kiddusha or song of praise, often described as like the voice of waters, is not homeless, but at Home, an anthem sung at the throne of God. This homeless voice is not joyous like the one song of nature discussed earlier; rather it rises as a collective threnody of all human wanderers who are themselves "far from home." It might well be that the voice attempts to speak Nothing, the message from eternity for which the poet would "need / Colours and words that are unknown to man." The poet can attempt to interpret and to translate the visionary experience, and he does. The scene *appears* to him as

> The perfect image of a mighty mind,
> Of one that feeds upon infinity,
> That is exalted by an under-presence,
> The sense of God, or whatso'er is dim
> Or vast in its own being. . . . (*Prelude* 13:69–73)

But as the immediacy of the vision yields to analysis, the language changes, resorting to simile (image of a mighty mind that feeds . . .) and abstraction (under-presence, sense of God, *or* whatso'er is dim). This is the language of metaphysical analysis, not the language of nature. If the mighty mind is the poet's, Wordsworth concludes, it is one with double vision, standing between, capable of observing the things of the natural world, and "seeing" the Nothings of the apocalyptic realms: His mind is "By sensible impressions not enthralled, / But quickened, rouzed, and made thereby more fit / To hold *communion* with the invisible world" (*Prelude* 13:103–05; emphasis supplied).

And here it is, a kind of Wordsworthian key: The mind is not "enthralled" by its transactions with nature through "sensible impressions" of things. Rather, those perceptions enliven the mind, rouse it, make it more fit "To hold communion with the invisible world." It is only through one's perceptions of nature, the visible world, the reaction of the mind to those impressions, and, most crucially, the language in which those perceptions are embodied, that one becomes able to "hold communion" with the "invisible world"—"to hold communion" suggesting both to talk intimately with, and to receive the Eucharist, thereby becoming one with the divine, the incarnate Word that preceded and created all things. In a Wordsworthian transformation of Pauline faith, "we understand that the worlds were framed by the word of God, so that things which are seen [the world of sensible impressions] were not made of things which do appear [i.e., they originate in thoughts, words, the (im)material and mystery of the 'invisible world']" (Heb. 11:3).

REVEALING NOTHING

> *Perhaps all the wisdom, and all truth, and all sincerity, are just compressed into that inappreciable moment of time in which we step over the threshold of the invisible.*
> —Joseph Conrad, *Heart of Darkness*

I want to return to Johnston's observation that in its apocalyptic mode Wordsworth's poetry is puzzling: "We are often at a loss to say what, if anything, has happened. . . ." And I want to reiterate a theme of these last two chapters: Wordsworth manipulates natural images and human language, using the techniques of negative theology and parapraxis, to compel them to represent the *un*-natural and *in*effable, to present "evidence of things not seen," that which would seem to be not only unrepresentable, but unspeakable. In this respect, it is proper to speak of a strange, idiosyncratic Wordsworthian faith sustained through the years of the Great Decade before his swerve to orthodoxy. It is a faith in the plot of human life, that the endless journey has purpose and goal; it is faith that there is mystery in the universe and in the mind inaccessible to the senses but that nevertheless constitutes a fit, a creative, fecund relationship like a marriage between them. It is faith, above all, that one's experiences have significance and, when read "with a worthy eye" and spoken well, offer evidence of the mystery of man. It is testimony to his genius that through the language of nature alone Wordsworth is able to take readers to the edge of an abyss and "reveal" to them that which is boundless and timeless, of first, and last, and midst, and without end, the never-was, the not-yet, the something ever more about to be. If one is at a loss to say what, if anything, has happened, it is not because nothing has happened; it is rather that the Wordsworthian linguistic probe has shown briefly into the unbodied, glorious mystery of mere being and nonbeing. One's response might well be, I heard Nothing and saw Nothing.

CONCLUSION

In these last two chapters, I have identified the several senses in which "apocalypse" is used in Wordsworthian scholarship: (1) to suggest a biblical intertextuality (especially to the Book of Revelation), identifying Wordsworth's representations of the biblical plot, his persistent theme of the kiddusha and its association with the Throne, the Merkabah and End-times; (2) to analyze the opposition of apocalypse and nature, and to explore the ways in which *apocalypse, imagination,* and *vision* become near synonyms for both Wordsworth and his readers, arguing that Wordsworthian apocalypse must be represented in the language of nature; and (3) to identify and analyze some of the poetic techniques by which Wordsworth adjusts the language of nature (especially in the poetry of the Great Decade) to serve his apocalyptic vision and to articulate an odd, parabiblical and largely unorthodox faith in words to embody and convey the unthought (the Nothing that is the self, neither being nor nonbeing), so as to provide "the substance of things hoped for, the evidence of things not seen."

These several concerns produce what I have called a pervasive apocalyptic mode to Wordsworth's persistent, if inconsistent, interrogation of the relationships between self or mind (and the geography of the mind) and nature, and among language, world, and thought. The result is a remarkable word-crafted revelation of a man and a universe, facing each other, imposing on each other, reciprocating beauty, depth, and power, terrified and terrifying, joyful and enjoying. The man is haunted among textual ruins by biblical ghosts whose ectoplasmic voices intrude, especially when mind and world are stopped dead in a spot of time, when world invades mind and mind invades world in a stunning coincidence that charges ordinary sights with extraordinary meaning and changes everything. The ghosts are scarcely recognizable: God as infinitude, as home, as under-presence, "or whatso'er is dim / Or vast in its own being"; Jesus as creative Word and prototype of all creators and creative words; John of Patmos peering at a divine throne through an open door into heaven; Paul as traveler on an endless way that leads along the road to Damascus; all the mystery implied in the paradox of faith: the insubstantial substance of things hoped for, the elusive evidence of things not seen—a definition leading one back to the divine mystery of the Word and of words, where darkness dwells, and "all the host / Of shadowy things," the holy, invisible (im)material from which worlds are framed and all "things which are seen."

Notes

1. I discuss this theme at length in chapter 8, "Wordsworthian Apocalyptics in Which Nothing Is Revealed."
2. The rather more orthodox religiosity of the later poetry is seldom at issue. In the chapters that follow, I offer analyses of the ways in which Wordsworth's changing spiritual orientation alters the nature of the biblical presence in the poems.
3. Unless otherwise specified, all references to the *Prelude* are to the 1805 version.
4. I discuss parables and their difficulties of interpretation in chapter 5, "Wordsworth's Prodigal Son."
5. Quotations from the Bible are from the Authorized King James Version.
6. I have chosen not to provide a separate analysis of Wordsworthian "prophecy." My decision is based on the fact that the subject is addressed here and there in other discussions, receiving considerable space in chapters 1, 4, 7, and 8.

CHAPTER 1. INTRODUCTION: POET IN A DESTITUTE TIME

1. Although many critics have provided useful insights, I am indebted in particular to M. H. Abrams' *Natural Supernaturalism;* Stephen Prickett's *Romanticism and Religion* and *Words and* The Word; and David P. Haney's *William Wordsworth and the Hermeneutics of Incarnation.*
2. As J. Hillis Miller has shown, Wordsworth's dream in Book 5 is a displacement of Descartes' dream, behind which "lies the Biblical, medieval, and Renaissance topos of the two books, the book of nature and the book of revealed Scripture" (*The Linguistic Moment* 93, n 32). Andrzej Warminski pays particular attention to the "two books" in the drowned man episode of Book 5.
3. Stephen Prickett offers a useful discussion of the history of the idea of the book of nature (*liber naturae*) and its currency in Wordsworth's time

(*Words and* the Word 123–48). In the late eighteenth and early nineteenth centuries, the metaphor of nature's book (and the language of nature) came to replace those from the music of the spheres and Newtonian physics (132), reflecting a pervasive Romantic concern with the power and functions of language. Just what the message of this text is, Prickett says, "Wordsworth is at pains to spell out . . . throughout his work from the *Lyrical Ballads* through *The Prelude* to *The Excursion*" (140).

4. Murray Roston, I believe, rather underestimates the biblical influence when he states that by the beginning of the Romantic period proper, the Bible as one among a variety of models, "still held a highly respected place, but it had, in a sense, served its turn, and it is to be discerned as a submerged current rather than as a mainstream in the writings of the romantic school itself" (172).

5. Edwin Stein asserts that "Wordsworth's poetry incorporated the English poetic tradition to a greater degree and in more ways than that of any poet before him" (vii), and finds the majority of Wordsworth's intertexts in Milton and, more broadly, in seventeenth- and eighteenth-century writers. Certainly Wordsworth's numerous and often overt allusions to and echoes of Milton have helped make a case for Milton as the greatest single influence upon Wordsworth. In his astute analysis of Wordsworthian-Miltonic intertextuality, J. Douglas Kneale argues that it is proper to make a distinction between *influence* and *intertextuality*, the former belonging to the history of ideas and the latter to rhetoric (27). From this view, Harold Bloom is speaking of influence, and not intertextuality, when he identifies in Milton, as Wordsworth's great precursor, in what is essentially a negative sense when he says of Wordsworthian memory that it is "a defense against time, decay, the loss of divinating power, and so finally a defense against death, whose other name is John Milton" (*Poetry and Repression* 53). Stein says that the evocations of scripture constitute "the only large group of echoes" outside this period, and points out that the King James version, which Wordsworth used, was essentially a seventeenth-century source (13).

6. As Roston points out, in Wordsworth the biblical influence is subtle. For example, in Wordsworth's lyric, "She dwelt among th' untrodden ways," "were it not for Wordsworth's own testimony to the biblical source, it would be difficult to argue that the simplicity of imagery and language was influenced by the biblical forms" (76). Bloom refers to this subtlety of allusion as "Wordsworth's characteristic *internalization* of allusion," remarking that "Internalization is at once the great Wordsworthian resource and the great Wordsworthian disaster" (*Poetry and Repression* 58).

7. Riffaterre's concept of the connective restores to texts the possibility of "newness" denied by Kristeva and others, and resuscitates the author declared by some to be dead. Harold Bloom almost denies that possibility in the "overpopulated world of literary language." He says, "Any poem is an inter-poem, and any reading of a poem is an inter-reading. A poem is

not writing, but *rewriting*, and though a strong poem is a fresh start, such a start is a starting-again" (*Poetry and Repression* 3).

8. Chief among these are M. H. Abrams, "English Romanticism: The Spirit of the Age" and *Natural Supernaturalism*; Roston, *Prophet and Poet*; and Prickett, *Words and* the Word, all of whom have demonstrated that Wordsworth's revolutionary poetics is pervaded by biblical influences. Coleridge was the first to claim the centrality of biblical texts in Wordsworth's poetics when, at the opening of chapter 14 of the *Biographica Literaria*, describing the joint enterprise of the *Lyrical Ballads*, he hints at Wordsworth's poetics by echoing the words of God to Isaiah (Is. 6:10) and of Jesus to his disciples concerning his teaching in parables (Mk. 4:11):

> Mr. Wordsworth . . . was to propose to himself as his object, to give the charm of novelty to things of every day, and to excite a feeling analogous to the supernatural, by awakening the mind's attention from the lethargy of custom, and directing it to the loveliness and the wonders of the world before us; an inexhaustible treasure, but for which . . . *we have eyes, yet see not, ears that hear not, and hearts that neither feel nor understand* (314; emphasis supplied).

9. Roston shows that whereas classicism dictated the laws of poetic composition and the criteria for judging poetic excellence in the Augustan age, Hebraism exerted a similar force for Romanticism. He identifies differences in style, including syntax, imagery, and levels of abstraction or generality, the greater generality in neoclassical verse influenced by periphrastic devices encouraged by the student's thesaurus, the *Gradus ad Parnassum* (Roston 80). Such dependence on periphrastic devices and what Roston calls "detached, controlled rhetoric" (38) had the effect of distancing the poet from both common language and direct expression of feeling. For the neoclassic poet or critic, literature was "an amusement for the leisured classes" (Roston 39).

10. This same complaint is evident in Wordsworth's *Essays upon Epitaphs*, wherein he stresses that "the first requisite . . . in an Epitaph is, that it should speak, in a tone which shall sink into the heart, the general language of humanity as connected with the subject of death—the source from which an epitaph proceeds—of death, and of life" (*Pr. W.* 2:57). Epitaphs can fail when one is "misled by false taste" or "not merely misled, but wholly laid asleep by the same power" (*Pr. W.* 2:75). Wordsworth identifies the problem endemic to the previous age as stemming from the "example of Pope, whose sparkling and tuneful manner had bewitched the men of letters, his contemporaries, and corrupted the judgment of the nation through all ranks of society" (*Pr. W.* 2:75). This severe indictment applies not only to epitaphs in verse, but to all the poetry of Pope and his contemporaries. Artificial form, expected style of diction, and epigrammatic wit—these "defile and clog" expression of feelings, imagination, and understanding (*Pr. W.* 2:98).

11. Frances Ferguson, among others, has pointed out the importance of the "Note to 'The Thorn'" to an understanding of Wordsworth's poetics, calling attention to its treatment of tautology and repetition (11). It is also important to a consideration of Wordsworth's central poetic principle—incarnation, to be discussed in chapter 2. Furthermore, as Ruth apRoberts argues, biblical language may well be the "real language of men"—simple rural people whose language is influenced by the only books they know: the Bible and the liturgy (135).

12. Coleridge's argument appears in chapter 17 of the *Biographia Literaria* (*The Oxford Authors: Samuel Taylor Coleridge* 333–45).

13. Many critics have acknowledged Wordsworth's role in constituting the modern view of literature and of its place in the world. Don H. Bialostosky, for instance, says that Wordsworth "authorized a progressive and theoretically self-conscious enterprise of literary study" (xiii), and declares Wordsworth one of the "founding fathers" of the trope by which the "enterprise of 'literature'" is grounded in a "constitution" (1). Jonathan Arac claims that "Wordsworth did more than anyone else to establish the vocation of literature" and our culture's "idea of the literary critic" (3).

14. I have in mind, among others, Frances Ferguson, Paul de Man, and David P. Haney, to whose analyses I shall return in chapter 2.

15. Another sort of power in words is seen in this language from Book 7 of the *Prelude*: "Oh wondrous power of words, how sweet they are / According to the meaning which they bring" (121–2). By contrast, their power is differently understood in the 1850 revision: "O, wond'rous power of words, by simple faith / Licensed to take the meaning that we love!" (119–20). The earlier description invests words with a history to which human beings are subject, while the later description is almost Humpty Dumptyesque—allowing the user to assign meaning to the words used.

16. Percy admires Lowth, calling him the "best Critic of the age" (vi), and approving his methods of exposition. Percy is impatient with traditional readings of the Song of Solomon that, giving little attention to the "literal sense," build structures of interpretation "without a foundation, which, however fair and goodly to the view, will be blown down by the slightest breath of true criticism." He argues that "the first principles of figurative composition require, that the metaphorical sense and the proper, the allegory and its literal meaning, the apologue and its moral, the parable and its spiritual application, should be clearly distinguished from each other. To jumble and confound them is contrary to the rules of all good writing, and indeed of common sense" (v–vi).

17. "Two-sidedness" is Prickett's term. He finds, for example, that Blake's objection to "Tintern Abbey" lay in what seemed to him an attempt to fuse Platonic and Naturalistic systems. "Are there any 'half-way houses' in philosophy?" Prickett asks, and responds that for some this awareness of a "two-sidedness, an ambiguity in Wordsworth's experience of Nature" is of "the profoundest religious significance" (*Romanticism and Religion* 85–6).

18. While Abrams' view of a secularizing impulse in Wordsworth is the prevalent one, still Prickett speaks for a significant minority. For example, when Easterlin raises the "question of Romantic religion," she assumes, as does Prickett, a religious impulse in Wordsworth. She is interested in the "transcendent experiences, metaphysical concerns, and conflicting beliefs" in Wordsworth's poetry and argues that "Wordsworth on occasion seeks to structure belief, traditionally structured in the social sphere by dogma and participation in group ritual, through the private act of poetic composition" (9). Watson joins Prickett and Easterlin in assuming an essentially religious Wordsworth: Wordsworth's poetry "concerns itself with fundamental truths of religious and human life" (4). Coleridge is less assertive in his description of Wordsworth's project in the *Lyrical Ballads,* suggesting merely religious analogy: Wordsworth's object was "to give the charm of novelty to things of every day, and to excite a feeling *analogous to the supernatural,* by awakening the mind's attention from the lethargy of custom, and directing it to the loveliness and the wonders of the world before us; an inexhaustible treasure" (314; emphasis supplied).

19. Wordsworth originally intended the story, written in 1800, for inclusion in *Michael* (which I argue in chapter 4 is a retelling of Luke 15); he cut it from *Michael* and included it in the *Prelude* (1804, 1805) and then cut it entirely in the period of 1816 to 1819 (*Prelude* 278 n. 3).

CHAPTER 2. THE WORD AS BORDERER:
INCARNATIONAL POETICS—THE THEORY

1. Ferguson suggests something of what I will discuss below as Wordsworth's nondualistic theory: "The attempt to make language an object of speculation and investigation so thoroughly conflates subject with object—and means with ends—that the possibility of fixed objects of knowledge and fixed knowing subjects disappears" (7).

2. In his chapter 5, "Wordsworth's Epitaphic Mode," Ferguson finds that the epitaph leaves "stylistic traces" in the poetry and that it is virtually omnipresent (155). Further, "the epitaph in Wordsworth is less a genre than a mode of thought," a mode that supports Wordsworth's "effort to expand the community of the living and the dead" (166–7).

3. In Wordsworth's semiotics, he joins a tradition that Umberto Eco traces to the Stoics, a tradition that recognizes a number of sign systems and acknowledges that language, while only one of them, "is a primary modeling system, through which the other systems are expressed" (32). Horst Ruthrof and Eco both speak of the metaphor as a *semiotic* phenomenon, whose venue is not restricted to language, but includes other sign systems, such as, for example, oneiric images (Ruthrof 23). Furthermore, "verbal metaphor itself often elicits references to visual, aural, tactile, and olfactory" images and systems of signs (Eco 89).

4. In his chapter 2 of *Semiotics and the Philosophy of Language*—"Dictionary vs. Encyclopedia"—Eco argues that production and interpretation of signs depend not on dictionary meanings, but on the virtually limitless resources of one's cultural and personal encyclopedias.

5. In Book 6 of the *Prelude,* Wordsworth offers an interesting paean to "geometric science," wherein he claims that he drew from this source "a sense of permanent and universal sway," the recognition of a changeless "Surpassing life" which exists outside "space and time" (6:150–5). Euclid's *Elements* (or Newton's *Principia Mathematica*), therefore, suggests in Book 5 the book of nature, through or in which one can sense or "read" the eternal, the immortal, the supernatural.

6. One understanding of *sign* is that "Something is a sign because it is interpreted as a sign of something by some interpreter" (Eco, *Semiotics* 15). Many things are recognized as signs because of what Eco calls the "cultural and personal encyclopedias" that have created a partially textual, partially experiential, web of namings and meanings. A strong intertextual element is present in the cultural encyclopedia. As the cultural code is being overturned or called into question, it continues to exert its influence alongside new interpretations and understandings. (*Sunrise* and *sunset,* for example, are difficult "readings" to see beyond; Eco uses the example of the sacred heart, of which Pope Pius XII spoke "as a 'natural symbol' of Divine Love," suggesting that it is a symbol "that was 'natural' only for those who, with an unconscious semiotic sensitivity, identified nature with encyclopedia" [146].)

7. Of this sort of linguistic invention, Eco remarks, "It is evident that we use linguistic expressions or other semiotic means to name 'things' first met by our ancestors; but it is also evident that we frequently use linguistic expressions to describe and to *call into life 'things' that will exist only after and because of the utterance of our expressions*" (*Semiotics* 76; emphasis supplied).

8. Thomas (26) quotes as an important text the first draft of this passage from the Alfoxden notebook, written in third person, but otherwise virtually unchanged in the 1805 *Prelude,* and little changed in the 1850 *Prelude.*

9. It is worth noting that Ferguson's analysis tends to retain the separability of the constituents, rather than their "intermixture," while recognizing a Wordsworthian difference from representational theories: "the relationship between words and things and thoughts which underlies representational schemes of language shifts to become a relationship between things and word-things and thoughts because of Wordsworth's concern with the interest of the mind in words 'as *things,* active and efficient'" (15–6).

10. While Bewell uses the term "resurrection" to describe a theme of the "Intimations Ode," I believe that a more accurate term is "reincarnation," a subject to which I shall return later.

11. The original epigraph of the "Intimations Ode," from Virgil's Fourth Eclogue, "*paulo maiora canamus*" ("Let us sing a nobler song"), is in itself an

exhortation suggesting the need to revise existing "songs," or accounts—specifically of life, growth, and death.

12. While Jonathan Wordsworth claims that the poet's "preoccupations do not suddenly change when he accepts the doctrine of an afterlife" (after 1806), he does experience that well-acknowledged "falling-off," a "slackening tension" (34). Wordsworth's later poems at times reveal a drift or indeed a shift toward a traditionally crafted heaven and eternity, where existence has been verbally rescued from natural dualities, as in the heaven of Revelation, where "death will be no more; neither shall there be mourning nor crying nor pain any more" (21:4). By contrast, in the Wordsworthian borderland of the earlier poems, his confinement in the natural assimilates life and death to each other, and implicates suffering in both.

13. I shall have more to say on the Lockean-Hartleian epistemology and Wordsworth's modification thereof in chapter 8, pp. 182–4 below.

14. In the *Prelude,* Wordsworth calls the written works of humans—their breathings—"powers," only less "Than Nature's self which is the breath of God" (5:215–22).

15. Both author and reader are figured in the maddened Arab-Quixote figure who appears in the dream episode of the *Prelude,* Book 5. He is, as Miller points out, a composite figure of author (*Don Quixote* is purportedly written by an Arab) and reader. Wordsworth says that the Arab-Quixote figure is "crazed." The madness is language induced, for conflated in this lunatic are Cervantes, an author concerned for the fragility of books, and his creature, Don Quixote, maddened by reading romances (*The Linguistic Moment,* Miller 91–2).

16. Biblical references to the body as clothing include Job's statement to God: "Thou hast clothed me with skin and flesh"; but also, Jesus' rhetorical question to the disciples insisting on a distinction between clothing and body: "Is not life more than food, and the body more than clothing?" (Mt. 6:25).

17. It seems to take a poet in an intermediate condition to observe and fix in language the intermediate being. As M. H. Abrams points out, Wordsworth in a manuscript of the "Prospectus" "described himself, the 'transitory being that beheld / This vision,'" as a borderer "living a double life": "In part a Fellow-citizen, in part / An Outlaw, and a borderer of his age" (*Natural Supernaturalism* 68). It is only from this precarious borderland in the doubleness of insider/outcast that other border states and dwellers—themselves transitory beings, conditions, and truths—can be embodied in verse that abides like the thorn in the stark terrain of indeterminacy.

18. Both Haney and Jonathan Wordsworth have discussed this rejected passage—Haney in conjunction with incarnational poetics, remarking "to attain this sort of identity [as living statue] is to become the kind of 'thing' to which words aspire" (77); Jonathan Wordsworth, in conjunction with "border visions" (1–2). Both call attention to the fact that the

horse is described as "an amphibious work of Nature's hand," a word of Greek origin meaning "living a double life."

19. As an aside, I think in this context of Wordsworth's "The Child is Father of the Man," a mysterious claim that echoes the elements of the opening of John.

20. The Greek *logos* used in the Johannine text was complex, with a "tendency . . . to acquire associations from Plato's demiurge in the *Timaeus* which make it function more like a gerund, or verbal, than a noun." For this reason, early translators were "frustrated by the inadequacy of any single Latin word to convey the complexity and transitive, dynamic power they feel to be expressed in the Johannine Logos." The Vulgate settles for *verbum,* a noun, for the Greek *logos* with its verbal characteristics. (Jeffrey 460).

21. Jesus' temptation in the desert adds a further metaphoric dimension to the word/body/bread complex in connection with life and death. When tempted to speak to the stones, to "command these stones to become loaves of bread," Jesus responds, "Man shall not live by bread alone, but by every word that proceeds from the mouth of God" (Mt. 4:3–4). The linguistic mysteries of the Incarnation have certainly intrigued other poets in other times. An early example occurs in "The Sacrament of the Altar," in which an anonymous fifteenth-century poet explores the inherent paradox of Christ's announcement through his world-altering metaphor ("this [bread] is my body"). The poem plays on the contradictory qualities between sign and referent, seeming and being, death and life, twoness and oneness: "It semes white and is red; / It is quike and semes dede; / It is fleshe and semes bred; / It is on and semes too; / It is God body and no mo." As in Wordsworth's poetics, the last line is irresolvably ambiguous, holding conflicting truths in endless play.

22. I am indebted to Ruthrof for calling to my attention this remarkable and, I would have to say, rather "Wordsworthian" theory advanced by a modern language philosopher (120–32).

23. In the *Essays upon Epitaphs,* de Man finds, Wordsworth depicts life as a journey, one that is "interrupted, but not ended, by death" (*Rhetoric of Romanticism* 74), a view that must be seen as rather traditional; whereas, during the years when Wordsworth's poetics was being framed in the practice (that is, before 1806), death was variously depicted, at times with radical and mind-eradicating transformative power, robbing the individual of spirit, force, hearing, and sight, as in "A Slumber did my Spirit seal."

24. The linguistic borderland is hospitable to, but is not to be identified with, the "visionary" experience of which Jonathan Wordsworth speaks, a "border" phenomenon marked by obscurity of perception, by "certain words and states," by "solitude and silence . . . together with that kind of stillness that is opposed to fixity" (17).

CHAPTER 3. THE WORD AS BORDERER:
OF CLOTHING AND INCARNATION—THE PRACTICE

1. Quotations are from Wordsworth's contribution to "The Three Graves" printed as Parts I and II in *Coleridge's Complete Poetical Works* (1:269–75). See Stephen Maxwell Parrish's recapitulation of the attribution of the parts of the poem (90–1).

2. One legend has it that it is unsafe to sit beneath a hawthorn on certain sacred days, while another has it that one is wise to shelter beneath a hawthorn in a storm as a safeguard against lightning (the narrator's impulse in "The Thorn"), while still another claimed that to bring its flowers into the house brought death (Cavendish 8:1134–5; Rees and Rees 174–6).

3. Priscilla Gilman suggests that the "deep irony which is the paradox of 'The Thorn'" is that "in being the most thing-like, most literal, the thorn is least readable or knowable" (40). I concur with the spirit of this claim, only demurring as to the claim that the thorn is "most literal." As suggested, the thorn (or hawthorn) carries a history of cultural and intertextual meanings from which it cannot be extricated.

4. For the alternative readings, see W. J. B. Owen, "'The Thorn' and the Poet's Intention," 16 n.6.

5. That in his credulity the narrator represents humanity in general is supported by John O. Hayden, who argues for the influence upon Wordsworth of Erasmus Darwin's *Zoonomia,* which treats various forms of mental disorder. One species of mania identified by Darwin—credulitas— "seems to be an almost universal mental problem rather than a form of outright insanity." Hayden quotes Darwin to this effect: "Life is short, opportunities of knowledge rare; our senses are fallacious, our reasonings uncertain, mankind therefore struggles with perpetual error from the cradle to the coffin" (72).

6. Like Parrish (102–5) and Bewell (169), I find the presence of Martha problematic. She seems a human metaphor for a natural object, and as such is intriguingly two-sided, suggestive of Wordsworthian dream metaphor: she is thorn and woman, or crag and woman, neither and both at once.

7. It is common to reverse this tropological process, seeing the thorn, hill, and pond as "symbols" for the human figures and events. Gilman, for example, finds that "the small thorn functions as a symbol of [the] baby, not quite alive, nor quite dead" (40). Nevertheless, assuming as I do that the thorn is the poem's focus, the "baby" (if there was a baby, which is not at all clear) or Martha herself (if she is not indeed a crag) is more satisfactorily seen as a symbol for the thorn. Parrish puts it this way: "Martha's presence in the poem surely illustrates one law: that when a credulous old seaman catches sight in a storm of a suggestively-shaped tree hung with

moss and later crams his head with village gossip, then his imagination can turn the tree into a woman, the brightly-colored moss into her scarlet cloak, and the creaking of the branches into her plaintive cry" (105).

8. Making a different sort of point, G. Kim Blank also notices that the thorn "stands . . . like a tombstone," in a paradoxical condition of youth and age, life and death (116).

9. Harold Bloom calls the passage in *The Borderers* from which this quotation is taken "extraordinary lines that form the credo of all of Wordsworth's own early poetry" (247). While the claim is sweeping and has not been tested, certainly "The Thorn" manifests this sort of credo, embodying the permanence of suffering in the knotted joints of the thorn.

10. In addition to the Persephone myth, Eilenberg finds that this "un-Wordsworthian" Nature "presents himself as the linguistic creature of an earlier literary tradition," with Chaucerian, Spenserian, and Miltonic antecedents—the product, along with Lucy, of "origins more literary than natural" (125–6). By contrast, and in my view mistakenly, Alan Bewell finds that the poem is a "consolatory fiction that seeks to explain her sudden death at the age of 'three.'" I believe that this is a common misreading—that the child dies at age three. The poem states that it is at that age that Nature appropriates the child, who lives to the age when her "virgin bosom swell[s]." Bewell, in contrast to my reading, finds further that death in the poem "is not portrayed as a Grim Reaper, but instead as 'Nature,' a benevolent parental figure . . ." (204). Wordsworth's Nature is akin to Plotinus' nature, cited by Coleridge, for whom not language but thought is creative: "The words of Plotinus, in the assumed person of nature. . . . With me the act of contemplation makes the thing contemplated, as the geometricians contemplating describe lines correspondent; but I not describing lines, but simply contemplating, the representative forms of things rise up into existence" (*Biographia Literaria,* Book 12). Here thought becomes thing without passing through language ("description").

11. Others have noticed the "almost divine force" of Nature's words "as the poet perceives them" (Eilenberg 131; Hartman 159).

12. The now-often-ignored grammatical rule is that one says "I shall" in nonemphatic contexts, but "I will" to show certainty and determination. Conversely in third person, the usage is reversed: "He (she/it/they) will" (nonemphatic), as opposed to the emphatic "He (she/it/they) shall." Everything Nature dictates is thus linguistically emphatic and determined.

13. Parrish recapitulates the critical claims (1–2). Eilenberg, too, considers the problem: She says that "The poem makes the poet . . . extraneous. . . . [T]he little the poet has to say is too much. Nature has usurped his voice as fatally as he has Lucy's." Nevertheless, a bit later she offers a confusing recantation: "It is not clear whether Nature gets into the poem because he is too powerful for the poet to keep out or because the poet has sponsored his appearance" (132).

14. Speaking of "I travelled among unknown men," Margaret Drabble observes that the "effect of [the poem] is to bring together, in some curiously

indirect way, the country and the girl, England and Lucy. England, to the poet, is Lucy; to him at least the two things mean the same. In missing one, he misses the other; in discovering the depth of his love for one, he discovers the depth of his love for the other" (66). She finds as well that "the identification of the girl and the country" are even more pronounced in "She dwelt among the untrodden ways" (67). My analysis of "Three years she grew" would suggest that this claim should be extended to include that poem and perhaps might appropriately describe the other Lucy poems as well. In a similar vein Eilenberg observes that Lucy of "Three years she grew" "diffuses into the abstract landscape" (129).

15. Bewell finds that the footprints that stop in the middle of the bridge indicate that "Lucy Gray" is an Enoch myth: "the poem is about the 'translation' of Lucy Gray in both a spiritual and a textual sense; it shows how an original, mysterious event comes, through successive retellings and interpretations, to serve as an 'intimation of immortality'" (204–5). At the same time, however, he finds that there are hints of an Orpheus/Eurydice myth in her solitary singing, "as if she were both the dead Eurydice and the poet Orpheus, continually bringing herself back from the Underworld through song, on the one condition that she 'never look[s] behind'" (205).

16. The single tree and the cornerstone of this borderland are evocative of the Clipping Tree and the cornerstone that remain at the end of *Michael*.

17. For example, in each case God (Jove or Yahweh) finds the world corrupt: Jove observes that "All men have joined in Hell's conspiracy" (37); Yahweh finds that "the wickedness of man was great in the earth" (Gen. 6:5). Both deities decide to eliminate humankind by means of a flood. In each case, however, the destruction is not complete, as certain exemplary people are spared: Deucalion and Pyrrha survive Jove's flood; Noah and his family survive Yahweh's flood.

18. Cynthia Chase also notices a "repetition" in the Boy of Winander episode, as the "text subtly invokes conceptions of depth and immersion." Her point, however, is that the repetition serves to disconnect, rather than connect, the episodes of the boy and the drowned man, wherein "one feels a loss of resonance" between the two (16–7).

19. While my discussion identifies and interprets in light of my argument certain revisions the passage undergoes over time, Peter J. Manning and Susan J. Wolfson, writing from different perspectives, offer detailed analyses of Wordsworth's revisions.

20. *Plain,* suggesting "without embellishment or decoration, simple or bare" provides a more striking contrast with the shell of the 1850 *Prelude,* which is described as "so beautiful in shape, / In colour so resplendent" (90–1).

21. Wordsworth would no doubt have known of the fish anagram for Jesus: ICHTHUS: *Iesous Christos Theou Huios Sotor* (Jesus Christ, Son of God, Savior) (J. C. Cooper 68), in connection with which the fish "came to be taken as a symbol of profound life, of the spiritual world that lies under the world of appearances, the fish representing

the life-force surging up" (Cirlot 107). St. Paul refers to Jesus as the "last Adam" who was "made a quickening soul"—in contrast to the "first Adam," a man made of earth who was made a "living soul" by the breath of God (1 Cor. 15:45). The first Adam, the man of earth, brings death to all; Jesus, the second Adam, brings life to all: "In Christ shall all be made alive" (1 Cor. 15:22).

22. Elsewhere Wordsworth seems to recommend a similar textual screen as he advises the poet to extend her range of sensibilities by developing "the habit of looking at things through the steady light of words," and he seems to reiterate the recognition of the *Essays upon Epitaphs* that words are connected with life and death: as clothing they act as counterspirit to madden and vitiate; as incarnations, they, like the Word, can "uphold, and feed, and leave in quiet" : "to speak a little metaphysically, words are not a mere vehicle, but they are powers either to kill or to animate." (*Letters* 437)

CHAPTER 4. HOW AWESOME IS THIS PLACE!
WORDSWORTH'S POEMS ON THE NAMING OF PLACES

1. I shall consider only the five poems composed in the ten month period between December, 1799, and October, 1800, and published together as *Poems on the Naming of Places* in *Lyrical Ballads* (1800).

2. Wordsworth read Lowth's *Lectures* perhaps as early as March 1798, and by September 30, 1800. He may have had access to Coleridge's notes on the *Lectures* by late in 1796 (Wu 89). See especially Lowth's *Lectures* X and XI for his discussion of the forms of allegory.

3. This inherent "spirit" of place, when unnamed, may, as in the 1799 *Prelude* passage cited below, be perceptible as an undefined uncanniness to an awakened imagination. In the cited passage, for example, it may present itself as a sense of extreme "visionary dreariness" experienced by the child William.

4. In biblical etymological tales, places and persons are typically given names suggesting acts; by contrast, Wordsworth typically, but not always, names places with personal names. In the former instance, the narrative preserves the personal name; in the latter, the "little incidents" that prompted the naming.

5. Discussing Wordsworth's emphasis on a temporal, as opposed to a spatial, dimension in the dialectic between self and nature, Paul de Man claims that for Wordsworth "the movements of nature are . . . instances of . . . endurance within a pattern of change," of "a metatemporal, stationary state" whose essence remains unchanged while the "outward aspects" are subject to "apparent" change and decay. Given Wordsworth's temporal focus, the Wordsworthian self is subject to the "temptation" "to borrow . . . the temporal stability that it lacks from nature, and to de-

vise strategies by means of which nature is brought down to a human level while still escaping from 'the unimaginable touch of time'" (196–7). My claim is that the most powerful of these strategies is the *textual* fusion of self and nature, self and place, through the processes of naming and narrating.

6. David Collings notices the gesture toward memory and the oral tradition, but not Wordsworth's textual insurance in the written poem. He says, referring to lines from *Michael,* that "These lines extend and revise the 'Poems on the Naming of Places'; to signify a memory in a more or less permanent fashion, one must not only substitute a name or sign for it but must also find a second self, another mind that can remember when one is gone" (159).

7. Also see Revelation 1:15: "And his feet like unto fine brass, as if they burned in a furnace; and his voice as the sound of many waters."

8. The association of the wheels with voice has resulted in a tendency to understand that the wheels are words, as Stephen Prickett points out, "even, specifically, a manifestation of the 'Word' or *logos*" (172).

9. Because the numbering of months was different for Ezekiel than for Wordsworth, Ezekiel's fourth month and fifth day refer to what would be July 31 by a modern Western calendar; his mysterious "thirtieth year" apparently does not refer to his own age, but perhaps to the last year of Israel's final Jubilee cycle (Rosenberg 195, 204).

10. The winged beings surrounding the divine throne in Ezekiel's vision and in Revelation appear to have captured Wordsworth's imagination, for they recur with some frequency in his poems, suitably disguised. For instance, in *Home at Grasmere,* Wordsworth has a vision reminiscent of that in "It was an April morning," evocative of both Ezekiel and Revelation, wherein the poet looks about him at the sights of Grasmere and thinks "Of Sunbeams, Shadows, Butterflies and Birds, / Angels and winged Creatures that are the Lords / Without restraint of all which they behold." Here Wordsworth uses the word *Creatures* (the term used in Ezekiel and Revelation for the winged beings surrounding the throne), connects them with angels, and reacts to the thought of all these winged beings by "stir[ring] in Spirit" (25–35). The winged beings appear to serve in these texts not only as suggestive of the divine presence, but actually as metonyms for the divine. They recur in Book 6 of the *Prelude* in the vision that succeeds Wordsworth's crossing of the Alps. During this visionary experience he apprehends the divine in the voices and acts of nature perceived as a remarkable unity that is imagined as features of one face, and "Characters of the great apocalypse" (a synonym for revelation), appearing in conjunction with Wordsworth's paraphrase of Milton's description of God in *Paradise Lost* 5:165:

Tumult and peace, the darkness and the light,
Were all like workings of one mind, the features

Of the same face, blossoms upon one tree,
Characters of the great apocalypse,
The types and symbols of eternity,
Of first, and last, and midst, and without end. (1805, 6:550–72; emphasis
   supplied)

The biblical beings are singers, as are the "living things" in "It was an
April morning." These winged creatures, these characters of the great
apocalypse, repeat, "Holy, holy, holy, is the Lord God Almighty, / who was
and is and is to come" (Rev. 4:8), a refrain ironically echoed in
Wordsworth's "Of first, and last, and midst, and without end." I shall
have more to say about this passage and the song, or kiddusha, of the
cherubim in chapter 7.

11. There is some indication that the poems are arranged so as to suggest a
   sort of Shepherd's Calendar in the progress of a year—from April, to
   summer, to fall, and back to spring and summer, but I do not know how
   to interpret this possibility.

12. Miller's essay on Wordsworth is one of the finest pieces of Wordsworthian criticism I know. His comments on Wordsworth's rocks, focused
   on the symbolism of Book 5 of the *Prelude,* are invaluable.

13. In chapter 20 of the *Biographia Literaria,* Coleridge refers to lines 53–65
   as an "imitation of Drayton," if they "be not a coincidence" (376). If
   the echoing laughter of Wordsworth's poem was suggested to him by
   Drayton's echoing speech, this fact would offer yet further evidence
   that the *Poems on the Naming of Places* are carefully crafted and "literary,"
   not merely personal history. Furthermore, this halting of the narrator
   by something associated with or to be identified with the imagination,
   figured in the rock, "this trap of the imagination," is similar to that
   imagination as "unfathered vapour" that stops Wordsworth dead in his
   tracks in the Simplon Pass episode of Book 6 of the *Prelude.*

14. The notion of loving communion, in connection with both solitude and
   height, may invite a reading of the "Eminence" as phallic. While I do
   not exclude this reading, I have chosen not to explore its implications
   here.

15. In *Home at Grasmere,* Wordsworth acknowledges himself as a type of Adam
   in Paradise, although actually more favored than Adam, asking,

What Being, therefore, since the birth of Man
Had ever more abundant cause to speak
Thanks. . . .
      [S]urpassing grace
To me hath been vouchsafed; among the bowers
Of Blissful Eden this was neither given,
Nor could be given, possession of the good
Which had been sighed for" (117–26)

CHAPTER 5. WORDSWORTH'S PRODIGAL SON:
MICHAEL AS PARABLE AND AS METAPARABLE

This chapter was first published as "Wordsworth's Prodigal Son: *Michael* as Parable and as Metaparable." *The Wordsworth Circle* 28:2 (spring 1997) 109–119.

1. Bewell's term, "anthropological paradigm," refers to Wordsworth's speculations about human origins, the origins of language and poetry, the evolution of religion, and the relationship of primitive to modern humanity, in which process Wordsworth "consistently drew upon and transformed the anthropological methods he inherited from the Enlightenment" (45). In *Michael,* as elsewhere in his poetry, the two paradigms—anthropological and biblical—are woven together into the fabric of the text. In this discussion, however, I have had to restrict attention to the biblical models.

2. The parabolic trait of expressing the mysterious and lofty in mundane language explains the difficulty sometimes encountered in the poem—Fox's objection to the blank verse, for example, but also Susan Eilenberg's objection that "there are passages in which the poet attempts to give objects a significance they seem not to deserve, passages in which he fails to maintain a balance between the humble and the elevated" (16). Parable has no choice but to give objects arbitrary and elevated significance; it is the process by which it works.

3. Wordsworth's reference to letter and spirit occurs in a passage of the *Prelude* (1850 8:293–7) in which he discusses the Michael-like "shepherds" the poet observed as a youth. His allusion is to 2 Cor. 3:6, which speaks of the new covenant and interpretation "not of the letter, but of the spirit; for the letter killeth, but the spirit giveth life." This notion, as Jeffrey points out, became central to biblical exegesis, and later to the reading of secular literature, distinguishing between a literal interpretation and a figurative signification; in a figurative sense, the letter covers the spirit as the chaff covers grain. It is useful "that the mystery be covered in the wrapping of the letter" (446). It is interesting that Wordsworth does not confine the concepts of letter and spirit to a reading of biblical and secular texts per se, but applies them as well to a reading of Nature (*Pr. W., Essays upon Epitaphs* 2:51).

4. Chapters 7 and 8 will explore at some length this matter of the no-thing, and the linguistic devices through which it is "revealed."

5. The birth of Aphrodite is recounted by Hesiod in *Theogony,* a text from which Milton drew imagery for *Paradise Lost.* According to Hesiod, the unborn Kronos castrates his father, Uranos ("Heaven"), because he will not let his children emerge from their mother, Ge ("Earth"). The discarded members fall into the sea and spread a "circle of white foam from the immortal flesh." Within the circle "grew a girl"—Aphrodite, "foam born" (ll. 147–200).

6. Dorothy Wordsworth uses "The Sheepfold" to refer both to the ruin of a sheepfold that she and William visited and to the poem that would later be titled *Michael*. Her repeated observation that William labored "at the Sheepfold" reveals both the ambiguity and the early focus of the composition. (See Dorothy Wordsworth, *Journals* 44–8.)

7. It is possible that Michael's role in *Paradise Lost*—to expel Adam and Eve from "the Paradise of God"—and to reveal the future to Adam (11:104–14) echoes as well in Wordsworth's text: Wordsworth's Michael does, in fact, drive Luke from the family home and into the fallen world, where he goes astray.

8. Susan Eilenberg notices this tendency throughout the second volume of the *Lyrical Ballads*, where property, as she says, "becomes increasingly a figure for poetry." I agree, but would argue that the convention with which Wordsworth is already working here is that to which he will turn again in the *Prelude*, as described by J. Hillis Miller in his analysis of Book 5 (*The Linguistic Moment* 59–113 passim; see note 11 below). Hence land is not merely a figure for poetry; it is poetry, the second book from the divine author. The human "author" is a latecomer, superimposing his text on an already existing one.

9. Wordsworth apparently recognized the parallel linguistic functions of parable and dream, for the dream in Book 5 serves as a sort of reverse parable. By "reverse," I mean that a contrast can be seen in the direction of representation. Whereas the parable begins in a domestic, this-worldly scene that points to some other place, other persons, and metaphoric meanings, the dream begins in an unnamed elsewhere, its figures and objects pointing to entities in this world. Michael's this-worldly stones are parabolic text; the dream's stone is a this-worldly text.

10. That Wordsworth's concerns were more poetic than political is a view shared as well by Susan Eilenberg, who suggests that "the reality of economic hardship only partially explains Wordsworth's interest in the theme [of property]" as it runs through *Michael* and other poems (13).

11. See Miller's discussion of Wordsworth's allusion to the stone "rescued," rather than "refused" by the bard "for some rude beauty of its own" (*The Linguistic Moment* 82, 112). The parable of *Michael* is likewise "Homely and rude." The word *rude*, which recurs in these two passages, comes originally from the Latin *rudus*, meaning "broken stone." Wordsworth's "rude" tale of *Michael* is a tale *of* stone and a tale *in* stone. As Miller sees it, Wordsworth rescues the stone of "rude beauty," to inscribe an epitaph, at once the stone's and his own, in this way transferring, Miller says, "the poet himself into language" (*The Linguistic Moment* 111–2). I would add that this sort of inscription—literal or figurative—provides both the poet and his poem the sort of "adamantine," impenetrable, stony permanence that the narrator longs for in Book 5 of the *Prelude* (28–48) and appropriates to himself in the rude heap of Michael's text.

CHAPTER 6. *WORDSWORTH'S SONG OF SONG'S:*
"NUTTING" AS MYSTICAL ALLEGORY

This chapter was first published as "Wordsworth's Song of Songs: 'Nutting' as Mystical Allegory," *The Wordsworth Circle* 30:1 (winter 1999) 36–47.

1. The word *garden* in this passage, as Giamatti points out, is a translation of the Hebrew *pardês,* from the Persian pairidaêza, which meant a royal park, orchard, or garden, a word used only three times in the Hebrew Bible (11). These verses (from the Authorized King James Version) are even more explicit about the sexual aggression of the lover in the Revised Standard Version: "You are stately as a palm tree, / and your breasts are like its clusters. / I say I will climb the palm tree / and lay hold of its branches" (S. of S. 7:7–8).

2. In this respect, as Harold Bloom reminds us, Wordsworth joins a tradition of allegorical readings of scripture and of Christian commentators on the sensuous imagery of the Song of Songs, authors who "charted the mystic way as a sustained and arduous spiritual journey and quest," culminating in a "spiritual marriage," which "sometimes is set forth in metaphors of physical lovemaking or even of violent sexual assault" (*Natural Supernaturalism* 50). Vaughan's overt reference to the Song occurs as a gloss on the closing lines, citing the verse, spoken by the beloved, "Arise O North, and come thou South-wind, and blow upon my garden, that the spices thereof may flow out" (4:16).

3. Roberts W. French shows that "Nutting" calls Milton's Garden of Eden, Satan, and Eve into the work. He has argued convincingly that "Nutting" "echoes *Paradise Lost* in significant ways" (42).

4. See Prickett's "'Types and Symbols of Eternity': The Poet as Prophet" and his chapter 3, "Poetry and prophecy: The language of the Great Code" in *Words and* the Word.

5. James Doleman, speaking of traditional readings of the Song of Songs, points out that "throughout most of the Jewish and Christian traditions, the Song of Songs has been read allegorically," commenting that there is debate, however, about whether the allegorization succeeded or preceded its entry into the canon (727). Doleman offers a review of the main readings of the Song as allegory in exegetical and literary treatments from the Council of Jamnia (ca. 90 B.C.E.) through the mainstream of European literature, including such British authors as Chaucer, Marvell, Spenser, and Milton (727–9). My emphasis upon the influence of Robert Lowth's *Lectures on the Sacred Poetry of the Hebrews* (1787) arises from the fact that, although without doubt Wordsworth knew much of the intertextual tradition of the Song, Lowth's study provided a current theoretical basis for reading biblical texts as literature, for analyzing the poetry of the Bible as poetry, and for making biblical poetry available as models for modern poetry.

6. What Lowth and Wordsworth offer are versions of the theory of accommodation, seen in an early form in St. Augustine's *City of God* (15.25) and in Milton, for example in *Paradise Lost* (5, 571–73). The theory holds that God uses the language of humans in a figurative sense to accommodate himself to human finitude, as Milton's Raphael explains to Adam, by "lik'ning spiritual to corporal forms."

7. One may not be persuaded by Lowth's traditional explanation, which ascribes the tendency to represent spiritual matters in sexual terms to divine intent, rather than human exigency. The tendency to merge the sexual and the spiritual may, as Georges Bataille asserts, have a "natural" basis. Bataille argues that humans experience eroticism and individual love, but express its extreme (often literary) forms as, on the one hand, sadism and, on the other, divine love (167–71).

8. See Paul de Man, chapter 4, "Autobiography as De-Facement," where he makes a case that autobiography is not a genre, but a "figure of reading or of understanding that occurs, to some degree, in all texts . . . [w]hich amounts to saying that any book with a readable title page is, to some extent, autobiographical" (70).

9. For this text, see *P. W.* 2:504–6.

10. The word *nut* had sexual connotations, being used colloquially to mean the glans penis. An English proverb had it that "He may be gott by an Apple and lost by a Nut," encapsulating the story of the Garden of Eden and the Fall and associating it with both nuts and sexual behavior (OED under "nut").

11. The incest theme argued by Johnston may find some support here. If there were incestuous impulses on either Dorothy's or William's part, Wordsworth's reading of the Song would clearly have made the phrase, "my sister, my spouse," resonate in personal ways.

12. An opposite effect obtains in *Fasti*, in which Ovid makes the garden of love the domain of the virgin Flora, a nature goddess, who is raped by Zephyr, then married by him, after which she lives a fecund and happy existence "in the fields that are my / dower [where] I have a fruitful garden" (Giamatti 42–3). Laura Claridge approaches the transformation of "Nutting" from another direction, suggesting that in Wordsworth's "Nutting," "Desire moves toward transforming its object," a process to which she refers as "a paradigm of destruction" (39).

13. A similar process is apparent in "Three years she grew in sun and shower," wherein Lucy, the poet's beloved, gradually absorbs and is absorbed and transformed into various aspects of nature; finally ceasing to be as a separate entity, she becomes "a virgin scene," as in "Nutting."

14. Frances Ferguson also finds for "Nutting" a textual background: "The original text (as it emerges in lines 4–14) is imperfectly conned from books of romance" (73). I agree that the poem invites a comparison of the youth's quest with that of the knight of romance, but my argument will be that another and closer fit is with that of the pilgrim.

15. Wordsworth employs this same phrase, "stately height," to describe Lucy in "Three years she grew," a poem that in other respects resonates with "Nutting."

16. Percy's translation is very close to that of the King James Authorized Version. There the beloved says, "Awake, O northwind, and come thou, south; blow upon my garden, that the spices thereof may flow out. Then let my beloved come into his garden, and eat his delicious fruits" (Percy 22–3).

17. It is instructive to compare "Nutting" with "To M. H.," one of the *Poems on the Naming of Places*, composed approximately one year later, for both can be seen as spousal verses or epithalamia and both are set in a paradisal, hidden, and difficult-of-access "nook." Like Paradise and the grove in "Nutting," "To M. H." has its own version of the fountain of life, a pool like a well; and as in the Song and in Vaughan's poem, sun and wind come here as blessings. The nook of "To M. H." is one that "was made by Nature for herself"; it is called by Mary's name and is therefore identified with the prospective bride; and it like the "dear nook" of "Nutting" is virginal—unvisited and unknown: "The travellers know it not, and 'twill remain / Unknown to them; but it is beautiful." As in "Nutting," the speaker is fearless of a rival.

CHAPTER 7. WORDSWORTHIAN APOCALYPTICS:
DEFINITIONS AND BIBLICAL INTERTEXTS

1. Taylor explains that *parapraxis* is a Freudian term, "involv[ing] a failure, slip, error, or mistake"; parapraxical writing "involves the inscription of the boundary, threshold, margin, or limit" (224) and is "unavoidably tropological" (225). In parapraxical writing, however, each trope is "de trop," an excess pointing not to polysemy, but entailing "a strange 'anasemia,' which both escapes and engenders discourse." The "absence of univocity," Taylor explains, "leaves parapraxical writing irreducibly duplicitous; its meaning is indeterminate, its sense undecidable. Such indeterminacy and undecidability harbor an obscurity that cannot be dispelled" (226).

2. As Robinson explains,

   All literature can easily be read as apocalyptic, whether because the images of apocalypse have permeated culture so deeply as to be virtually ubiquitous, or because, as Frank Kermode suggests in *The Sense of an Ending* (1967), the classic narrative structure, rising action—climax—denouement, seems to have been modeled on the apocalypse. Kermode argues, in fact, that narrative literature and apocalyptic are both grounded in a human need for closure, for a "sense of an ending." ("Literature and Apocalyptic" 360)

3. For Goldsmith, the end of time, explicit in Revelation and implicit in apocalypse, serves political ends—either revolutionary or, more often, conservative: "The idea of the end of history has often been bound up with the promise of an *aesthetic* space relieved of historical determinants. It is in this sense that one might call 'apocalyptic' any locus or activity (textual, cognitive, or metaphysical) in which historical contingency is not supposed to figure significantly, in which, in other words, history is said to have come to an end" (2). In Goldsmith's analysis, a key theme of Revelation is the silencing of multiple voices in the victory of the Logos over the linguistically promiscuous Whore of Babylon.

4. I do not mean to suggest that even here Wordsworth is, strictly speaking, orthodox, only more orthodox in his treatment of the biblical plot than that found in the *Prelude*.

5. Paul Ricoeur, following Frye and Kermode, takes up the matters of poetics and eschatology, of poetic structure and closure, and biblical history and Apocalypse, observing that in Western tradition the "myth of the Apocalypse . . . has most contributed to structuring these expectations, by giving the term 'fiction' a range that overflows the domain of literary fiction." It is theological, historical-political, and epistemological "by way of the theory of models," and literary "by way of the theory of the plot." He notices that this congruence may be explained by the fact that the move from Apocalypse, "the cosmic stance," to a poetic one "finds some justification in the fact that the idea of the end of the world comes to us by means of the text [Revelation] that, in the biblical canon received in the Christian West . . . concludes the Bible (*Time and Narrative* 2:23).

6. David Wood observes that the concern with time is pervasive as well in philosophy, remarking that philosophy's texts, its attempts to make sense, are also apocalyptically colored by the sense of existing in time, a "pervasive and hydra-headed problem" ("Introduction," *On Paul Ricoeur* 1). Underscoring this claim, Woods remarks that "Much philosophy reads like the construction of sea-walls against . . . [time]. For time is the destroyer not just of all that we are proud of, even pride itself, it threatens the realization of many a philosophical ideal. Time is the possibility of corruption at the deepest level. And yet without organized temporal extension, there would be nothing to be corrupted. Time makes as well as breaks. Time giveth and it taketh away" ("Introduction," *On Paul Ricoeur* 1).

7. Recognizing the "pervasiveness of time" and the "pervasiveness of language" as vital dimensions of "all our philosophical reflections on the world," David Wood leaves open the question of whether language is constitutive of time. Nevertheless, he acknowledges that if "what we commonly call language is already caught up in certain temporal valuations, then bringing language onto the scene is not quite as innocent as it seems" ("Introduction," *On Paul Ricoeur* 2–3).

8. In the foregoing description, I am indebted to Stephen Goldsmith's fine account of the confrontation of Babel and the Logos. See his "Language beyond History" in *Unbuilding Jerusalem* (56–72).

9. In the *Poetics,* Aristotle claims that for the poet the "greatest thing by far is to be a master of metaphor," for it is "a sign of genius" and "implies an intuitive perception of the similarity in dissimilars" (1459a).

10. The similarity of this "sentiment" to the "presence," or "sense sublime," of "Tintern Abbey" (95–6) is suggested in the fact that a superseding of the natural senses occurs. Nevertheless, if the physical senses can be overcome by inner sense, the reverse is also true. Wordsworth discusses later in the *Prelude* a "twofold frame of body and of mind"; the physical senses he calls the "outward sense." Their transports are "Not of the mind—vivid but not profound." When outward sense is given full reign, the effect is "To lay the inner faculties asleep" (11:170–94).

11. See discussion of these complexities in chapter 3, pp. 68–71.

12. The articulate or speaking trumpet has its prototype in Revelation: "The first voice which I heard was as it were of a trumpet talking with me; which said, Come up hither, and I will shew thee things which must be hereafter" (4:1).

13. Compare 1 Thessalonians 4:16: "For the Lord himself shall descend from heaven with a shout, with the voice of the archangel, and with the trump of God: and the dead in Christ shall rise first. . . ."

14. One of the remarkable aspects of Wordsworth's dream is its willingness to raise the terrifying question, "Everything stops; what then?" Speaking of works "imagining total annihilation," Robinson notices that they are rare. He asks, "What would motivate a writer to tell the story of the destruction of all human life with nothing to follow, no rebirth, no denourment of any kind? And what narrative point of view would allow that story to be told to its end? . . . [W]ho would tell the story?" (379).

15. The epigraph appears on the fly-leaf of D. L. Moody's Bible.

16. Lyotard has argued this point—that the figural (the visual matter of the dream) "transgresses the law of discourse" and "refuses to respect the invariant spacing and rules of substitution which define the system of language" (Bennington 91).

17. In Freudian terms, there would be evidence that if the dream is "real," it has undergone extensive revision—"secondary revision," a psychical function of dreams that is "akin to waking thoughts," and which interprets dreams and disguises their "true significance" before "they are submitted to waking interpretation" (Freud 490). A crucial aspect of such secondary revision is logico-linguistic—making narrative sense of a seemingly senseless assortment of visual images or, in Lyotard's sense, figures.

18. A similarly orthodox treatment of the kiddusha and Merkabah appears in the 1850 *Prelude* (14:181–7), a passage composed perhaps in the period from 1816 to 1819.

CHAPTER 8. WORDSWORTHIAN APOCALYPTICS
IN WHICH NOTHING IS REVEALED

1. Wordsworth himself analyzes the inevitability of representing the boundless in the form of natural images. Speaking of the child's interrogation of the whence and whither of human life on observing a running stream and asking, "Towards what abyss is it in progress?," Wordsworth notices that the "*spirit* of the answer, though the word might be sea or ocean, accompanied perhaps with an image gathered from a map, or from the real object in nature—these might have been the *letter,* but the *spirit* of the answer must have been *as* inevitably,—a receptacle without bounds or dimensions;—nothing less than infinity" (*Pr. W., Essays upon Epitaphs* 2:51). Hartman may be leaning toward this position when he claims that whatever Wordsworth's apocalyptic impulses, and whatever "imagination's source," the "end as poetry is the nature all recognize, and still a nature that leads beyond itself. [Wordsworth] seeks his earthly paradise not 'beyond the Indian mount' but in the real Abyssinia—any mountain-valley where poetry is made" (*Wordsworth's Poetry* 67; 69). Still Hartman does not distinguish between nature and the language of nature. The crucial point is to say how "nature [can lead] beyond itself," and my response is that it may do so only through the poet's crafting of the language of nature.

2. Burke's argument has been most helpful to me. His intention is a broad one: to demonstrate that the "whole problem of negativity in language . . . has its analogue in 'negative theology,' by defining God in terms of what he is not, as when God is described in words like 'immortal,' 'Immutable,' 'infinite,' 'unbounded,' 'impassive' and the like" (22). I found it useful to apply Burke's insights to understanding Wordsworth's use of negatives in apocalyptic representations not simply as "negative theology," for they do not necessarily implicate God. They do nevertheless provide a means for the poet to pursue the fugitive god through a Newtonian universe in order to express previously unarticulated metaphysical or psychological phenomena for which positive terms of nature prove inadequate. I came to see Wordsworth's practice as one in which he combines the techniques of the negative way with parapraxical writing.

3. Coleridge's famous dismissal of Hartleian theory is in Book 7 of the *Biographia Literaria:* "According to this hypothesis the disquisition, to which I am at present soliciting the reader's attention, may be as truly said to be written by Saint Paul's church as by me; for it is the mere motion of my muscles and nerves; and these again are set in motion from external causes equally passive, which external causes stand themselves in interdependent connection with everything that exists or has existed. Thus the whole universe co-operates to produce the minutest stroke of every letter, save only that I myself, and I alone, have nothing to do with it, but merely the causeless and effectless beholding of it when it is done" (219). Wordsworth, too, explicitly dismisses Hartleian thought when he denies

that one can "class the cabinet [a Lockean-Hartleian metaphor for mind] / Of . . . sensations." Radical empiricism argued for the origin of thoughts in experience, i.e., sensations; Wordsworth replies that it is a "Hard task to analyse a soul," for any particular thought "Not in a mystical and idle sense, / But in the words of reason deeply weighed—/ Hath no beginning" (*Prelude* 2:228–36).

4. Bloom argues against the attempt to analyze this process of reciprocity, which is, he says, "like a conversation that never stops, and cannot therefore be summed up discursively or analyzed into static elements" (*Visionary Company* 132).

5. Warminski is obviously speaking of the poet when he continues, "But if one reading does not (merely) cancel the other, then their binding simultaneity is certainly problematic. *The memory that binds them together would be the memory of the time of writing* . . ." (987; emphasis supplied).

6. Bloom finds that the chief actors in the scene are "the weather and the eminence . . . which is located at an Oedipal crossroads" (*Ruin the Sacred Truths* 134). Certainly the atmosphere and setting are extremely suggestive, but the boy's act of attempting to see focuses its themes and ironies.

7. My claim is different from that of Johnston. Speaking of "A Night-Piece," Johnston observes, "As is so often his wont, Wordsworth here describes his soul 'Remembering how she felt, but what she felt / Remembering not . . .'" (13). My claim concerns not memory, but language. Wordsworth's obscurity is attributable to the limitations of natural human language—a "few weak words"—to articulate essentially un-, sub-, or supernatural experiences, thoughts, and insights.

8. The OED offers this definition of *endowment*: "A 'gift', power, capacity or other advantage with which a person is endowed by nature or fortune," a definition that supports the sense of person, the imagination depicted in the passage as separate, autonomous, and powerful.

9. The terms "literal" and "mental" travelers are Hartman's. He depends on the 1850 version of this passage for his argument that the poet learns that "Unless he can respect the natural (which includes the temporal) order, his song, at least as narrative, must cease. Here Imagination, not Nature . . . defeats Poetry." He continues, "This conclusion may be verified by comparing the versions of 1805 and 1850. The latter replaces 'Before the eye and progress of my Song' with a more direct metaphorical transposition. Imagination is said to rise from the mind's abyss 'Like an unfathered vapour that enwraps, / At once, some lonely traveller'" (*Wordsworth's Poetry* 46). Yet, it seems, Hartman depends on the deleted 1805 language to make his point about Poetry. What the 1850 version adds does not equal what it omits.

10. This power, fatherless and homeless in the 1805 version, is, in the 1850 version, altered significantly when it is provided a place of origin in "the mind's abyss," evocative of the description of the mind's depths in the "Prospectus" to *The Excursion* as "The darkest pit of lowest Erebus" (36).

11. As Hegel puts the matter, "Nothing is generally opposed to Something; but Something is an already determinate existent distinguished from another Something: such a Nothing opposed to Something, therefore, such a negation of Something, is a determinate Nothing [the God of negative theology]. Here, however, Nothing must be taken in its indeterminate simplicity" (95). Wordsworth's passage conforms to what Michel de Certeau names a "rhetoric of withdrawal," implicated in "mystic speech," whose secrets must be "torn from them" along with the confession of their "impotence." Mystical speech establishes "a space where change serves as a foundation and saying loss is another beginning. . . . [T]he mystic poem is connected to the *nothing* that opens the future, the time *to come*, and more precisely, to that single work, 'Yahweh,' which forever makes possible the self-naming of that which induces departure" (cited in Taylor 225–6).

12. The traveler is in this respect like the Platonic child in "Intimations Ode," who brings into the natural world the light (the clouds of glory) by which he sees. Although the light begins to yield to "shades of the prison-house," the soul "beholds the light, and whence it flows" and "by the vision splendid / Is on his way attended" (67, 69, 73–4).

Works Cited

Abrams, M. H. *Natural Supernaturalism: Tradition and Revolution in Romantic Literature.* New York and London: W. W. Norton and Company, 1971.

apRoberts, Ruth. *The Biblical Web.* Ann Arbor: The University of Michigan Press, 1994.

Arac, Jonathan. *Critical Genealogies: Historical Situations for Postmodern Literary Studies.* New York: Columbia University Press, 1987.

Bataille, Georges. *The Accursed Share: An Essay on General Economy.* Vol. 2. Tr. Robert Hurley. New York: Zone Books, 1991.

Bennington, Geoffrey. *Lyotard: Writing the event.* New York: Columbia University Press, 1988.

Bewell, Alan. *Wordsworth and the Enlightenment: Nature, Man, and Society in the Experimental Poetry.* New Haven and London: Yale University Press, 1989.

Bialostosky, Don H. *Wordsworth, dialogics, and the practice of criticism.* Cambridge: Cambridge University Press, 1992.

Bigley, Bruce. "Multiple Voices in 'Nutting': The Urbane Wordsworth." *Philological Quarterly* 70 (fall 1991): 433–52.

Blank, G. Kim. *Wordsworth and Feeling: The Poetry of an Adult Child.* Madison, NJ: Fairleigh Dickinson University Press, 1995.

Bloom, Harold. *Poetry and Repression: Revisionism from Blake to Stevens.* New Haven and London: Yale University Press, 1976.

———. *Ruin the Sacred Truths: Poetry and Belief from the Bible to the Present.* Harvard University Press: Cambridge and London, 1989.

———. *The Ringers in the Tower: Studies in Romantic Tradition.* Chicago and London: The University of Chicago Press, 1971.

———. *The Visionary Company: A Reading of English Romantic Poetry.* 2nd ed. Ithaca, NY, 1971.

———. *The Western Canon: The Books and School of the Ages.* New York, San Diego, London: Harcourt Brace & Company, 1994.

———and Lionel Trilling, eds. *Romantic Poetry and Prose.* New York: Oxford University Press, 1973.

Bradley, A. C. *Oxford Lectures on Poetry.* 2nd ed. London: Macmillan and Company Limited, 1955.

Burke, Kenneth. *The Rhetoric of Religion: Studies in Logology.* Berkeley: University of California Press, 1970.

Bushnell, John P. "'Where is the Lamb for a Burnt Offering?': Michael's Covenant and Sacrifice." *The Wordsworth Circle* 2.4 (autumn 1981): 246–52.

Butler, Bishop Joseph. *Analogy of Religion, Natural and Revealed, to the Constitution and Course of Nature.* New York: Harper & Brothers, Publishers, 1852.

Cavendish, Richard, ed. *Man, Myth & Magic: The Illustrated Encyclopedia of Mythology, Religion and the Unknown.* 21 vols. North Billmore, NY: Marshall Cavendish Corporation, 1995.

Chase, Cynthia. *Decomposing Figures: Rhetorical Readings in the Romantic Tradition.* Baltimore and London: The Johns Hopkins University Press, 1986.

Cirlot, J. E. *A Dictionary of Symbols.* 2nd ed. Tr. Jack Sage. New York: Philosophical Library, 1971.

Claridge, Laura. *Romantic Poetry: The Paradox of Desire.* Ithaca and London: Cornell University Press, 1992.

Coleridge, Samuel Taylor. *The Complete Poetical Works.* Ernest Hartley Coleridge, ed. 2 vols. Oxford: Oxford University Press, Clarendon Press, 1912.

———. *The Oxford Authors: Samuel Taylor Coleridge.* Ed. H. J. Jackson. Oxford and New York: Oxford University Press, 1985.

Collings, David. *Wordsworthian Errancies: The Poetics of Cultural Dismemberment.* Baltimore and London: The Johns Hopkins University Press, 1994.

Cooper, J. C. *An Illustrated Encyclopaedia of Traditional Symbols.* London: Thames and Hudson, 1978.

Cooper, Lane, ed. *A Concordance to the Poems of William Wordsworth.* New York: Russell & Russell, 1965.

Crawford, Rachel. "The Structure of the Sororal in Wordsworth's 'Nutting.'" *Studies in Romanticism* 31 (summer 1992): 197–211.

de Man, Paul. *Blindness and Insight: Essays in the Rhetoric of Contemporary Criticism.* 2nd Edition, Rev. Intro. Wlad Godzich. Minneapolis: University of Minnesota Press, 1983.

———. *The Rhetoric of Romanticism.* New York: Columbia University Press, 1984.

De Quincey, Thomas. *The Collected Writings.* Ed. David Masson. 14 vols. London: A. & C. Black, 1896–97.

De Selincourt, Ernest, ed. *The Poetical Works of William Wordsworth.* Oxford: The Clarendon Press, 1952.

Dolar, Mladden. "'I Shall Be with You on Your Wedding-Night': Lacan and the Uncanny." *October* 58 (fall 1991): 5–23.

Doleman, James, "Song of Songs," in David Lyle Jeffrey, ed. *A Dictionary of Biblical Tradition in English Literature.* Grand Rapids, MI: William B. Eerdmans Publishing Company, 1992: 727–30.

Drabble, Margaret. *Wordsworth.* New York: Arco Publishing Company, Inc., 1969.

Drury, John. "Luke" in *The Literary Guide to the Bible.* Ed. Robert Alter and Frank Kermode. Cambridge, MA: The Belknap Press of Harvard University Press, 1987: 418–39.

Dryden, John. *Essays of John Dryden.* W. P. Ker, ed. 2 vols. New York: Russell & Russell, 1961.

Easterlin, Nancy. *Wordsworth and the Question of "Romantic Religion."* Lewisburg, PA: Bucknell University Press; London: Associated University Presses, 1996.

Eco, Umberto. *Kant and the Platypus: Essays on Language and Cognition.* Tr. Alastair McEwen. New York, San Diego, London: Harcourt Brace & Company, 1999.

————. *Semiotics and the Philosophy of Language.* Bloomington: Indiana University Press, 1984.

Eilenberg, Susan. "Wordsworth's 'Michael': The Poetry of Property." *Essays in Literature* 15.1 (spring 1988): 13–25.

Ferguson, Frances. *Wordsworth: Language as Counter-Spirit.* New Haven and London: Yale University Press, 1977.

French, Roberts W. "Wordsworth's Paradise Lost: A Note on 'Nutting.'" *Studies in the Humanities* V, 1 (Jan. 1976): 42–5.

Freud, Sigmund. *The Interpretation of Dreams.* Tr. and ed., James Strachey. New York: Basic Books, Inc., Publishers, 1959.

Gaull, Marilyn. *English Romanticism: The Human Context.* New York and London: W. W. Norton & Company, 1988.

Genette, Gérard. *The Architext: An Introduction.* Tr. Jane E. Lewin. Foreword Robert Scholes. Berkeley, Los Angeles, and Oxford: University of California Press, 1992.

Giamatti, A. Bartlett. *The Earthly Paradise and the Renaissance Epic.* New York and London: W. W. Norton & Company, 1966.

Gill, Stephen, ed. *The Oxford Authors: William Wordsworth.* Oxford and New York: Oxford University Press, 1984, 1987.

————. *William Wordsworth, A Life.* Oxford: Clarendon Press, 1989.

Gilman, Priscilla. "'To Kill and Bury the Poor Thorn Forever': 'The Thorn' and Mant's Simpliciad." *The Wordsworth Circle* 27:1 (winter 1996): 37–41.

Goldsmith, Stephen. *Unbuilding Jerusalem: Apocalypse and Romantic Representation.* Ithaca and London: Cornell University Press, 1993.

Graves, Robert. *The White Goddess: A historical grammar of poetic myth.* Amended and Enlarged Ed. New York: Farrar, Straus and Giroux, 1949.

Haney, David P. *William Wordsworth and the Hermeneutics of Incarnation.* University Park: The Pennsylvania State University Press, 1993.

Hartley, David. *Observations on Man, His Frame, His Duty And His Expectations.* 2 vols. London, 1749.

Hartman, Geoffrey. *Saving the Text: Literature/Derrida/Philosophy.* Baltimore and London: The Johns Hopkins University Press, 1981.

————. *Wordsworth's Poetry, 1787–1814.* New Haven and London: Yale University Press, 1964.

Hayden, John O. *William Wordsworth and the Mind of Man: The Poet as Thinker.* New York: Bibli O'Phile Publishing Company, 1992.

Hegel, G. W. F. *Science of Logic.* 2 vols. Tr. W. H. Johnston and L. G. Struthers. London: George Allen & Unwin Ltd., 1929.

Heidegger, Martin. *Poetry, Language, Thought.* Tr. Albert Hofstadter. New York: Harper & Row, Publishers, 1971.

Hilton, Nelson. "Blakean Zen," *Romanticism, A Critical Reader.* Ed. Duncan Wu. Cambridge: Basil Blackwell Ltd, 1995.

Izenberg, Gerald N. *Impossible Individuality: Romanticism, Revolution, and the Origins of Modern Selfhood, 1787–1802.* Princeton, NJ: Princeton University Press, 1992.

Jeffrey, David Lyle, ed. *A Dictionary of Biblical Tradition in English Literature*. Grand Rapids, MI: William B. Eerdmans Publishing Company, 1992.

Johnston, Kenneth R. *The Hidden Wordsworth: Poet, Lover, Rebel, Spy*. New York and London: W. W. Norton & Company, 1998.

————. "The Idiom of Vision," in *New Perspectives on Coleridge and Wordsworth: Selected Papers from the English Institute*. Ed. Geoffrey H. Hartman. New York and London: Columbia University Press, 1972: 1–39.

Kermode, Frank. *The Sense of an Ending: Studies in the Theory of Fiction*. New York: Oxford University Press, 1967.

Kneale, J. Douglas. *Monumental Writing: Aspects of Rhetoric in Wordsworth's Poetry*. Lincoln and London: University of Nebraska Press, 1988.

Kristeva, Julia. *In the Beginning Was Love: Psychoanalysis and Faith*. Tr. Arthur Goldhammer. New York: Columbia University Press, 1987.

Landy, Francis. "The Song of Songs," in *The Literary Guide to the Bible*. Robert Alter and Frank Kermode, ed. Cambridge, MA: The Belknap Press of Harvard University Press, 1987: 305–19.

Lessa, Richard. "Wordsworth's *Michael* and the Pastoral Tradition." *University of Toronto Quarterly* 53.2 (winter 1983/4): 181–94.

Levinson, Marjorie. "Spiritual economics: a reading of 'Michael,'" in *Wordsworth's Great Period Poems: Four Essays*. London and New York: Cambridge University Press, 1986: 58–79.

Lowth, Robert. *Lectures on the Sacred Poetry of the Hebrews*. 2 vols. Tr. G. Gregory. London: J. Johnson, 1787. Repr. Hildesheim: Georg Olms Verlag, 1969.

Magnuson, Paul. "The Articulation of 'Michael'; or, Could Michael Talk?" *The Wordsworth Circle* 13.2 (spring 1982): 72–9.

Manning, Peter J. "Reading Wordsworth's Revisions: Othello and the Drowned Man." *Studies in Romanticism* 22 (spring 1983): 3–28.

Marin, Louis. *Food for Thought*. Tr. Mette Hjort. Baltimore and London: The Johns Hopkins University Press, 1989.

Miller, J. Hillis. "The Critic as Host." *Theory Now and Then*. Durham, NC: Duke University Press, 1991: 143–70.

————. *The Disappearance of God: Five Nineteenth-Century Writers*. Cambridge, MA: The Belknap Press of Harvard University Press, 1963.

————. *The Linguistic Moment from Wordsworth to Stevens*. Princeton, NJ: Princeton University Press, 1985.

————. "Parable and performative in the Gospels and modern literature" in *Tropes, Parables, Performatives: Essays on Twentieth Century Literature*. Durham, NC: Duke University Press, 1991: 135–150.

Milton, John. *Paradise Lost* and *Paradise Regained*. Ed. Christopher Ricks. New York and Toronto: The New English Library Limited, London, 1968.

Moorman, Mary. *William Wordsworth, The Early Years, 1770–1803*. Oxford: Clarendon Press, 1957.

Newton, Isaac. *Newton's Philosophy of Nature: Selections from his Writings*. H. S. Thayer, ed. New York: Hafner Publishing Company, 1953.

Ovid. *The Metamorphoses*. Tr. and intro. Horace Gregory. New York and Scarborough, Ontario: New American Library, 1958.

Owen, W. J. B. "'The Thorn' and the Poet's Intention." *The Wordsworth Circle* 8:1 (winter 1977): 3–17.

Page, Judith W. "'A History / Homely and Rude': Genre and Style in Wordsworth's 'Michael.'" *Studies in English Literature, 1500–1900*, 29.4 (autumn 1989): 621–36.

Parker, Reeve. "Finishing off 'Michael': Poetic and Critical Enclosures. *Diacritics*, 17.4 (winter, 1987): 53–64.

Parrish, Stephen Maxfield. *The Art of the* Lyrical Ballads. Cambridge, MA: Harvard University Press, 1973.

Patrides, C. A. "*Paradise Lost* and the Language of Theology." *Bright Essence: Studies in Milton's Theology*. Ed. W. B. Hunter, et al. Salt Lake City: University of Utah Press, 1971.

Percy, Thomas. *The Song of Solomon, Newly translated from the Original Hebrew: with a Commentary and Annotations*. London: R. and J. Dodsley, 1769.

Plato. *The Republic*, in *Dialogues of Plato*. Ed. J. D. Kaplan. Jowett Translation. New York: Pocket Books, 1950.

Prickett, Stephen. *Romanticism and Religion: The Tradition of Coleridge and Wordsworth in the Victorian Church*. Cambridge: Cambridge University Press, 1976.

———. "'Types and Symbols of Eternity': The Poet as Prophet," *Centrum* 1, I (1981): 19–35.

———. *Words and* The Word: *Language, poetics and biblical interpretation*. Cambridge: Cambridge University Press, 1986.

Rapaport, Herman. *Heidegger & Derrida: Reflections on Time and Language*. Lincoln and London: University of Nebraska Press, 1989.

Rees, Alwyn, and Brinley Rees. *Celtic Heritage: Ancient Tradition in Ireland and Wales*. London: Thames and Hudson, 1961.

Ricoeur, Paul. *Time and Narrative*. 3 vols. Trans. Kathleen Laughlin and David Pellauer. Chicago: University of Chicago Press, 1984–1988.

Riffaterre, Michael. "Compulsory reader response: the intertextual drive." *Intertextuality: Theory and Practices*. Ed., Michael Worton and Judith Still. Manchester and New York: Manchester University Press, 1990: 56–78.

Robinson, Douglas. "Literature and Apocalyptic," in *The Encyclopedia of Apocalypticism*. 3 vols. Stephen J. Stein, ed. New York: The Continuum Publishing Company, 1998: 3:360–91.

Rosenberg, Joel. "Jeremiah and Ezekiel," in *The Literary Guide to the Bible*. Ed. Robert Alter and Frank Kermode. Cambridge, MA: The Belknap Press of Harvard University Press, 1987.

Roston, Murray. *Poet and Prophet: The Bible and the Growth of Romanticism*. Evanston, IL: Northwestern University Press, 1965.

Rowe, M. W. "The Underthought in Wordsworth's 'Nutting.'" *English* 44.178 (spring 1995): 17–23.

Ruthrof, Horst. *Pandora and Occam: On the Limits of Language and Literature*. Bloomington and Indianapolis: Indiana University Press, 1992.

Stein, Edwin. *Wordsworth's Art of Allusion*. University Park and London: The Pennsylvania State University Press, 1988.

Taylor, Mark C. *Tears*. Albany: State University of New York Press, 1990.

Thomas, Keith G. *Wordsworth and Philosophy: Empiricism and Transcendentalism in the Poetry.* Ann Arbor and London: UMI Research Press, 1989.

Tracy, David. "Metaphor and Religion: The Test Case of Christian Texts" in *On Metaphor.* Ed. Sheldon Sacks. Chicago and London: The University of Chicago Press, 1979: 89–104.

Turbayne, Colin Murray. *The Myth of Metaphor.* Rev. ed. Columbia: University of South Carolina Press, 1970.

Warminski, Andrzej. "Facing Language: Wordsworth's First Poetic Spirits." *Diacritics* 17 (winter 1987): 18–31.

———. "Missed Crossings: Wordsworth's Apocalypses," *M.L.N.* 99 no. 4–5 (Sep.–Dec., 1984): 983–1006.

Watkins, Daniel P. *Sexual Power in British Romantic Poetry.* Gainesville: University Press of Florida, 1996.

Watson, J. R. *Wordsworth's Vital Soul: The Sacred and Profane in Wordsworth's Poetry.* Atlantic Highlands, NJ: Humanities Press, 1982.

Wolfson, Susan J. "The Illusion of Mastery: Wordsworth's Revisions of 'The Drowned Man of Esthwaite,' 1799, 1805, 1850." *PMLA* 99 (1984): 917–35.

Wood, David. "Introduction: Interpreting narrative" *On Paul Ricoeur.* London and New York: Routledge, 1991: 1–19.

Wordsworth, Dorothy. *Journals of Dorothy Wordsworth: The Alfoxden Journal 1798, The Grasmere Journals 1800–1803.* 2nd ed. Intro. Helen Darbishire. Ed. Mary Moorman. New York and London: Oxford University Press, 1976.

Wordsworth, Jonathan. *William Wordsworth: The Borders of Vision.* Oxford: Clarendon Press, 1982.

Wordsworth, William. *The Letters of William and Dorothy Wordsworth: The Later Years.* Ed. Ernest de Selincourt. Oxford: Clarendon Press, 1939.

———. *Literary Criticism of William Wordsworth.* Ed. Paul M. Zall. Lincoln: University of Nebraska Press, 1966: 90–126.

———. *The Poetical Works of William Wordsworth.* Ed. Ernest de Selincourt. 5 vols. Oxford: Clarendon Press, 1940–49.

———. "Preface" to *Lyrical Ballads, with Other Poems (1800)* in *Literary Criticism of William Wordsworth.* Ed. Paul M. Zall. Lincoln: University of Nebraska Press, 1966: 15–32.

———. *The Prelude, 1799, 1805, 1850.* Ed. Jonathan Wordsworth, M. H. Abrams, and Stephen Gill. New York and London: W. W. Norton & Company, 1979.

———. *The Prose Works of William Wordsworth.* Ed. W. J. B. Owen and Jane Worthington Smyser. 3 vols. Oxford: Clarendon Press, 1974.

———. *Works.* Ed. Stephen Gill. Oxford and New York: Oxford University Press, 1984.

Wu, Duncan. *Wordsworth's Reading, 1770–1799.* Cambridge: Cambridge University Press, 1993.

Zall, Paul M., ed. *Literary Criticism of William Wordsworth.* Lincoln: University of Nebraska Press, 1966.

Index